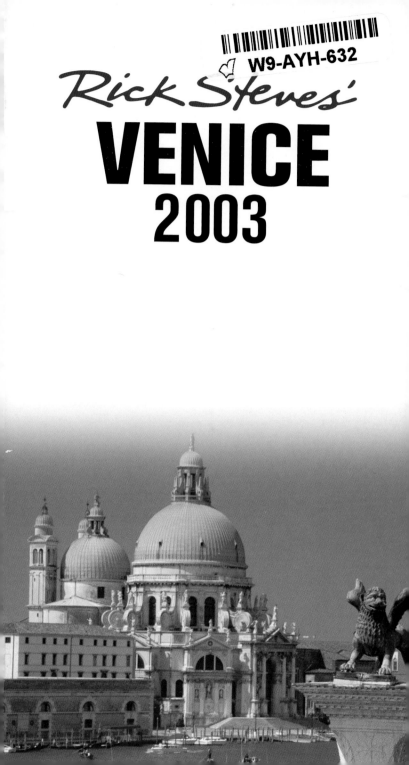

Rick Steves'
VENICE
2003

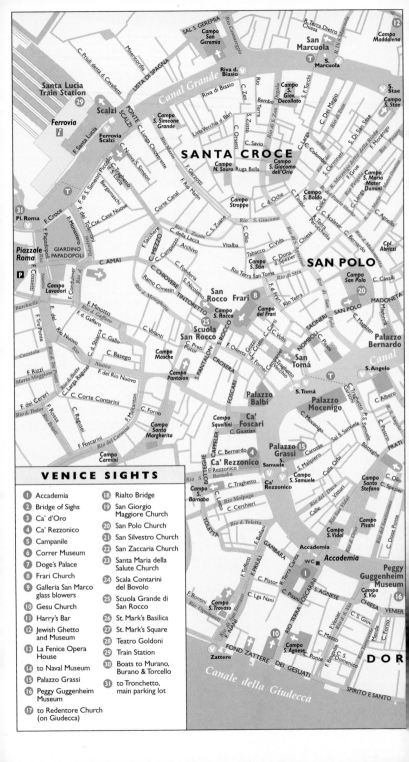

VENICE SIGHTS

1. Accademia
2. Bridge of Sighs
3. Ca' d'Oro
4. Ca' Rezzonico
5. Campanile
6. Correr Museum
7. Doge's Palace
8. Frari Church
9. Galleria San Marco glass blowers
10. Gesu Church
11. Harry's Bar
12. Jewish Ghetto and Museum
13. La Fenice Opera House
14. to Naval Museum
15. Palazzo Grassi
16. Peggy Guggenheim Museum
17. to Redentore Church (on Giudecca)
18. Rialto Bridge
19. San Giorgio Maggiore Church
20. San Polo Church
21. San Silvestro Church
22. San Zaccaria Church
23. Santa Maria della Salute Church
24. Scala Contarini del Bovolo
25. Scuola Grande di San Rocco
26. St. Mark's Basilica
27. St. Mark's Square
28. Teatro Goldoni
29. Train Station
30. Boats to Murano, Burano & Torcello
31. to Tronchetto, main parking lot

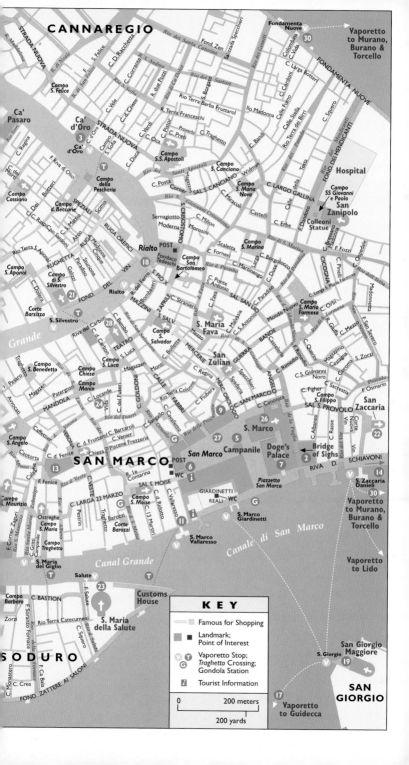

VENICE
2003

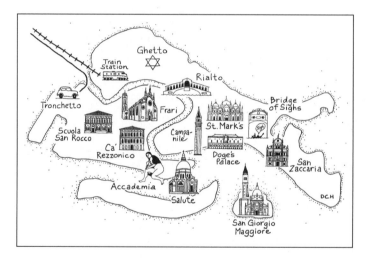

by Rick Steves & Gene Openshaw

AVALON
TRAVEL

Other ATP travel guidebooks by Rick Steves

Avalon Travel Publishing, 1400 65th Street, Suite 250, Emeryville, CA 94608
Text copyright © 2002 by Rick Steves. All rights reserved.
Maps copyright © 2002 Europe Through the Back Door. All rights reserved.

Photos are used by permission and are the property of the original copyright owners.

Printed in the U.S.A. by R.R. Donnelley. First printing October 2002.
Distributed by Publishers Group West

Portions of this book were originally published in *Rick Steves' Mona Winks*
© 2001, 1998, 1996, 1993, 1988 by Rick Steves and Gene Openshaw and in
Rick Steves' Italy © 2002, 2001, 2000, 1999, 1998, 1997, 1996, 1995 by Rick Steves.

ISBN 1-56691-483-3
ISSN 1538-1595

For the latest on Rick's lectures, guidebooks, tours, and public television series, contact
Europe Through the Back Door, Box 2009, Edmonds, WA 98020, 425/771-8303, fax
425/771-0833, www.ricksteves.com, or e-mail: rick@ricksteves.com.

Europe Through the Back Door Editors: Risa Laib, Lauren Mills,
    Cameron Hewitt, Jill Hodges
Avalon Travel Publishing Editor: Mia Lipman
Avalon Travel Publishing Series Manager: Kate Willis
Research Assistance: Heidi Sewell
Copy Editor: Leslie Miller
Indexer: Stephen Callahan
Production & Typesetting: Kathleen Sparkes, White Hart Design
Cover & Interior Design: Janine Lehmann
Maps & Graphics: David C. Hoerlein, Rhonda Pelikan, Zoey Platt
Photography: Elizabeth Openshaw, Dominic Bonuccelli, Andrea Johnson,
    Karen Kart, Rick Steves, Gene Openshaw
Front cover photo: Zodiac Clock at St. Mark's, Venice, Italy;
    copyright © Trip/B. Gadsby
Front matter color photos: p. i, Narrow Canal, Venice, Italy; copyright © William
    Manning; p. iv, Grand Canal, Venice, Italy; copyright © Dominic Bonuccelli

CONTENTS

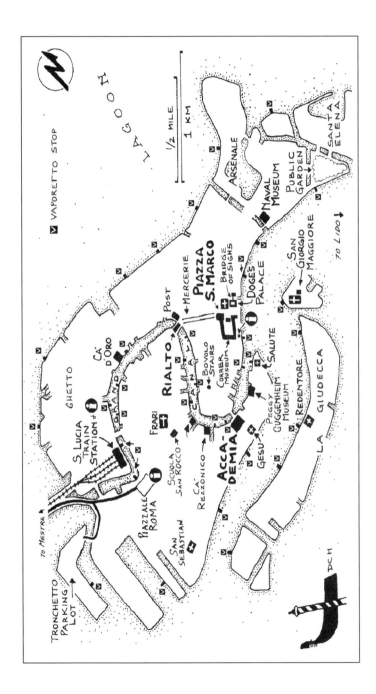

INTRODUCTION

Engineers love Venice—a completely man-made environment rising from the sea, with no visible means of support. Romantics revel in its atmosphere of elegant decay, seeing the peeling plaster and seaweed-covered stairs as a metaphor for beauty in decline. And first-time visitors are often stirred deeply, awaking from their ordinary lives to a fantasy world unlike anything they've ever seen before.

Those are strong reactions, considering that Venice today can, frankly, also be an overcrowded, prepackaged, and tacky tourist trap. But Venice is unique. Built on a hundred islands with wealth from trade with the East, its exotic-looking palaces are laced together by sun-speckled canals. The car-free streets suddenly make walkers feel big, important, and liberated.

By day, it's a city of museums and churches, packed with great art, all within a half-hour's walk. Cruise the canals on a vaporetto water-bus. Climb towers for stunning seascape views. Shop for local crafts (such as glass and lace), high fashions, or tacky souvenirs for Uncle Eric. Linger over lunch, trying to crack a local crustacean with weird legs and antennae. Sip valpolicella wine at a café on St. Mark's Square as the orchestra plays "New York, New York."

At night, when the hordes of day-trippers have gone, another Venice appears. Dance across a floodlit square. Glide in a gondola through quiet canals while music echoes across the water. Pretend it's Carnevale time, don a mask—or just a clean shirt—and become someone else for a night.

This Information Is Accurate and Up-to-Date

This book is updated every year. Most publishers of guidebooks can afford an update only every two or three years (and even then, it's often by letter). Since this book is selective, we can personally update it annually. Even so, things change. But if you're traveling with the current edition of this book, we guarantee you're using the most up-to-date information available (for the very latest, visit www.ricksteves.com/update). This book will help you have an inexpensive, hassle-free trip. Your trip costs about $10 per waking hour. Your time is valuable. This guidebook saves lots of time.

Welcome to Our Venice City Guide

This book is organized this way:

Orientation includes tourist information and public transportation. The "Planning Your Time" section offers a suggested schedule with thoughts on how to best use your limited time.

Sights provides a succinct overview of Venice's most important sights, arranged by neighborhood, with ratings: ▲▲▲—Don't miss; ▲▲—Try hard to see; ▲—Worthwhile if you can make it; No rating—Worth knowing about.

The **Self-Guided Tours** lead you through Venice's most important sights, with tours of the Grand Canal, St. Mark's Square, St. Mark's Basilica, Doge's Palace, Correr Museum, Accademia, Scuola San Rocco, Frari Church, Ca' Rezzonico (Museum of 18th-Century Venice), Peggy Guggenheim Museum, La Salute Church, and San Giorgio Maggiore.

The **St. Mark's to Rialto Walk** takes you on a less touristy route between these two major landmarks. The **Rialto to Frari Church Walk** leads you from the Rialto Bridge to the Frari Church's exquisite art, with interesting stops (Rialto Market, local pub, and a mask-making shop) en route. The **St. Mark's to San Zaccaria Walk** takes you behind the basilica to a historic church and a seldom-seen view of the famous Bridge of Sighs.

Day Trips covers nearby sights: Padua, Vicenza, Verona, and Ravenna.

Sleeping is a guide to our favorite budget hotels, conveniently located near St. Mark's Square, the Rialto Bridge, and the Accademia—all near the sights in this compact city.

Eating offers restaurants ranging from inexpensive eateries to splurges, with an emphasis on good value.

Venice with Children, Shopping, and **Nightlife** contain our best suggestions on those topics.

Transportation Connections covers connections by train and plane, laying the groundwork for your smooth arrival and departure.

Venetian History fills you in on the background of this fascinating city.

The **appendix** includes telephone tips, a climate chart, a list of festivals, and Italian survival phrases.

Throughout this book, when you see a ✪ in a listing, it

Tips for Tackling Our Self-Guided Tours

Soaking up the sights can be hard work. Our self-guided tours are designed to help make your visits to Venice's finest museums meaningful, fun, fast, and painless. To make the most of our tours, read the tour the night before your visit, and call ahead to make sure the hours and costs have not changed.

When you arrive at the sight, use the overview map to get the lay of the land and the basic tour route. Expect a few changes—paintings can be on tour, on loan, out sick, or shifted at the whim of the curator. Even museum walls are often moved. To adapt, pick up any available free floor plans as you enter, ask an information person to glance at this book's maps to confirm they're current, or if you can't find a particular painting, just ask any museum worker. Point to the photograph in this book and ask, "*Dov'è?*" ("Where?").

We cover the highlights. You might want to supplement with an audioguide, dry-but-useful recorded descriptions in English (about $5), or a guided tour (usually $6 or more). Tours in English are most likely to occur during peak season. The quality of a tour depends on the guide's knowledge, fluency, and enthusiasm.

Museums have their rules; if you're aware of them in advance, they're no big deal. Keep in mind that many sights have "last entry" times 30–60 minutes before closing. Guards usher people out before the official closing time. Cameras are normally allowed in museums, but no flashes or tripods (without special permission). A handheld camera with ASA-400 film and an F-2 aperture will take a fine picture (or buy slides at the museum bookstore). Video cameras are usually allowed. For security reasons, you're often required to check even small bags. Every museum has a free checkroom at the entrance. They're safe. Prepare to stash anything that you can't bear to part with in a purse or pocket.

At the museum bookshop, thumb through the biggest guidebook (or scan its index) to be sure you haven't overlooked something that is of particular interest to you. If there's an on-site cafeteria, it's usually a good place to rest and have a snack or light meal. Museum WCs are free and generally clean.

means that the sight is covered in much more detail in one of our tours—a page number will tell you just where to look to find more information.

Browse through this book and choose your favorite sights. Then have a great trip! You'll become your own guide with our tours. Traveling like a temporary local, you'll get the absolute most out of every mile, minute, and dollar. You won't waste time on mediocre sights because, unlike other guidebooks, this one covers only the best. Since your major financial pitfall is lousy, expensive hotels, we've worked hard to assemble the best accommodations values.

Trip Costs

Six components make up your trip costs: airfare, surface transportation, room and board, sightseeing/entertainment, shopping/miscellany, and gelato.

Airfare: Don't try to sort through the mess. Find and use a good travel agent. A basic, round-trip United States–Venice (or even cheaper, Milan) flight should cost $700–1,000, depending on where you fly from and when (cheapest in winter). Always consider saving time and money in Europe by flying "open jaw" (into one city and out of another).

Surface Transportation: Venice's sights are within walking distance of each other, but vaporetto boat rides are cheap (under $3) and fun time-savers. For a one-way trip between Venice's airport and the city, allow $2.50 by bus, $9 by speedboat, or $70 by water taxi (for details, see Transportation Connections, page 238).

The cost of round-trip, second-class train transportation to day trip destinations is affordable ($15 to Padua; about $40 to Vicenza; around $30 to Verona; and about $40 to Ravenna).

Room and Board: You can thrive in Venice on $80 a day per person for room and board. This allows $10 for lunch, $20 for dinner, and $50 for lodging (based on 2 people splitting the cost of a $100 double room that includes breakfast). If you've got more money, we've listed great ways to spend it. Students and tightwads can enjoy Venice for as little as $40 a day ($20 for a bed, $20 for meals and snacks). But budget sleeping and eating require the skills covered later in this chapter (and in greater detail in *Rick Steves' Europe Through the Back Door*).

Sightseeing and Entertainment: Figure about $6–9 per major sight (Accademia, Doge's Palace), $3–5 for smaller ones (museums, climbing church towers), and $20 or more for splurge experiences (e.g., tours, concerts). A gondola ride costs $55 (by day) or $80 (at night); split the cost—go with a pal. An overall average of $30 a day for Venice works for most. Don't skimp here.

After all, this category directly powers most of the experiences all the other expenses are designed to make possible.

Shopping and Miscellany: Figure $1 per postcard, coffee, and soft drink and $2 per gelato. Shopping can vary in cost from nearly nothing to a small fortune. Good budget travelers find that this category has little to do with assembling a trip full of lifelong and wonderful memories.

Exchange Rate

We've priced things throughout this book in the euro currency.

> 1 euro (€) = about $1.

Just like the dollar, one euro is broken down into 100 cents. You'll find coins ranging from 1 cent to 2 euros, and bills ranging from 5 euros to 500 euros.

Prices, Times, and Discounts

The opening hours and telephone numbers listed in this book are accurate as of mid-2002—but once you pin Venice down, it jiggles. Always get the latest listing of sights (including hours and entry fees) at a local tourist information office. Any guidebook to Italy starts to yellow even before it's printed. Because of that, prices in this book are approximate.

In Venice—and in this book—you'll use the 24-hour clock. It's the same through 12:00 noon, then keep going—13:00, 14:00.... For anything over 12, subtract 12 and add p.m. (14:00 is 2:00 p.m.).

Discounts for sights are not listed in this book because they are generally limited to European residents and countries that offer reciprocal deals (the U.S. doesn't). Young people can get some price breaks in Venice by buying a "Rolling Venice" Youth Discount Pass (see page 24).

When to Go

Venice's best travel months (and busiest, most expensive months) are May, June, September, and October. Between November and April, you can expect mild winter weather, some flooding (particularly March and Nov), and generally none of the sweat and stress of the tourist season (except during the Carnevale festival—Feb 21–March 4 in 2003 and Feb 13–24 in 2004).

Venice's summers are more temperate than Italy's scorching inland cities. Venetian temperatures hit the high 70s and 80s in summer and drop to the 30s and 40s in winter. Spring and fall can be cool, and many hotels do not turn on their heat. Many

mid-range hotels come with air-conditioning (usually only oper-
ates June–Sept), worthwhile for people who wilt in summer heat.
(See climate chart in the appendix.)

Red Tape, Business Hours, and Banking

You need a passport but no visa or shots to travel in Italy.

Business Hours: Traditionally, Italy uses the siesta plan.
People work from about 8:00 to 13:00 and from 15:30 to 19:00,
Monday through Saturday. Many businesses have adopted the
government's new recommended 8:00 to 16:00 workday.
In tourist areas, shops are open longer. Shoppers interested in
pursuing VAT refunds (the tax refunded on large purchases
made by non-EU residents) can refer to page 232.

Banking: You'll want to spend local hard cash. The fastest way
to get it is by using plastic: your ATM, credit, or debit card at a cash
machine (Bancomat). Bring some traveler's checks only as a backup.

To get a cash advance from a bank machine, you'll need a
four-digit PIN (numbers only, no letters, 7-digit PIN won't work)
with your bank card. Before you go, verify with your bank that
your card will work.

Visa and MasterCard are more commonly accepted than
American Express. Bring two cards in case one is demagnetized,
eaten by a machine, or rejected by a temperamental cash machine.
(If your card is rejected, try again, and request a smaller amount;
some cash machines won't let you take out more than about €150—
don't take it personally.) Just like at home, credit or debit cards
work easily at larger hotels, restaurants, and shops, but smaller
businesses prefer payment in hard cash.

Regular banks have the best rates for cashing traveler's
checks. For a large exchange, it pays to compare rates and fees.
The Bank of Sicily (Banca di Sicilia) consistently has good rates
(there's one in Venice, a block off Campo San Bartolomeo in
the direction of St. Mark's Square). Banking hours are generally
from 8:30 to 13:30 and from 15:30 to 16:30 Monday through
Friday, but can vary wildly. Banks are slow; simple transactions
can take 15–30 minutes. Post offices and train stations usually
change money if you can't get to a bank.

Use a money belt (order online at www.ricksteves.com or
call 425/771-8303 for our free newsletter/catalog). Thieves target
tourists. A money belt provides peace of mind and allows you to
carry lots of cash safely.

Don't be petty about changing money. The greatest avoidable
money-changing expense is wasting time every few days to return
to a bank. Change a week's worth of money, get big bills, stuff
them in your money belt, and travel!

Travel Smart

Many people travel through Italy thinking it's a chaotic mess. They feel any attempt at efficient travel is futile. This is dead wrong—and expensive. Italy, which seems as orderly as spilled spaghetti, actually functions well. Only those who understand this and travel smart can enjoy Italy on a budget.

Buy a phone card and use it for reservations and double-checking hours of sights. (We've included phone numbers for this purpose.) Enjoy the friendliness of the local people. Ask questions. Most locals are eager to point you in their idea of the right direction. Pack along a pocket-size notebook to organize your thoughts. Those who expect to travel smart, do.

Museums and sights, especially large ones, usually stop admitting people 30–60 minutes before closing time (last entry for the Doge's Palace is 90 min before closing).

Sundays have the same pros and cons as they do for travelers in the United States: Sightseeing attractions are generally open, though some churches in Venice are closed in the morning to sightseers. Shops and banks are closed. City traffic is light. Rowdy evenings are rare on Sundays. Saturdays are virtually weekdays with earlier closing hours.

Hotels in Venice are usually booked up on Carnevale (Feb 21–March 4 in 2003), Easter (April 20 in 2003), April 25, May 1, in August, and on Fridays and Saturdays. Religious holidays and train strikes can catch you by surprise anywhere in Italy.

Really, this book can save you lots of time and money. But to have an "A" trip, you need to be an "A" student. Read it all before your trip; note the time-saving tips and the days when museums are closed. If you save St. Mark's Basilica for Sunday morning, you've missed the gondola. You can sweat in line at the Doge's Palace, or buy your Museum Card at the nearby Correr Museum and zip right though the Doge's Palace turnstile. Day-tripping to Verona or Vicenza on Monday, when most sights are closed, is bad news. A smart trip is a puzzle—a fun, doable, and worthwhile challenge.

Tourist Information

Venice has several tourist information offices (abbreviated TI in this book); for a list, see page 20.

Before your trip, contact the nearest Italian TI in the United States and briefly describe your trip and request information. You'll get the general packet and, if you ask for specifics (city map, calendar of festivals, etc.), an impressive amount of help. If you have a specific problem, they're a good source of sympathy.

Contact the office nearest you...

In New York: 630 Fifth Ave. #1565, New York, NY 10111,

brochure hotline 212/245–4822, 212/245–5618, fax 212/586–9249, e-mail: enitny@italiantourism.com.

In Illinois: 500 N. Michigan Ave. #2240, Chicago, IL 60611, brochure hotline 312/644–0990, 312/644–0996, fax 312/644–3019, e-mail: enitch@italiantourism.com.

In California: 12400 Wilshire Blvd. #550, Los Angeles, CA 90025, brochure hotline 310/820–0098, 310/820–1898, fax 310/820–6357, e-mail: enitla@earthlink.net.

Web sites on Venice: www.govenice.org (Venice tourist information), www.veniceforvisitors.com, www.meetingvenice.it, and www.aguestinvenice.com.

Web sites on Italy: www.italiantourism.com (Italian Tourist Board in the U.S.), www.museionline.it (museums in Italy, in English), and www.fs-on-line.com (train info and schedules).

Recommended Guidebooks

For most travelers, this book is all you need. The well-researched Access guide (which combines Venice and Florence) and the colorful Eyewitness guide (on Venice and the Veneto) are popular with travelers. Eyewitness is fun for its great, easy-to-grasp graphics and photos, and it's just right for people who want only factoids. But the Eyewitness books are relatively skimpy on content and they weigh a ton. (Their new "Top 10 Venice" book, heavy on top 10 lists, is lighter weight.) You can buy Access or Eyewitness guides in Venice (no more expensive than in the U.S.) or simply borrow them for a minute from other travelers at certain sights to make sure you're aware of that place's highlights. If you'll be traveling elsewhere in Italy, consider *Rick Steves' Italy 2003*.

In Venice, local guidebooks are cheap and give you a map and a decent commentary on the sights (sold at kiosks).

Rick Steves' Books and Videos

Rick Steves' Europe Through the Back Door 2003 gives you budget travel skills on minimizing jet lag, packing light, planning your itinerary, traveling by car or train, finding budget beds without reservations, changing money, avoiding rip-offs, outsmarting thieves, hurdling the language barrier, staying healthy, taking great photographs, using your bidet, and much more. The book also includes chapters on 35 of Rick's favorite "Back Doors," six of which are in Italy.

Rick Steves' Country Guides are a series of eight guidebooks that cover: Italy; Great Britain; Ireland; Spain/Portugal; France; Germany/Austria/Switzerland; Scandinavia; and the Best of Europe. All are updated annually and come out in December (*Best of Europe* in Jan).

Rick Steves' City Guides include this book, Florence, Rome, Paris, London, and—new for 2003—*Rick Steves' Amsterdam, Bruges & Brussels*. These handy, easy-to-pack guidebooks offer thorough coverage of Europe's greatest cities, complete with extensive self-guided tours through the greatest museums. They're updated annually and come out in December and January.

Rick Steves' Europe 101: History and Art for the Traveler (with Gene Openshaw, 2000), which gives you the story of Europe's people, history, and art, is heavy on Italy's ancient, Renaissance, and modern histories. Written for smart people who were sleeping in their history and art classes before they knew they were going to Europe, *101* helps resurrect the rubble.

Rick Steves' Mona Winks: Self-Guided Tours of Europe's Top Museums (with Gene Openshaw, 2001) gives you fun, easy-to-follow self-guided tours of Europe's 25 most exhausting, important museums and cultural sites. All of the *Mona Winks* chapters on Venice are included in this Venice guidebook. But if you'd like similar coverage for the great museums in Florence (Uffizi Gallery and Bargello), Rome (Forum, Colosseum, National Museum of Rome, St. Peter's Basilica, Vatican Museum, and the Borghese Gallery), Madrid, Paris, London, and Amsterdam, *Mona*'s for you.

In Italy, a phrase book is as fun as it is necessary. *Rick Steves' Italian Phrase Book* (1999) will help you meet the people and stretch your budget. It's written by a monoglot who, for 25 years, has fumbled through Italy struggling with all the other phrase books. Use this fun and practical communication aid to make accurate hotel reservations over the telephone, have the man in the deli make you a sandwich, and ask for a free taste of cantaloupe-flavored gelato at the *gelateria*.

Rick's public television series, *Rick Steves' Europe*, started airing a new season of 14 shows—with five on Italy, including one on Venice—in the fall of 2002. Between the new series and the earlier *Travels in Europe* series (more than 80 shows total), Rick has hosted and written 15 half-hour shows on Italy. These air throughout the United States on public television stations. Each episode is also available on an information-packed home video (order online at www.ricksteves.com or call us at 425/771-8303 for our free newsletter/catalog).

Rick Steves' Postcards from Europe (1999), an autobiographical book, packs 25 years of travel anecdotes and insights into the ultimate 2,000-mile European adventure. Through his guidebooks, Rick shares his favorite European discoveries with you. In *Postcards*, he introduces you to his favorite European friends. Half of the book is set in Italy: Venice, Florence, Rome, and the Cinque Terre.

All of Rick Steves' books are published by Avalon Travel Publishing (www.travelmatters.com).

Maps

The maps in this book, designed and drawn by Dave Hoerlein, are concise and simple. Dave is well-traveled in Venice and Italy and has designed the maps to help you orient quickly and get to where you want to go painlessly. In Venice, any TI or your hotel will have free maps (better maps are sold at newsstands). For a longer Italy trip, consider our new Rick Steves' Italy Planning Map. With sightseeing destinations listed prominently, it's designed for the traveler (get our free newsletter/catalog by calling 425/771-8303 or order online at www.ricksteves.com).

Tours of Venice and Italy

Travel agents will tell you about normal tours of Italy, but they won't tell you about ours. At Europe Through the Back Door, we offer one-week getaways to **Venice,** to **Florence,** and to **Rome** (departures Oct–April, 20 people maximum). Our 20-day **Best of Italy** tour, featuring all of the biggies and a few of our favorite "back doors" (April–Oct, 24 people), and our new 15-day **Village Italy** adventure, which laces together intimate towns (April, Sept, and Oct, 20 people), come with two great guides and a big, roomy bus. For more information, call 425/771-8303 or visit www.ricksteves.com.

Transportation

Your transportation concerns in Venice are limited to vaporetto boats, covered in the Orientation chapter. If you have a car, stow it at Tronchetto (in Venice) or Mestre (on the mainland). For arrival and departure information, see the Transportation Connections chapter. For specifics on traveling throughout Italy by train or car, see *Rick Steves' Italy 2003*.

Telephones, Mail, and E-mail

Smart travelers use the telephone every day to confirm hotel reservations, check opening hours, and phone home.

Phone Cards: There are two kinds of phone cards—official Italian phone cards that you insert into the phone instead of coins, and long-distance scratch-off PIN cards that can be used from virtually any phone (you dial a toll-free number and enter your PIN code).

Insertable Italian phone cards are sold in varying denomin-ations at tobacco shops, post offices, and machines near phone booths (many phone booths indicate where the nearest phone-card sales outlet is located). Rip off the perforated corner to "activate" the card before you insert it into the phone.

PIN cards, sold at small newsstand kiosks and hole-in-the-wall long-distance phone shops, are usually the least expensive way to call back to the United States (about 10 min/€1). Since you don't insert these cards into a phone, you can use them from most phones, including the one in your hotel room (if it's set on pulse, switch it to tone). Because there are so many brand names, just ask for an international telephone card (*carta telefonica prepagate internazionali*, pron. KAR-tah teh-leh-FOHN-ee-kah pray-pah-GAH-tay in-ter-naht-zee-oh-NAH-lee); specify that you want a card for making calls to America or Canada to avoid getting the PIN cards that are only good within particular regions in Italy.

The orange SIP public telephones are everywhere and take cards or coins. About a quarter of the phones are broken (which could explain why so many Italians carry cell phones). The rest of the phones work reluctantly. Dial slowly and deliberately, as if the phone doesn't understand numbers very well. Often a recorded message in Italian will break in, brusquely informing you that the phone number does not exist (*non-esistente*), even if you're dialing your own home phone number. Dial again with an increasing show of confidence, in an attempt to convince the phone of your number's existence. If you fail, try a different phone. Repeat as needed.

When spelling out your name on the phone, you'll find *a* (pronounced "ah" in Italian), *i* (pronounced "ee"), and *e* (pronounced "ay") are confusing to Americans. Say "*a*, Aosta," "*e*, Empoli," and "*i*, Italia" to clear up that problem. If you plan to access your voice mail from Italy, be advised that you can't always dial extensions or secret codes once you connect (you're on vacation—relax).

Dialing within Italy: Italy has a direct-dial phone system (no area codes). To call anywhere within Italy, just dial the number. For example, the number of one of our recommended Venice hotels is 041-522-7131. To call it from the Venice train station, dial 041-522-7131. If you call it from Rome, it's the same: 041-522-7131.

Italian phone numbers vary in length; a hotel can have, say, a 10-digit phone number and an 11-digit fax number.

Italy's toll-free numbers start with 800 (like U.S. 800 numbers, though in Italy you don't dial a "1" first). In Italy, you can dial these 800 numbers—called *freephone* or *numero verde* (green number)—free from any phone without using a phone card or coins.

Dialing International Calls: When calling internationally, dial the international access code (00 if you're calling from Europe, 011 from the U.S. or Canada), the country code of the country

you're calling (39 for Italy; see appendix for list of other countries), and the local number. To call the Venice hotel from the
United States, dial 011 (the U.S. international access code), 39
(Italy's country code), then 041-522-7131. To call the ETBD
office from Italy, we dial 00 (Europe's international access code),
1 (the U.S. country code), 425 (Edmonds' area code), and 771-
8303. European time is six/nine hours ahead of the East/West
Coasts of the United States.

Hotel-room phones are reasonable for calls within Italy (the
faint beeps stand for €0.10 phone units) but a terrible rip-off for
calls to the United States (unless you use a PIN card or your hotel
allows toll-free access to your calling card service—see below).

Calling Card Services: While still convenient, these services,
such as AT&T, MCI, and Sprint, are no longer a good value. It's
much cheaper to call the United States using a PIN card or Italian
phone card, but some people prefer to use their easier, pricier
calling cards. Each card company has a toll-free number in each
European country (for Italy: AT&T—tel. 172-1011, MCI—tel.
172-1022, Sprint—tel. 172-1877), which puts you in touch with an
English-speaking operator. The operator takes your card number
and the number you want to call, puts you through, and bills your
home phone number for the call. Oddly, you need to use a small-
value coin or Italian phone card to dial the toll-free number. The
cheapest of the lot, MCI charges about $2.50 per minute with no
surcharges. Sprint and AT&T charge about the same per minute,
but tack on hefty surcharges and fees (if you get an answering
machine, it can cost you $7–8 to say, "Hi, sorry I missed you.").
For less than 25 cents, call first with a coin or European phone
card to see if the answering machine is off or if the right person's
at home. It's outrageously expensive to use a calling card to make
calls between European countries; it's far cheaper to simply call
direct using a phone card purchased in Italy.

Cell Phones: Affluent travelers like to buy cell phones
(about $70 on up) in Europe to use for making local and interna-
tional calls. The cheaper phones generally work only if you're
making calls from the country where you purchased it (e.g., a
phone bought in Italy won't work in France). Pricier phones
allow you to call from any country, but it'll cost you about $40
per country to outfit the phone with the necessary chip and pre-
paid phone time. If you're interested, stop by any European shop
that sells cell phones (you'll see an array of phones prominently
displayed in the store window). Depending on your trip and
budget, ask for a phone that works only in that country or one
that can be used throughout Europe. And if you're really on a
budget, skip cell phones and use PIN cards instead.

Mail: Mail service is miserable throughout Italy. Postcards get last priority. If you must have mail stops, consider a few pre-reserved hotels along your route or use American Express offices. Most American Express offices in Italy will hold mail for one month. This service is free to anyone using an AmEx card (and available for a small fee to others). Allow 14 days for U.S.-to-Italy mail delivery, but don't count on it. Federal Express makes pricey two-day deliveries. Phoning is so easy that we've completely dispensed with mail stops. If possible, mail nothing precious from Italy.

E-mail: E-mail use among Italian hoteliers is increasing. We've listed e-mail addresses when possible. Drab little cyber-cafés are popular in big cities like Venice.

Tipping

Tipping in Italy isn't as automatic and generous as it is in the United States, but for special service, tips are appreciated, if not expected. As in the United States, the proper amount depends on your resources, tipping philosophy, and the circumstance, but some general guidelines apply.

Restaurants: Check the menu to see if the service is included (*servizio incluso*—generally 15 percent); if not, a tip of 5–10 percent is typical (for details, see page 214).

Taxis: To tip the cabbie, round up. For a typical ride, round up to the next euro on the fare (to pay a €13 fare, give €14); for a long ride, to the nearest 10 (for a €75 fare, give €80). If the cabbie hauls your bags and zips you to the airport to help you catch your flight, you might want to toss in a little more. But if you feel like you're being driven in circles or otherwise ripped off, skip the tip.

Special Services: It's thoughtful to tip a couple of euros to someone who shows you a special sight and who is paid in no other way (such as the man who shows you an Etruscan tomb in his backyard). Tour guides at public sites sometimes hold out their hands for tips after they give their spiel; if I've already paid for the tour, I don't tip extra, though some tourists do give a euro or two, particularly for a job well done. I don't tip at hotels, but if you do, give the porter a euro for carrying bags and leave a couple of euros in your room at the end of your stay for the maid if the room was kept clean. In general, if someone in the service industry does a super job for you, a tip of a couple of euros is appropriate . . . but not required.

When in doubt, ask. If you're not sure whether (or how much) to tip for a service, ask your hotelier or the TI; they'll fill you in on how it's done on their turf.

Culture Shock—Accepting Italy as a Package Deal

We travel all the way to Italy to enjoy differences—to become temporary locals. You'll experience frustrations. Certain truths that we find "God-given" or "self-evident," such as cold beer, ice in drinks, bottomless cups of coffee, hot showers, body odor smelling bad, and bigger being better, are suddenly not so true. One of the benefits of travel is the eye-opening realization that there are logical, civil, and even better alternatives. A willingness to go local ensures that you'll enjoy a full dose of Italian hospitality.

If there is a negative aspect to the image Italians have of Americans, it is that we are big, loud, aggressive, impolite, rich, and a bit naive. While Italians, flabbergasted by our Yankee excesses, say in disbelief, "*Mi sono cadute le braccia!*" ("I throw my arms down!"), they nearly always afford us individual travelers all the warmth we deserve.

Send Us a Postcard, Drop Us a Line

If you enjoy a successful trip with the help of this book and would like to share your discoveries, please fill out and send the survey at the end of this book to Europe Through the Back Door, Box 2009, Edmonds, WA 98020. We personally read and value all feedback. Thanks in advance—it helps a lot.

For our latest travel information on Italy, tap into our Web site at www.ricksteves.com. To check on any updates for this book, go to www.ricksteves.com/update. Rick's e-mail address is rick@ricksteves.com. Anyone is welcome to request a free issue of our Back Door quarterly newsletter.

Judging from all the happy postcards we receive from travelers who have used this book, it's safe to assume you'll enjoy a great, affordable vacation—with the finesse of an independent, experienced traveler.

From this point, "we" (your coauthors) will drop our respective egos and become "I."

Thanks, and *buon viaggio!*

BACK DOOR TRAVEL PHILOSOPHY
From *Rick Steves' Europe Through the Back Door*

Travel is intensified living—maximum thrills per minute and one of the last great sources of legal adventure. Travel is freedom. It's recess, and we need it.

Experiencing the real Europe requires catching it by surprise, going casual . . . "Through the Back Door."

Affording travel is a matter of priorities. (Make do with the old car.) You can travel—simply, safely, and comfortably—anywhere in Europe for $80 a day plus transportation costs. In many ways, spending more money only builds a thicker wall between you and what you came to see. Europe is a cultural carnival and, time after time, you'll find that its best acts are free and the best seats are the cheap ones.

A tight budget forces you to travel close to the ground, meeting and communicating with the people, not relying on service with a purchased smile. Never sacrifice sleep, nutrition, safety, or cleanliness in the name of budget. Simply enjoy the local-style alternatives to expensive hotels and restaurants.

Extroverts have more fun. If your trip is low on magic moments, kick yourself and make things happen. If you don't enjoy a place, maybe you don't know enough about it. Seek the truth. Recognize tourist traps. Give a culture the benefit of your open mind. See things as different but not better or worse. Any culture has much to share.

Of course, travel, like the world, is a series of hills and valleys. Be fanatically positive and militantly optimistic. If something's not to your liking, change your liking. Travel is addictive. It can make you a happier American, as well as a citizen of the world. Our Earth is home to six billion equally important people. It's humbling to travel and find that people don't envy Americans. They like us, but, with all due respect, they wouldn't trade passports.

Globetrotting destroys ethnocentricity. It helps you understand and appreciate different cultures. Travel changes people. It broadens perspectives and teaches new ways to measure quality of life. Many travelers toss aside their hometown blinders. Their prized souvenirs are the strands of different cultures they decide to knit into their own character. The world is a cultural yarn shop. And Back Door travelers are weaving the ultimate tapestry. Come on, join in!

ORIENTATION

The island city of Venice is shaped like a fish. Its major thorough-fares are canals. The Grand Canal winds through the middle of the fish, starting at the mouth where all the people and food enter, passing under the Rialto Bridge, and ending at St. Mark's Square (Piazza San Marco). Park your 21st-century perspective at the mouth and let Venice swallow you whole.

Venice is a car-less kaleidoscope of people, bridges, and odor-less canals. The city has no real streets, and addresses are hope-lessly confusing. There are six districts (see map on page 17): San Marco (most touristy), Castello (behind San Marco), Cannaregio (from the train station to the Rialto), San Polo (other side of the Rialto), Santa Croce, and Dorsoduro. Each district has about 6,000 address numbers. Luckily it's easy to find your way, since many street corners have a sign pointing you to (*per*) the nearest major landmark, such as San Marco, Accademia, Rialto, and Ferrovia (train station). To find your way, navigate by landmarks, not streets. Obedient visitors stick to the main thoroughfares as directed by these signs and miss the charm of backstreet Venice.

Planning Your Time

Venice is remarkably small. Nearly all your sightseeing is within a 20-minute walk of the Rialto Bridge or St. Mark's Square. Two key considerations: Maximize your evening magic and avoid the midday crowds around St. Mark's Basilica and the Doge's Palace (for tips on crowd control, see the Daily Reminder on page 18). Venice itself is its greatest sight. Make time to wander, explore, shop, and simply be.

Venice in One (Busy) Day

9:00   Walk from St. Mark's Square to Frari Church (following
       2 of my self-guided walks: St. Mark's to Rialto, and

Venice's Districts

Rialto to Frari Church), making time to enjoy the Rialto market action.

11:00   Tour Frari Church.

12:00   Lunch near the Frari, then catch the vaporetto (boat) back to St. Mark's to wander and shop.

14:30   Correr Museum (both the Museum Card—and the pricier Museum Pass—include the Doge's Palace, too).

15:30   St. Mark's Basilica.

16:30   Doge's Palace.

18:00   Go up the Campanile bell tower for city view (long lines at midday, should be O.K. by now).

18:30   Pub dinner (crawl or stay put and munch).

20:00   Gondola ride.

21:00   Enjoy the dueling orchestras with a drink on St. Mark's Square.

Venice in Two Days

Day 1

9:00   Walk from St. Mark's Square to Frari Church (connecting my self-guided walks: St. Mark's to Rialto, and Rialto to Frari Church), stopping at the Rialto market to browse.

11:00   Tour Frari Church.

12:00   Tour Ca' Rezzonico (Museum of 18th-Century Venice) or Scuola San Rocco (if you prefer Tintoretto to Casanova).

13:00   Lunch in Dorsoduro neighborhood, then take the vaporetto back to St. Mark's Square to wander and shop.

Daily Reminder

Sunday: The Church of San Giorgio Maggiore (on island near St. Mark's Square) hosts a Gregorian Mass at 11:00. The Rialto market consists mainly of souvenir stalls today (fish and produce sections closed). These sights are open only in the afternoon: Frari Church (13:00–18:00, closed Sun in Aug) and St. Mark's Basilica (14:00–17:00). It's a bad day for a pub crawl, as most pubs are closed.

Monday: All sights are open except for the Rialto fish market, Dalmatian School, Palazzo Mocenigo (textiles), and Torcello Museum (on Torcello island). The Accademia and Ca d'Oro (House of Gold) close early in the afternoon (14:00). Don't side-trip to Verona or Vicenza today; most sights are closed.

Tuesday: All sights are open except the Peggy Guggenheim Museum, Ca' Rezzonico (Museum of 18th-Century Venice), and the Lace Museum (on Burano island).

Wednesday: All sights are open except the Glass Museum (on Murano island).

Thursday/Friday: All sights are open.

Saturday: All sights are open (Peggy Guggenheim Museum until 22:00 April–Oct) except the Jewish Museum.

Notes: The Accademia is open earlier (daily at 8:15) and closes later (19:15 Tue–Sun) than most sights in Venice. Some sights close earlier off-season (e.g., Doge's Palace; Correr Museum; the Campanile; and St. Mark's Museum, Treasury, and Golden Altarpiece).

Churches: Modest dress is recommended at churches and required at St. Mark's Basilica—no bare shoulders, shorts, or short skirts. Some churches are closed to sightseers on Sunday morning (e.g., St. Mark's Basilica and Frari Church) and many are closed from roughly 12:00 to 15:00 Monday through Saturday (e.g., La Salute and San Giorgio Maggiore).

Crowd Control: Crowds can be a serious problem only at the Accademia (to minimize crowds, go early or late); St. Mark's Basilica (consider reserving online at www.alata.it); Campanile bell tower (go late—it's open until 21:00 in the summer); and the Doge's Palace. For the Doge's Palace, you have three options for avoiding the ticket-sales line: Buy your Museum Card or Museum Pass at the Correr Museum (then step right up to the Doge's Palace turnstile, skipping the long line); visit the Doge's Palace at 17:00 (if it's April–Oct) when lines disappear; or book a "Secret Itineraries" tour (see page 64).

15:00	Correr Museum (both the Museum Card and Museum Pass cover Doge's Palace).
16:00	St. Mark's Basilica.
17:00	Doge's Palace.
19:00	Go up the Campanile bell tower for city view (long lines midday, should be O.K. by now).
20:00	Dinner.
22:00	Enjoy the dueling orchestras with a drink on St. Mark's Square.

Day 2

9:00	Shopping or exploring.
11:00	Cruise Grand Canal.
13:00	Lunch (pizza near Accademia Bridge?).
14:00	Tour Accademia, explore Dorsoduro neighborhood, visit La Salute Church or Peggy Guggenheim Museum.
17:00	Commence pub crawl, eating dinner along the way.
20:00	Gondola ride.

Venice in Three (or Four) Days

Day 1

9:30	St. Mark's Basilica and Square.
11:00	Correr Museum (Museum Card and Museum Pass include Doge's Palace).
12:00	Shop, wander, and have lunch in St. Mark's area.
16:00	Doge's Palace.
18:00	Ascend Campanile bell tower.
19:00	Gondola ride.
20:00	Dinner.

Day 2

9:00   Walk from St. Mark's Square to Frari Church (connect
        my self-guided walks: St. Mark's to Rialto and Rialto
        to Frari Church), allowing time to experience the
        Rialto market scene.
11:00 Tour Frari Church.
12:00 Tour Scuola San Rocco for Tintoretto.
13:00 Lunch.
14:00 Tour Ca' Rezzonico (Museum of 18th-Century Venice).
15:00 Explore Dorsoduro, the neighborhood around the
        Accademia.
17:00 Tour Accademia.
18:00 Cruise Grand Canal in vaporetto.

Day 3

9:00   Explore lagoon by vaporetto or tour boat, visiting
        Burano and Torcello. Art-lovers may prefer
        touring the Venice Biennale International Art
        Exhibition (March–Nov, see page 257).
15:00 Take San Zaccaria Walk and catch a vaporetto to visit
        San Giorgio Maggiore.
17:00 Commence pub crawl.
21:00 Savor a drink with the dueling orchestras on
        St. Mark's Square.

Day 4

Side-trip to Padua and/or Verona.

Arrival in Venice

For a rundown on Venice's train station and airport, see Transportation Connections, page 238.

Tourist Information

There are TIs at the train station (daily 8:00–20:00, crowded and
surly); at St. Mark's Square (Mon–Sat 9:45–15:15; with your back
to St. Mark's, it's in far left corner of square); and near St. Mark's
Square vaporetto boat stop on the lagoon (daily 9:00–18:00, sells
vaporetto tickets, rents audioguides at €3.65/hr for self-guided
walking tours). Smaller offices are at Tronchetto, Piazzale Roma,
and the airport. For a quick question, save time by phoning 041-
529-8711. Web sites on Venice: www.govenice.org (official TI
site), www.veniceforvisitors.com, and www.meetingvenice.it.

   At any TI, pick up a free city map and the free *Leo* bimonthly
magazine, which comes with an insert, *Leo Bussola*, listing museum
hours, exhibitions, and musical events (in Italian and English).

Confirm your sightseeing plans. Ask for the fine brochures outlining three offbeat Venice walks. The free periodical entertainment guide *Un Ospite di Venezia* (a monthly listing of events, nightlife, museum hours, train and vaporetto schedules, emergency telephone numbers, and so on) is available at the TI or fancy hotel reception desks (www.aguestinvenice.com).

Maps: The €3.10 Venice map on sale at postcard racks has much more detail than the TI's free map, but the "Illustrated Venice Map" by Magnetic North is by far the best ever (€6.20, listing nearly every shop, hotel, and restaurant). Also consider the little guidebook (sold alongside the postcards), which comes with a city map and explanations of the major sights.

Helpful Hints

Venice is expensive for locals as well as tourists. The demand is huge, supply is limited, and running a business is costly. Things just cost more here; everything must be shipped in and hand-trucked to its destination. Perhaps the best way to enjoy Venice is to just succumb to its charms and blow a lot of money.

Get Lost: Accept the fact that Venice was a tourist town 400 years ago. It was, is, and always will be crowded. While 80 percent of Venice is, in fact, not touristy, 80 percent of the tourists never notice. Hit the backstreets.

Venice is the ideal town to explore on foot. Walk and walk to the far reaches of the town. Don't worry about getting lost. Get as lost as possible. Keep reminding yourself, "I'm on an island, and I can't get off." When it comes time to find your way, just follow the directional arrows on building corners or simply ask a local, "*Dov'è San Marco?*" ("Where is St. Mark's?") People in the tourist business (that's most Venetians) speak some English. If they don't, listen politely, watching where their hands point, say "*Grazie*," and head off in that direction. If you're lost, pop into a hotel and ask for their business card—it comes with a map and a prominent "you are here."

Take Breaks: Grab a cool place to sit down, relax, and recoup from sightseeing—meditate in a pew in an uncrowded church or buy a cappuccino and a fruit cup in a café.

Etiquette: Walk on the right and don't loiter on bridges. Picnicking is technically forbidden (keep a low profile). Dress modestly. Men should keep their shirts on. When visiting St. Mark's Basilica or other major churches, men, women, and even children should cover their knees and shoulders (or risk being turned away).

Water: Venetians pride themselves on having pure, safe, and tasty tap water piped in from the foothills of the Alps; you can actually see the mountains from Venice bell towers on crisp, clear winter days.

Pigeon Poop: If bombed by a pigeon, resist the initial response to wipe it off immediately—it'll just smear into your hair. Wait until it dries and flake it off cleanly.

Passes for Venice

To help control (and confuse?) its flood of visitors, Venice now offers cards and passes that cover some museums and/or transportation. For most visitors, the simple Museum Card (for the Doge's Palace and Correr Museum) or Museum Pass will do.

Note that none of these cards or passes cover some of Venice's important attractions—the sights within St. Mark's Basilica, the Campanile, Accademia, Peggy Guggenheim Museum, Scuola Grande di San Rocco, and the Frari Church.

Museum Cards and Museum Pass: The main **Museum Card** covers the museums of St. Mark's Square: Doge's Palace, Correr Museum, and two museums accessed from within the Correr—the National Archaeological Museum and the Monumental Rooms of Marciana National Library (€9.50, called "*Museum Card per i Musei di Piazza San Marco*," valid for 3 months; purchase it at the Correr Museum, then use your card at the Doge's Palace to bypass the long line).

The pricier **Museum Pass** includes the St. Mark's Square museums listed above, plus Ca' Rezzonico (Museum of 18th-Century Venice), Mocenigo Palace museum (textiles and costumes), Casa Goldoni (home of the Italian playwright), and museums on the islands—Murano's Glass Museum and Burano's Lace Museum (€15.50, valid for 3 months).

Venice also (pointlessly) offers a couple of other Museum Cards: €8 for the museums of the 18th-century (called "*Museum Card per area del Settecento*"; the museums are Ca' Rezzonico, Casa Goldoni, and Palazzo Mocenigo) and €6 for the island museums (called "*Museum Card per i musei delle isole*," covering Murano's Glass Museum and Burano's Lace Museum).

Are the Museum Cards and Passes worth it? If you want to see just the Correr Museum and Doge's Palace, get the Museum Card that covers these sights. If you want to add Ca' Rezzonico (€6.70 entry), you'll save money by getting the Museum Pass. With a Museum Card or Pass (sold at participating museums), you'll breeze past any lines.

Venice Cards: Personally, I'd skip these, but here's the information. These cards include Venice's public transportation, the few public toilets, and, if you get the "orange" version, some sights.

The **Blue Venice Card** covers all your vaporetto and *traghetto* (gondola crossing of Grand Canal, normally €0.40) rides—plus entry to public toilets: 1 day–€11, 3 days–€23,

7 days–€41; cheaper for "Juniors" under 30. (If all you want is a vaporetto pass, you can get a 24-hour pass for €9.30 at any vaporetto dock; described under Getting Around Venice, below.)

The **Orange Venice Card**, which also includes transportation and toilets, gets you into the museums covered by the Museum Pass. It's like getting a Blue Venice Card and a Museum Pass for 1 day–€26, 3 days–€43, and 7 days–€58; cheaper for "Juniors" under 30.

Hefty supplements—which vary depending on which card and how many days you get—cover transportation to and from Marco Polo Airport and parking at San Giuliano car park with transportation to the city center.

Venice only issues 30,000 cards a day. You must reserve your card at least 48 hours in advance by going online (see www .venicecard.it for details) or calling tel. 011-30-041-271-4747 from the U.S. or tel. 899-909-090 within Italy. Pay for the card when you pick it up at one of many offices around Venice.

Note that you don't need a Venice Card of any color to enter the city. A Museum Card or Museum Pass makes the most sense for most travelers.

Services

Money: ATMs are plentiful and the easiest way to go. Bank rates vary. I like the Banca di Sicilia, a block toward St. Mark's Square from Campo San Bartolomeo. The American Express change desk is just off St. Mark's Square (see "Travel Agencies," below). Non-bank exchange bureaus, such as Exacto, will cost you $10 more than a bank for a $200 exchange. A 24-hour cash machine near the Rialto vaporetto stop exchanges U.S. dollars and other currencies at fair rates (when it's not out of order).

Travel Agencies: If you need to get train tickets, pay supplements, or make reservations, avoid the time-consuming trip to the crowded station by using a downtown travel agency.

Kele & Teo Viaggi e Turismo is good and handy (CC for train tickets only, Mon–Fri 8:30–19:00, Sat 9:00–19:00, Sat afternoon and Sun no train tickets available, at Ponte dei Bareteri on the Mercerie midway between Rialto and St. Mark's Square, tel. 041-520-8722, e-mail: incoming@keleteo.com).

American Express books flights, sells train tickets, and makes train reservations (travel agency: Mon–Fri 9:00–17:30, closed Sat–Sun; change desk: Mon–Sat 7:00–19:30, closed Sun; about 2 blocks off St. Mark's Square at 1471, en route to Accademia, tel. 041-520-0844).

Rip-offs, Theft, and Help: While pickpockets work the crowded main streets, docks, and vaporetti (wear your money belt and carry your daybag in front), the dark, late-night streets of Venice are safe. A service called Venezia No Problem tries to help tourists who've been mistreated by any Venetian business (toll-free tel. 800-355-920, for complaints only, not for information).

"Rolling Venice" Youth Discount Pass: This worthwhile €2.60 pass gives those under 30 discounts on sights and transportation, plus information on cheap eating and sleeping. In summer, they may have a kiosk in front of the train station (July–Sept daily 8:00–20:00). Their main office, near St. Mark's Square, is open year-round (Mon–Fri 9:00–14:00, closed Sat–Sun, from American Express head toward St. Mark's Square, first left, first left again through "Contarina" tunnel, follow white sign to Commune di Venezia and see the sign, Corte Contarina 1529, 3rd floor, tel. 041-274-7651).

Church Services: The **San Zulian Church** (the only church in Venice that you can actually walk around) offers a Mass in English at 9:30 on Sunday (May–Sept, 2 blocks toward Rialto off St. Mark's Square). Gregorians would enjoy the sung Gregorian Mass on Sundays at 11:00 (plus Mon–Sat at 8:00) at **San Giorgio Maggiore Church** (on island of San Giorgio Maggiore, visible from Doge's Palace, catch vaporetto #82 from "San Marco M.V.E." stop, located 200 meters east of St. Mark's Square, at third bridge along waterfront; see page 148). Call 041-522-7827 to confirm times.

Laundry: There is a self-service launderette (open daily) and two full-service laundries (both closed Sat–Sun).

The modern, cheap **Bea Vita** self-serve *lavanderia* is across the canal from the train station (daily 8:00–22:00, from station go over bridge, take first right, first left, first right).

At either of the following full-service laundries, you can get a nine-pound load washed and dried for €16—confirm price carefully. Drop it off in the morning and pick it up that afternoon. (Call to be sure they're open.) Don't expect to get your clothes back ironed, folded, or even entirely dry. **Lavanderia Gabriella** is near St. Mark's Square (Mon–Fri 8:00–19:00, closed Sat–Sun, 985 Rio Terra Colonne, from San Zulian Church go over Ponte dei Ferali, then take first right down Calle dei Armeni, tel. 041-522-1758). **Lavanderia S.S. Apostoli** is near the Rialto Bridge on the St. Mark's side (Mon–Fri 8:30–12:00 & 15:30–19:00, closed Sat–Sun, just off Campo S.S. Apostoli on Salizada del Pistor, tel. 041-522-6650).

Post Office: A large post office is off the far end of St. Mark's Square (on the side of square opposite St. Mark's Basilica, Mon–Sat 8:10–18:00, closed Sun, shorter hours off-season), and a branch is near the Rialto Bridge (on St. Mark's side, Mon–Fri 8:10–13:30, Sat 8:10–12:30, closed Sun).

Haircuts: I've been getting my hair cut at Coiffeur Benito for

15 years. Benito has been keeping local men and women trim for 25 years. He's an artist—actually a "hair sculptor"—and a cut here is a fun diversion from the tourist grind (€19.50 for women, €16.50 for men, Tue–Sat 8:30–13:30 & 15:30–19:30, closed Sun–Mon, behind San Zulian Church near St. Mark's Square, Calle S. Zulian Gia del Strazzanol 592A, tel. 041-528-6221).

Getting around Venice

By Vaporetto: The public transit system is a fleet of motorized bus-boats called vaporetti. They work like city buses except that they never get a flat, the stops are docks, and if you get off between stops, you may drown. For most, only two lines matter: #1 is the slow boat, taking 45 minutes to make every stop along the entire length of the Grand Canal; #82 is the fast boat that zips down the Grand Canal in 25 minutes, stopping mainly at Tronchetto (car park), Piazzale Roma (bus station), Ferrovia (train station), Rialto Bridge, San Tomá (Frari Church), the Accademia Bridge, and St. Mark's Square. Some #82 boats go only as far as Rialto—confirm with the conductor before boarding. Buy a €3.10 ticket ideally before boarding (at the booth at the dock) or from a conductor on board (before you sit down or you risk being fined). Families of three or more pay €2.60 per person. A round-trip (*andata e ritorno*) costs €5.20 (good for 2 trips within a day on any line).

A 24-hour pass (€9.30, cheaper for families) pays for itself in three trips. The cheaper "Itinerary Ticket" covers only stops on the Grand Canal and Murano, Burano, and Torcello (€7.75, valid for 12 hours). Also consider the 72-hour (€18.10) and one-week (€31) passes. It's fun to be able to hop on and off spontaneously. Technically, luggage costs the same as dogs—€3.10—but I've never been charged. Riding free? There's a 1-in-10 chance a conductor will fine you €20.

For vaporetto fun, take the Grand Canal Cruise (see page 37); avoid rush hour, when boats are packed heading to St. Mark's Square early in the day and packed heading to the train station late in the day. If you like joyriding on vaporetti, ride a boat around the city and out into the lagoon and back. Ask for the circular route—*circulare*, pronounced "cheer-koo-LAH-ray." It's usually the #51 or #52, leaving from the San Zaccaria vaporetto stop (near the Doge's Palace) and from all the stops along the perimeter of Venice.

By *Traghetto*: Only three bridges cross the Grand Canal, but *traghetti* (gondolas) shuttle locals and in-the-know tourists across the Grand Canal at several handy locations (see map on page 38; routes also marked on pricier maps sold in Venice). Take advantage of these time-savers. They can also save money. For instance, while most tourists take the €3.10 vaporetto to connect St. Mark's with

La Salute Church, a €0.40 *traghetto* does the job (free with Venice Blue or Orange Card). Most people stand while riding. *Traghetti* generally run from 6:00 until 20:00, sometimes until 23:00.

By Water Taxi: Venetian taxis, like speedboat limos, hang out at most busy points along the Grand Canal. Prices, which average €30 to €40 (about €75 to the airport), are a bit soft. Negotiate and settle before stepping in. For travelers with lots of luggage or small groups, taxi rides can be a worthwhile and time-saving convenience—and extremely scenic to boot.

Walking Tours of Venice

Audioguide Tours—The TI at the lagoon (near St. Mark's Square) rents audioguides for self-guided walking tours of Venice (2 hrs-€5, 24 hrs-€10, just punch the number of what you'd like described—exteriors only).

American Express Tours—AmEx runs a couple of basic multi-lingual tours daily (€24, 2 hrs, depart from AmEx office, about 2 blocks off St. Mark's Square in direction of Accademia, 9:00 tour visits St. Mark's Square and the Doge's Palace, 15:00 tour goes to the Frari Church and includes a gondola ride, tours some-times rushed and shallow, tel. 041-520-0844).

Classic Venice Bars Tour—Debonair local guide Alessandro Schezzini is a connoisseur of Venetian *bacaros*—classic old bars serving traditional *cicchetti* (local munchies). He offers evening tours that involve stopping and sampling a snack and a glass of wine at three of these. The fee (about €30 per person) includes wine, *cicchetti*, and a great insight into this local tradition (6–8 per group, tours don't depart without a minimum of 6 people so call a couple of days ahead to arrange and he'll match up smaller parties to form group, tel. & fax 041-534-5367, cellular 33-5530-9024, e-mail: venische@tiscalinet.it).

Venicescapes—Michael Broderick's private theme tours of Venice are intellectually demanding and beyond the attention span of most mortal tourists, but for the curious with stamina, he's enthralling. Michael's challenge: to help visitors gain a more solid understanding of Venice. For a description of all six of his itiner-aries, see www.venicescapes.org (book well in advance, 4–6-hr tour: €275 for 2, €50 per person after that, plus admissions and transportation, tel. 041-520-6361, e-mail: info@venicescapes.org).

Local Guides—Alessandro Schezzini gets beyond the clichés and into offbeat Venice (€90, 2.5 hrs, listed above in "Classic Venice Bars Tour"). Elisabetta Morelli is a good, licensed guide who can also provide tours in museums (€130, 2 hrs, tel. 041-526-7816, cellular 328-753-5220, e-mail: bettamorelli@inwind.it).

SIGHTS

Venice's greatest sight is the city itself. As well as seeing world-class museums and buildings, make time to wander narrow lanes, linger over a meal, or enjoy evening magic on St. Mark's Square.

In this chapter, Venice's most important sights have the shortest listings and are marked with a ⭐ (and page number). These sights are covered in much more detail in one of the tours included in this book.

Some of Venice's sights are covered by a €9.50 Museum Card; more are covered by the €15.50 Museum Pass. For details, see page 22.

One of Venice's most delightful sights—a gondola ride, worth ▲▲▲—is covered under Nightlife (see page 233).

San Marco District

▲▲▲**St. Mark's Square (Piazza San Marco)**—This grand square is surrounded by splashy, historic buildings and sights (described separately below)—St. Mark's Basilica, the Doge's Palace, Campanile bell tower, and Correr Museum. The square is filled with music, lovers, pigeons, and tourists by day and is your private rendezvous with the Middle Ages late at night. Europe's greatest dance floor is the romantic place to be.

For a slow and pricey evening thrill, invest €6.20 (plus €4 if the orchestra plays) in a beer or coffee at one of the elegant cafés with the dueling orchestras (see Caffè Florian, page 235). For the best people-watching and an unmatched experience, it's worth the small splurge. If all you have is €1, buy a bag of pigeon seed and become popular in a flurry. To get everything airborne, toss your sweater in the air.

The clock tower, a Renaissance tower built in 1496, marks the entry to the main shopping drag, called the Mercerie, which

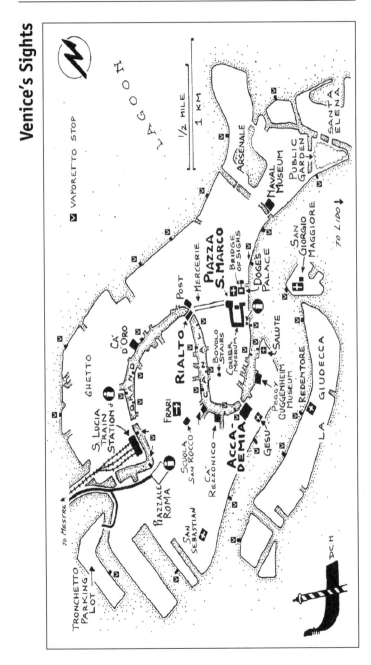

Venice's Sights

connects St. Mark's Square with the Rialto. From the piazza, you can see the bronze men (Moors) swing their huge clappers at the top of each hour. In the 17th century, one of them knocked an unsuspecting worker off the top and to his death—probably the first-ever killing by a robot. Notice the world's first "digital" clock on the tower facing the square (with dramatic flips every 5 min).

Venice's best TIs (and WCs) are on or near St. Mark's Square. One TI is on the square, the other on the lagoon. To find the TI on the square, stand with your back to the church and go to the far corner on your left; the office is tucked away in the arcade (daily 9:00–17:00); near this TI is a €0.50 WC open daily 8:00–21:00—it's a few steps beyond St. Mark's Square en route to the AmEx office and the Accademia; see *Albergo Diorno* sign marked on pavement). The other TI is on the lagoon (daily 9:00–18:00, walk toward the water by the Doge's Palace, go right; nearby WCs open daily 9:00–19:00). ✪ See St. Mark's Square Tour, page 45.

▲▲▲St. Mark's Basilica—Since about A.D. 830, the Basilica has housed the saint's bones. The church, built in Eastern style to underline Venice's connection with Byzantium (and thus protecting it from the ambition of Charlemagne and his Holy Roman Empire), is decorated with booty from returning sea captains—a kind of architectural Venetian trophy chest. The interior glows mysteriously with gold mosaics and colored marble.

To enter the church, modest dress is required even of kids (no shorts or bare shoulders). In peak season, there can be long lines of people waiting up to an hour to get into the church. People who ignore the dress code hold up the line while they plead fruitlessly with—or put on extra clothes under the watchful eyes of—the dress-code police. Consider reserving an entry time at www.alata.it.

Cost and Hours: Free, Mon–Sat 9:30–17:00, Sun 14:00–17:00, some areas close at 16:00 in winter. No photos are allowed inside. The church also includes a Treasury (€2.10, includes audioguide), Golden Altarpiece (€2.10), and Museum (which has the original bronze horses and a great view over St. Mark's Square, €1.60). Of the three, the Museum is best. The Treasury and Golden Altarpiece are interesting and historic, but neither is as much fun as two bags of pigeon seed. ✪ See St. Mark's Basilica Tour, page 53.

▲▲▲Doge's Palace (Palazzo Ducale)—The seat of the Venetian government and home of its ruling duke, or doge, this was the most powerful half-acre in Europe for 400 years. The Doge's Palace was built to show off the power and wealth of the republic and remind all visitors that Venice was number one. The doge lived with his family on the first floor near the halls of power. From his once lavish (now sparse) quarters, you'll follow the

Floods and a Dying City

Venice floods about 60 times a year—normally in March and November—when the wind blowing up from Egypt and high barometric pressure on the lower Adriatic Sea are most likely to combine to push water up to this top end of the sea. (There is no real lunar tide in the Mediterranean.)

Floods start in St. Mark's Square. The entry of the church is nearly the lowest spot in town. (You might see stacked wooden benches; when the square floods, these are put end to end to make elevated sidewalks). The measuring devices at the base of the outside of the Campanile bell tower (near the exit, facing St. Mark's Square) show the  current sea level (*livello marea*). When the water level rises one meter, a warning siren sounds. It repeats if a serious flood is imminent. Find the mark showing the high-water level from the terrible floods of 1966 (waist-level, on right).

In 1965, Venice's population was over 150,000. Since the flood of 1966 the population has been shrinking. Today the population is about 65,000 . . . and geriatric. Sad, yes, but imagine raising a family here: The fragile nature of the city means piles of regulations (no biking, and so on), and costs are high—even though the government is now subsidizing rents to keep people from moving out. You can easily get glass and tourist trinkets, but it's hard to find groceries. And floods and the humidity make house maintenance an expensive pain.

one-way tour through the public rooms of the top floor, finishing with the Bridge of Sighs and the prison. The place is wallpapered with masterpieces by Veronese and Tintoretto. Don't worry much about the great art. Enjoy the building.

Cost: Covered by the €9.50 Museum Card that includes admission to the Correr Museum and two museums within the Correr (see page 22 for details; ticket valid 3 months). Or you could buy a €15.50 Museum Pass which includes the above museums, Ca' Rezzonico, the island museums, and more (see page 22). If the line is very long at the Doge's Palace, buy your Museum Card or Pass at the Correr Museum across the square.

With that, you can go directly through the Doge's turnstile (push your way through the throngs).

Hours: April–Oct daily 9:00–19:00, Nov–March daily 9:00–17:00, last entry 90 minutes before closing.

Tours: Consider the €5.50 audioguide or the "Secret Itineraries Tour," which takes you into palace rooms otherwise not open to the public (€12.50, at 10:00 and 11:30 in English, 1.25 hrs, to make the mandatory reservation for the tour, call 041-522-4951 several days in advance). ✪ See Doge's Palace Tour, page 63.

▲▲**Correr Museum (Museo Civico Correr)**—This uncrowded museum gives you a good overview of Venetian history and art. The doge memorabilia, armor, banners, statues (by Canova), and paintings (by the Bellini family and others) re-create the festive days of the Venetian Republic. There are English descriptions and great St. Mark's Square views throughout (covered by €9.50 Museum Card or €15.50 Museum Pass, April–Oct daily 9:00–19:00, Nov–March 9:00–17:00, last entry 90 min before closing, enter at far end of square directly opposite church, tel. 041-522-5625). ✪ See Correr Museum Tour, page 76.

▲**Campanile (Campanile di San Marco)**—The dramatic bell tower was once half as tall—a lighthouse marking the entry of the Grand Canal and part of the original fortress/palace which guarded its entry. This tower crumbled into a pile of bricks in 1902, a thousand years after it was built. Ride the elevator 92 meters (300 feet) to the top of the reconstructed bell tower for the best view in Venice. For an ear-shattering experience, be on top when the bells ring (€6, June–Sept daily 9:00–21:00, Oct–May until 19:00). The golden angel at its top always faces into the wind. Beat the crowds and enjoy crisp morning air at 9:00.

Dorsoduro District

▲▲**Accademia (Galleria dell' Accademia)**—Venice's top art museum, packed with highlights of the Venetian Renaissance, features paintings by the Bellinis, Titian, Tintoretto, Veronese, Tiepolo, Giorgione, Testosterone, and Canaletto. It's just over the wooden Accademia Bridge. Expect long lines in the late morning because they allow only 300 visitors in at a time; visit early or late to miss crowds (€6.20 entry, Mon 8:15–14:00, Tue–Sun 8:15–19:15, shorter hours off-season, ticket window closes 45 minutes early, no photos allowed, tel. 041-522-2247). The dull audioguides (€3.60, €5.20 with 2 earphones, or €6 for a Palm Pilot) don't let you fast-forward to works you want to hear about; you have to listen to the whole spiel for each room. ✪ See Accademia Tour on page 89.

At the Accademia Bridge, there's a decent pizzeria canalside

(Pizzeria Accademia Foscarini; see "Eating," page 213); a public WC under it; and usually a classic shell game being played on top (study the system as partners in the crowd win big money).

▲▲**Peggy Guggenheim Museum**—This popular collection of far-out art, housed in the American heiress' former retirement palazzo, offers one of Europe's best reviews of the art styles of the first half of the 20th century. Stroll through cubism (Picasso, Braque), surrealism (Dalí, Ernst), futurism (Boccione), American abstract expressionism (Pollock), and a sprinkling of Klee, Calder, and Chagall (€6.50, April–Oct Wed–Mon 10:00–18:00, Sat until 22:00, closed Tue, audioguide-€4, guidebook-€18, free 15-minute tours given daily in English at 12:00 and 16:00, free baggage check, pricey café, photos allowed only in garden and terrace—a fine and relaxing perch overlooking Grand Canal, near Accademia, tel. 041-240-5411). The place is run (cheaply) by American interns working on art history degrees. ✪ See Peggy Guggenheim Museum Tour, page 130.

La Salute Church (Santa Maria delle Salute)—This impressive church with a crowned-shaped dome was built and dedicated to the Virgin Mary by grateful survivors of the 1630 plague (free, daily 9:00–12:00 & 15:00–17:30, tel. 041-522-5558 to confirm; 10-min walk from Accademia Bridge, or vaporetto stop: Salute, or cheap *traghetto* ride from near St. Mark's Square—catch between TI on lagoon and Harry's Bar). ✪ See La Salute Tour, page 143.

▲**Ca' Rezzonico (Museum of 18th-Century Venice)**—This grand Grand Canal palazzo offers the best look in town at the life of Venice's rich and famous in the 1700s. Wandering among furnishings from that most decadent century, you'll see the art of Tiepolo, Guardi, Canaletto, and Longhi (€6.70, April–Oct Wed–Mon 10:00–18:00, closed Tue and at 17:00 Nov–March, ticket office closes one hour before closing, €5.50-audioguide, easy vaporetto access via Ca' Rezzonico stop, tel. 041-241-0100). ✪ See Ca' Rezzonico Tour, page 118.

San Polo District

▲▲**Frari Church (Chiesa dei Frari)**—My favorite art experience in Venice is seeing art in the setting for which it was designed—at the Frari Church. The Franciscan "church of the brothers" and the art that decorates it is warmed by the spirit of St. Francis. It features the work of three great Renaissance masters: Donatello, Bellini, and Titian—each showing worshipers the glory of God in human terms (€2, Mon–Sat 9:00–18:00, Sun 13:00–18:00, closed Sun in Aug, last entry 15 min before closing, audioguides-€1.60/person or €2.60/double set, modest dress recommended, tel. 041-523-4864). ✪ See Frari Church Tour, page 112; if you'll

Water, Water Everywhere, But Not a Drop to Drink

Venice, while surrounded by water, originally had no natural source of drinking water. For centuries, locals collected water from the mainland with much effort and risk. Eventually, in the ninth century, locals devised a way to collect rainwater using town squares as catchment systems. Clay tubs were constructed under each square with a sand filtering system and channels directing water to a cistern at the center. Squares were paved at a slight slant so rainwater would drain through funnels and into the tub to be drawn by buckets from the neighborhood "well." Only then, with a safe local source of drinking water, could Venice's population begin to grow. Several thousand of these cisterns provided lagoon communities with drinking water right up until 1886 when an aqueduct was built (paralleling the railroad tracks across the lagoon) to bring in water from nearby mountains. Since then,

 the clay tubs have rotted out. Now, with a high tide, the floods show first on these grates that mark the low point of each town square. As you explore Venice, notice the marble grates and wells that grace nearly every square.

be walking to the church from the Rialto Bridge, see Rialto to Frari Church Walk, page 159.

▲▲**Scuola Grande di San Rocco**—Sometimes called "Tintoretto's Sistine Chapel," this lavish church (next to the Frari Church) has some 50 large, colorful Tintoretto paintings plastered to the walls and ceilings. The best paintings are upstairs, especially the *Crucifixion* in the smaller room. View the neck-breaking splendor with one of the mirrors (*specchio*) available at the entrance (€5.20, includes free and informative audioguide, daily 9:00–17:00, or see a concert here and enjoy the art as an evening bonus). ✪ See Scuola San Rocco Tour, page 102; also Rialto to Frari Church Walk, page 159.

For *molto* Tiepolo (by the son, not his more famous father), drop by the nearby Church of San Polo to see the 14 Stations of the Cross.

Cannaregio District

Jewish Ghetto—The word "ghetto" is Venetian for foundry, and was inherited by Venice's Jewish community when it was confined to the site of Venice's former copper foundries in 1516. Notice how an island—dominated by the Campo del Ghetto Nuovo square and connected with the rest of Venice by only three bridges—would be easy to isolate. While little survives from that time, in its day the square was densely populated, lined with proto-skyscrapers seven to nine stories high. This original ghetto becomes most interesting after touring the **Jewish Museum** (€3, June–Sept Sun–Fri 10:00–19:30, Oct–May Sun–Fri 10:00–17:30, closed Sat, English guided tours-€8, hourly 10:30–16:30, later in summer, Campo di Ghetto Nuovo, tel. 041-715-359).

Castello District

Dalmatian School (Scuola Dalmata dei San Giorgio)—This school (which means "meeting place") is a reminder that Venice was Europe's most cosmopolitan place in its heyday. It was here that the Dalmatian community (from the present-day region of Croatia) worshiped in their own way, held neighborhood meetings, and worked to preserve their culture. The chapel on the ground floor happens to have the most exquisite Renaissance interior in Venice, with a cycle painted by Carpaccio ringing the room (€3, Tue–Sat 9:30–12:30 & 15:30–18:30, Sun 9:30–12:30, closed Mon, between St. Mark's Square and Arsenale, on Calle dei Furlani, 3 blocks southeast of Campo San Lorenzo, tel. 041-522-8828).

Santa Elena—For a pleasant peek into a completely non-touristy, residential side of Venice, catch the boat from St. Mark's Square to the neighborhood of Santa Elena (at the fish's tail). This 100-year-old suburb lives as if there were no tourism. You'll find a kid-friendly park, a few lazy restaurants, and beautiful sunsets over San Marco.

Venice Lagoon

The island of Venice sits in a lagoon—a calm section of the Adriatic protected from wind and waves by the neutral breakwater of the *lido.* Four interesting islands hide out in the lagoon.

San Giorgio Maggiore is the dreamy island you can see from the waterfront by St. Mark's Square. The impressive church, designed by Palladio, features art by Tintoretto and a bell tower with oh-wow views of Venice (free entry to church, daily 9:30–12:30 & 15:30–18:30, closed Sun to sightseers during Mass, Gregorian Mass sung on Sun at 11:00, Mon–Sat at 8:00; €3 for bell tower lift, stops 30 min before church's closing time). To reach the island from

Venice Lagoon

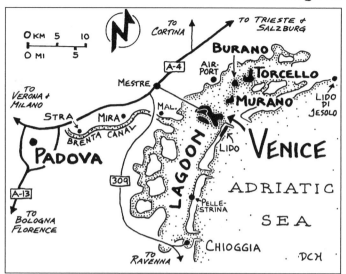

St. Mark's Square, take the five-minute vaporetto ride on #82, departing from the "San Marco (M.V.E.)" stop, 200 meters east of St. Mark's Square, at the third bridge along the waterfront (Note: This is not the same vaporetto stop as "San Marco.") ⭐ See San Giorgio Maggiore Tour, page 148.

The islands of **Murano, Burano,** and **Torcello** are reached easily, cheaply, and slowly by vaporetto. Pick up a free map of the islands from any TI. Depart from San Zaccaria dock nearest the Bridge of Sighs/Doge's Palace. Line #12 connects all three islands, or take #41 to Murano (get off at "Murano Colonna"), then #12 to the other islands. If you plan to visit even two of these islands, get a 24-hour €9.30 vaporetto pass or a 12-hour €7.75 "Itinerary Ticket" for convenience. Four-hour speedboat tours of these three lagoon destinations leave twice a day from the dock near the Doge's Palace—look for the signs and booth (€16, usually at 9:30 and 14:30; off-season 1/day at 14:30, tel. 041-523-8835 or 041-522-2159); the tours are speedy indeed, stopping for roughly 35 minutes at each island.

Murano, famous for its glass factories, has the Glass Museum, which displays the very best of 700 years of Venetian glassmaking and exhibits of ancient and modern glass art (Museo Vetrario, €4, covered by €15.50 Museum Pass, Thu–Tue 10:00–17:00, last entry 30 min before closing, closed Wed, tel. 041-739-586).

You'll be tempted by salesmen offering free speedboat shuttles from Piazza San Marco to Murano. If you're interested in glass, it's handy. You must watch the show, but then you're free to buy or escape and see the rest of the island. Numerous glass factories (*fabbrica* or *fornace*) offer demonstrations all over the island—check one out, and then wander up Via Fondamenta Vetrai toward the Glass Museum (Museo Vetrario). Get off the beaten path by taking the backstreets behind the Duomo on Calle di Conterie for a look at village Venezia. Head to the "Faro" vaporetto stop and take the #12 to either Burano or Torcello or the #41 back to San Zaccaria.

Burano, famous for its lace, is a sleepy island with a sleepy community—village Venice without the glitz. Lace fans enjoy the Lace Museum (Scuola di Merletti, €4.10, covered by €15.50 Museum Pass, Wed–Mon 10:00–17:00, closed Tue, tel. 041-730-034). The park next to Burano's only vaporetto dock is perfect for a waterfront picnic. While the main drag leading from the vaporetto stop into town is lined with shops and packed with tourists, simply wander to the far side of the island and the mood shifts. Explore to the right of the leaning tower for a peaceful yet intensely pastel, small-town lagoon world. Benches lining a little promenade at the water's edge make another tranquil picnic spot. As you head back to the dock, notice the marble tables on Campo Pescaria where the fish market used to be held. Hungry? Try the huge *bruschetta* at Bruschetteria al Vecio Pipa (daily 11:30–16:30, Fondamente San Mauro 397, tel. 041-730-045).

Torcello is dead except for its church, which claims to be the oldest in Venice (€5.20 for church, tower, and museum, daily 10:30–17:30 but museum closed Mon, tel. 041-730-761). It's impressive for its mosaics, but not worth a look on a short visit unless you really love mosaics and can't make it to Ravenna.

GRAND
CANAL
CRUISE

Take a joyride and introduce yourself to Venice by boat. Cruise the entire Canal Grande from Tronchetto (car park) or Ferrovia (train station) all the way to San Marco.

If it's your first trip down the Grand Canal, by all means, put this book away and just take it all in—Venice is a barrage on the senses that hardly needs a narration. But, on a later trip, these notes give the cruise a little meaning and help orient you to this great city.

Orientation
Cost: €3.10 for a vaporetto ticket (€2.60 per person for families of 3 or more) or €9.30 for a 24-hour pass (cheaper for families).
Hours: This ride has the best light and fewest crowds early or late. Sunset bathes the buildings in gold. Twilight is magic. After dark, chandeliers light up the building interiors.
Getting There: From Tronchetto (the bus and car park) or the Santa Lucia train station, catch vaporetto #1, which is ideal because it's slow (45 min). Although vaporetto #82 does the same route, it's too fast (25 min). If you take #82, be certain you're on a "San Marco via Rialto" boat because some boats don't go farther than the Rialto Bridge. (The conductor announces "Solo Rialto!" for boats going only as far as Rialto.)

Best seats are in the open air—in the front (you must stay seated), at the stern, or standing along the railing.
Information: Some city maps (on sale at postcard racks) have a handy Grand Canal map on the back.
Length of Our Tour: 45 minutes on vaporetto #1 or 25 minutes on vaporetto #82.
Starring: Palaces, markets, boats, bridges—Venice.

Grand Canal

Palaces Rising from the Sea

The Grand Canal is Venice's "Main Street." At over three kilometers (2 miles) long, nearly 50 meters (150 feet) wide, and nearly five meters (15 feet) deep, it's the biggest canal with the most impressive palaces. The canal is the remnant of a river that once spilled from the mainland into the Adriatic. The sediment it carried formed a delta that was eventually swallowed up by the sea, becoming a "lagoon."

Venice was built on the marshy islands of the former delta, sitting on pilings driven nearly five meters (15 feet) into the clay (alder wood worked best). About 40 kilometers (25 miles) of **canals** drain the city, dumping like streams into the Grand Canal.

Technically, there are only three canals: Grand, Giudecca, and Cannaregio. The other 45 "canals" are referred to as *rio* (rivers).

Venice is a city of **palaces**, dating from the days when Venice was the world's richest city. The most lavish formed a chorus line of elegance along the Grand Canal. Once painted in reds and blues, with black-and-white borders and gold-leaf trim, they made Venice a city of dazzling color. This cruise is the only way to really appreciate the palaces, approaching them at water level, which was their main entrance. Today, strict laws prohibit any changes in these buildings, so while landowners gnash their teeth, we can enjoy Europe's best-preserved medieval city—slowly rotting. Many of the grand buildings are now vacant. Others harbor chandeliered elegance above mossy, empty ground floors.

THE TOUR BEGINS

Start at the **train station** or **Tronchetto** car park. We'll orient by the vaporetto stops.

Venice's main thoroughfare is busy with all kinds of **boats:** taxis, police boats, garbage boats, ambulances, construction cranes, and even brown-and-white UPS boats. Venice's sleek, black, graceful **gondolas** are a symbol of the city. While used gondolas cost around €10,000, new ones run up to €30,000 apiece. Today, with over 400 gondoliers joyriding amid the churning vaporetti, there's a lot of congestion on the Grand Canal. Watch your vaporetto driver curse the (better-paid) gondoliers.

Ferrovia (vaporetto stop)

The **Santa Lucia train station** (on the left bank of the canal), one of the few modern buildings in town, was built in 1954. It's been the gateway into Venice since 1860, when the first station was built. "F.S." stands for "Ferrovie dello Stato," the Italian state railway system. The **bridge** at the station is the first of only three that cross the Canal Grande.

Opposite the station, atop the green dome of **San Simeone Piccolo** church, Saint Simon waves *ciao* to whoever enters or leaves the "old" city.

Riva di Biasio

Just past the Riva di Biasio stop, look left down the broad **Cannaregio Canal**. The twin pale-pink six-story "skyscrapers" are a reminder of how densely populated the world's original **ghetto** was. Set aside as the local Jewish quarter in 1516, the area (located behind the San Marcuola stop) became extremely crowded. This urban island developed into one of the most closely knit business and cultural quarters of all the Jewish communities in Italy, and gave us our word ghetto (from *getti*, the jets of the brass foundry located here). For more information, visit the Jewish Museum in this neighborhood (see page 34).

San Marcuola

The gray **Turkish Foundation** (right side, opposite the vaporetto stop), with its horseshoe arches and roofline of triangles-and-dingleballs, has an Islamic feel. Turkish traders in turbans docked here, unloaded their goods into the warehouse on the bottom story, then went upstairs for a home-style meal and a place to sleep. Venice in the 1500s was very cosmopolitan, welcoming every religion and ethnicity, so long as they carried cash.

Venice's **Casino** (left-hand side) is housed in the palace where German composer Richard *(The Ring)* Wagner died in 1883. See his distinct, strong-jawed profile in the white plaque on the brick wall. In the 1700s, Venice was Europe's Vegas, with casinos and prostitutes everywhere. Today, this elegant Casino welcomes men in ties and ladies in dresses.

San Stae

Opposite the San Stae stop, look for the **faded frescoes** (left bank, on lower story). Imagine the grand facades of the Grand Canal at their grandest. As colorful as the city is today, it's still only a sepia-toned snapshot of a Technicolor era.

Ca' d'Oro

The lacy **Ca' d'Oro**, or "House of Gold," (left bank, next to the vaporetto stop) is the best example of "Venetian Gothic" on the canal. Its three stories offer different variations on balcony design, topped with a spiny white roofline. Venetian Gothic mixes traditional French Gothic (pointed arches) with Byzantine styles (tall, narrow arches atop thin columns), filled in with Venice's unique frills (round medallions stamped with a four-leaf clover). Like all the palaces, this was originally painted and gilded to make it even more glorious than it is now. "Ca" means "house." Because only the house of the doge (Venetian ruler) could be called a palace ("palazzo"), all other palaces are technically "Ca."

Today the Ca' d'Oro is a museum but, other than temporary exhibits, there's little to see inside (€3, Mon 8:15–14:00, Tue–Sun 8:15–19:15, free peek through hole in door of courtyard).

Farther along, on the right, the outdoor arcade of the **fish and produce market** bustles with people in the morning but is quiet the rest of the day. This is a great scene to wander through—even though new European hygiene standards required a less-colorful remodeling job last year. Find the *traghetto* gondola ferrying shoppers—standing like Washington crossing the Delaware—back and forth.

The huge **post office** (left side, just before the Rialto Bridge), with *servizio postale* boats moored at its blue posts, was once the German Foundation, the branch office for German metal merchants. The building's top story has a rare sight in frilly Venice—square windows. Rising above the post office, you can see in the distance the golden angel of the Campanile (bell tower) at St. Mark's Square, where this tour will end.

As the canal bends, we pass beneath the impressive Rialto Bridge. Singing gondoliers love the acoustics here: "*O sole mio . . .*"

Rialto

A major landmark of Venice, the **Rialto Bridge** is lined with shops and tourists. Constructed in 1588, it's the third bridge built on this spot. With a span of 49 meters (158 feet) and foundations stretching 200 meters (650 feet) on either side, the Rialto was an impressive engineering feat in its day. Earlier Rialto Bridges could

open to let in big ships, but not this one. When this new bridge was completed, much of the Grand Canal was closed to shipping and became a canal of palaces. Locals call the summit of this bridge the "icebox of Venice" for its cool breeze. Tourists call it a great place to kiss.

Rialto, a separate town in the early days of Venice, has always been the commercial district, while San Marco was the religious and governmental center. Today, a winding street called the Mercerie connects the two, providing travelers with human traffic jams and a mesmerizing gauntlet of shopping temptations. The restaurants that line the canal feature great views, midrange prices, and low quality.

San Silvestro

On the left side, opposite the vaporetto stop, **two palaces stand side by side**, with stories the same height, creating the effect of one long balcony.

We now enter a long stretch of important **merchants' palaces**, each with proud and different facades. Since ships couldn't navigate beyond the Rialto Bridge (to reach the section of the Grand Canal you just came from), the biggest palaces—with the major shipping needs—lie ahead. Many feature the Roman palace design of twin towers flanking a huge set of central windows. These were showrooms designed to let in maximum sunlight.

Just after the San Silvestro stop, you'll see (on the right) the palace of a 15th-century **"captain general of the sea."** The Venetian equivalents of five-star admirals were honored with twin obelisks decorating their palaces. This palace flies three flags: of Italy (green-white-orange), the European Union (blue with ring of stars), and Venice (the lion).

Sant' Angelo

Notice how many buildings have a foundation of waterproof white stone (*pietra d'Istria*) upon which the bricks sit high and dry. Many canal-level floors are abandoned; the rising water level takes its toll. The **posts**—historically painted gaily with the equivalent of family coats of arms—don't rot under water. But the wood at the water-line does rot.

Look at how the rich marble facades are just a veneer covering no-nonsense brick buildings. Look up at the characteristic **funnel-shaped chimneys**. These forced embers through a loop-the-loop channel until they were dead—required in the days when stone palaces were surrounded by humble wooden buildings and a live spark could make a merchant's work-force homeless.

Take a deep whiff of

Venice. What's all this nonsense about stinky canals? All I smell is my shirt. By the way, how's your captain? Smooth dockings? To get to know him, stand up in the bow and block his view.

San Tomá

After the San Tomá stop, look down the side canal (on the right, before the bridge) to see the traffic light, the **fire station**, and the fireboats ready to go.

We now prepare to round the hairpin turn and double back toward St. Mark's. The impressive **Ca' Foscari** (right side) dominates the bend in the canal. Its four stories get increasingly ornate as they rise from the water—from simple Gothic arches at water level, to Gothic with a point, to Venetian Gothic arches topped with four-leaf clovers, to still more medallions and laciness that look almost Moorish. Wow.

Ca' Rezzonico

The grand, heavy, white **Ca' Rezzonico**, directly at the stop of the same name, houses the Museum of 18th-Century Venice. ⊕ See Ca' Rezzonico Tour, page 48. Across the canal is the cleaner and leaner **Palazzo Grassi**, which often showcases special exhibitions.

These days, when buildings are being renovated, huge murals with images of the building mask the ugly scaffolding. Corporations hide the scaffolding for the goodwill—and the publicity.

Accademia

The wooden **Accademia Bridge** crosses the Grand Canal and leads to the **Accademia Gallery** (right side), filled with the best Venetian paintings. The bridge was put up in 1932 as a temporary one. Locals liked it, so it stayed. Cruising under the bridge, you'll get a classic view of the domed La Salute Church ahead.

The low white building among greenery (on the right, between the bridge and the church) is the **Peggy Guggenheim Museum**. The American heiress "retired" here, sprucing up the palace that had been abandoned in mid-construction; the locals call it the "palazzo non finito." Peggy willed the city her fine collection of modern art. ⊕ See Peggy Guggenheim Museum Tour, page 130.

Next door, notice the early Renaissance building's flat-feeling facade with "pasted-on" Renaissance motifs. The Salviati building (with the fine mosaic) is a glass factory.

Just before the Salute stop (on the right), the house with the big windows and the red and wild Andy Warhol painting on the living-room wall (often behind white drapes) was lived in by rock-singer Mick Jagger. In the 1970s, this was notorious as Venice's rock-and-roll-star **party house**.

Salute

A crown-shaped dome supported by scrolls stands atop **La Salute Church** (daily 9:00–12:00 & 15:00–18:00). ⚫ See La Salute Tour, page 143. This Church of Saint Mary of Good Health was built to coax God into delivering them from the devastating plague of 1630 (which eventually killed about a third of the city's

population). It's claimed that more than a million trees were piled together to build a foundation reaching below the mud to the solid clay.

Much of the surrounding countryside was deforested by Venice. Trees were exported and consumed locally to fuel

the furnaces of Venice's booming glass industry, to build Europe's biggest merchant marine, and to prop up this city in the mud.

Across the canal (left side), several **fancy hotels** have painted facades that hint at the canal's former glory.

As the Grand Canal opens up into the lagoon, the last building on the right with the golden ball is the 16th-century **Customs House** (Dogana da Mar, not open to the public). Its two bronze Atlases hold a statue of Fortune riding the ball. Arriving ships stopped here to pay their tolls.

As you prepare to disembark at San Marco/Vallaresso, look from left to right out over the lagoon. On the left, a wide harbor-front walk leads past the town's most elegant hotels to the green area in the distance. This is the public garden, the largest of Venice's few parks, which hosts the Biennale art show. Farther in the distance is the **Lido**, the island with Venice's beach. It's tempting, with sand and casinos, but its car traffic breaks into the medieval charm of Venice.

The dreamy white church that seems to float is the architect Palladio's **San Giorgio Maggiore**. It's just a vaporetto ride away (#82 from San Marco M.V.E. dock). ⚫ See San Giorgio Maggiore Tour, page 148. Across the lagoon (to your right) is a residential island called **Giudecca**.

San Marco/Vallaresso

Get off at the San Marco/Vallaresso stop. Directly ahead is **Harry's Bar**. Hemingway drank here when it was a characteristic no-name *osteria* and the gondoliers' hangout. Today, of course, it's the overpriced hangout of well-dressed Americans who don't mind paying triple for their Bellinis (peach juice with Prosecco wine) to make the scene. St. Mark's Square is just around the corner.

ST. MARK'S SQUARE
TOUR

Piazza San Marco

Venice was once Europe's richest city, and the Piazzo San Marco was its center. As middleman in the trade between Asia and Europe, it reaped wealth from both sides. In 1450, Venice had 150,000 citizens (far more than Paris) and a gross "national" product 50 percent greater than the entire country of France.

The rich Venetians learned to love the good life—silks, spices, and jewels from the East, crafts from northern Europe, good food and wine, fine architecture, music, gaiety, and laughter. Venice was a vibrant city full of impressed visitors, painted palaces, and glittering canals. Five centuries after its "fall," Venice is all of these still, with the added charm of romantic decay. In this tour we'll spend an hour in the heart of this Old World superpower.

Orientation

Cost and Hours: If you ascend the Campanile (bell tower), it'll cost you €6 (June–Sept daily 9:00–21:00, Oct–May until 19:00).

Getting There: Signs all over town point to "San Marco"—both the square and the basilica, located where the Grand Canal spills out into the lagoon. Vaporetto stop: San Marco/Vallaresso.

Information: There are two tourist information offices. One TI is in the southwest corner of the Piazza; the other is along the waterfront at the San Marco/Vallaresso vaporetto stop.

In any given year, expect a famous building to be covered with scaffolding. Restoration is an ongoing process.

Cuisine Art: Pricier cafés with live music are on St. Mark's Square; cheaper bars are just off the square. The Correr Museum (far end of the square) has a quiet coffeeshop overlooking the crowded square.

Starring: Byzantine domes, Gothic arches, Renaissance arches... and the wonderful space they enclose.

Piazza San Marco

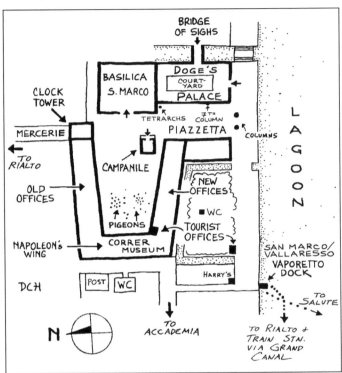

• *For an overview of this grand square and the buildings that surround it, view it from the far end of the square (away from St. Mark's Basilica).*

The Piazza—Bride of the Sea

St. Mark's Basilica dominates the square with its Byzantine-style onion domes and glowing mosaics. Mark Twain said it looked like "a warty bug taking a meditative walk." To the right of the basilica is its 100-meter-tall bell tower, or Campanile. Between the basilica and the Campanile, you can catch a glimpse of the pale pink Doge's Palace. Lining the square are the former government offices that administered the Venetian empire's vast network of trading outposts.

The square is big, but it feels intimate with its cafés and dueling orchestras. By day, it's great for people-watching and pigeon-chasing. By night, under lantern light, it transports you to another century, complete with its own romantic soundtrack. The Piazza

draws Indians in saris, English
nobles in blue blazers, and
Nebraskans in shorts. Napoleon called the Piazza "the
most beautiful living room in
Europe." Napoleon himself
added to the intimacy by building the final wing, opposite the
basilica, that encloses the square.

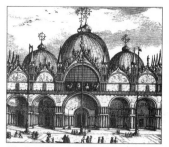

For architecture buffs, here
are three centuries of styles, bam, side by side, *uno due tre*, for
easy comparison:

(1) On the left side (as you face the basilica) are the "Old"
offices, built in 1530 in solid, column-and-arch Renaissance style.

(2) The "New" offices (on the right), from a century later, are
a little heavier and more ornate, mixing arches, columns, and statues in the Baroque style.

(3) Napoleon's wing is neoclassical—a return to simpler, more
austere classical columns and arches. Napoleon's architects tried to
make his wing bridge the styles of the other two. But it turned out a
little too high for one side and not enough for the other. Nice try.

Imagine this square full of water, with gondolas floating
where people now sip cappuccinos. That happens every so often
at very high tides (*acqua alta*), a reminder that Venice and the sea
are intertwined.

Venice became Europe's richest city from its trade with northern Europeans, Turkish Muslims, and Byzantine Christians. Here
in St. Mark's Square, the exact center of this East–West axis, we
see both the luxury and the mix of Eastern and Western influences.

• *The tourist information office is nearby, in the corner of Napoleon's*
Wing. With Venice's inconsistent opening hours, it's wise to confirm
your sightseeing plans here. Behind you (southwest of the piazza), you'll
find the public WC, a post office, and the American Express office.

Now approach the basilica. If it's hot and you're tired, grab a shady
seat at the foot of the Campanile. Watch out for pigeon speckle.

St. Mark's Basilica—Exterior

The facade is a crazy mix of East and West. There's sculpture
from Constantinople, columns from Alexandria, and capitals
from Sicily. The mosaics are an Eastern style, designed by Venetians but executed by Greek craftsmen. The doorways are massive Romanesque (European) arches but lined with marble
columns from Eastern Byzantine buildings. The upper story
has some pointed Gothic-style arches, while the whole affair is
topped by Greek domes with their onion-shaped caps.

The columns alone show the facade's variety—purple, green, gray, white, yellow, some speckled, some striped horizontally, some vertically, some fluted, all topped with a variety of different capitals.

What's amazing isn't so much the variety as the fact that the whole thing comes together in a bizarre sort of harmony. St. Mark's remains simply the most interesting church in Europe, a church that (paraphrasing Goethe) "can only be compared with itself."

⭐ For more on the basilica, inside and out, see St. Mark's Basilica Tour, page 53.

• *Facing the basilica, turn 90 degrees to the left to see...*

The Clock Tower

Two bronze Moors (African Muslims) stand atop the clock tower. (They only gained their ethnicity when the metal darkened over the centuries.) At the top of each hour they swing their giant clappers. The dial shows the 24 hours, the signs of the zodiac, and, in the blue center, the phases of the moon. Above the dial is the world's first digital clock, which changes every five minutes. The clock tower retains some of its original coloring of blue and gold, a reminder that, in centuries past, this city glowed with color.

An alert winged lion, the symbol of St. Mark and the city, looks down on the crowded square. He opens a book that reads *"Tibi Marcus"* or "Peace to you, Mark." As legend goes, these were the comforting words an angel spoke to the stressed evangelist during a stormy night he spent here on the island, assuring him he would find serenity. Eventually, his body found its final resting place inside the basilica, and now his lion symbol is everywhere. (Find 4 in 20 seconds. Go.)

Venice's many lions express the city's various mood swings through history—triumphant after a naval victory, sad when a favorite son has died, hollow-eyed after a plague, smiling when the soccer team wins. The pair of lions squatting between the clock tower and

Escape from St. Mark's Square

Crowds getting to you? Here are some relatively quiet areas near St. Mark's Square.

• **Correr Museum**—Sip a cappuccino in the café of this uncrowded history museum in a building overlooking St. Mark's Square (enter at the far end of the Piazza). ✪ See Correr Museum Tour, page 76.

• **Giardinetti Reali**—A small park along the waterfront west of the Piazzetta (facing the water, turn right).

• **Isle of San Giorgio Maggiore**—The dreamy island you see from the Piazzetta (catch vaporetto #82 from the "San Marco M.V.E." stop, located about 200 meters east of St. Mark's Square; facing the water, turn left). ✪ See San Giorgio Maggiore Tour, page 148.

• **Il Merletto**—A lace shop in a small chapel (near northwest corner of St. Mark's Square, on Sotoportego del Cavalletto).

• **La Salute Church**—This cool, quiet church in a quiet neighborhood is a five-minute ride by vaporetto #1 or *traghetto*—both leave from the San Marco/Vallaresso stop. ✪ See La Salute Tour, page 143.

basilica have probably been photographed being ridden on by every Venetian child born since the dawn of cameras.

The Campanile

The original Campanile (camp-ah-NEE-lay), or bell tower, was a marvel of 10th-century architecture until the 20th century (1902), when it toppled into the center of the piazza. It had groaned ominously the night before, sending people scurrying from the cafés. The next morning...crash! The golden angel on top landed right at the basilica's front door, standing up.

The Campanile was rebuilt 10 years later complete with its golden angel which always faces the breeze. You can ride a lift to the top for the best view of Venice. Notice the photo of the crumpled tower on the wall just before you enter the elevator. The view on top is glassed in, stuffy, and crowded at times, but worth it.

• *The small square between the basilica and the water is* ...

The Piazzetta

This "Little Square" is framed by the Doge's Palace on the left, the Old Library on the right, and the waterfront of the lagoon. In former days, the Piazzetta was closed off to the public for a few hours a day so that government officials and big-

wigs could gather in the sun to strike shady deals.

The pale pink Doge's Palace is the epitome of the style known as "Venetian Gothic." Columns support traditional, pointed Gothic arches, but with a Venetian flair—they're curved to a point, ornamented with a trefoil (three-leaf clover), and topped with a round medallion of a quatrefoil (four-leaf clover).

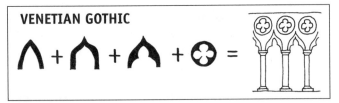

VENETIAN GOTHIC

The two large 12th-century columns near the water were looted from Constantinople. Mark's winged lion sits on top of one. His body (nearly 5 meters long, or 15 feet) predates the wings, and is over 2,000 years old.

The other column holds St. Theodore, the former patron saint who was replaced when they got hold of Mark. I guess stabbing crocodiles in the back isn't classy enough for an upwardly mobile world power.

These columns were used to string up and torture criminals so the public could learn its lessons vicariously. A poor baker who was beheaded here was later found to be innocent, and he's remembered today with a memorial—a dim red light about 12 meters (40 feet) up on the side of St. Mark's Basilica that faces the Piazzetta.

Venice was the "Bride of the Sea" because she was dependent on sea trading for her livelihood. This "marriage" was celebrated

annually by the people. The doge, in full regalia, boarded a ritual boat (his "Air Force One") here at the edge of the Piazzetta and sailed out into the lagoon. There a vow was made, and he dropped a jeweled ring into the water to seal the marriage. (I always think of that image whenever the café orchestras play the theme from *Titanic*.)

In the distance, on an island across the lagoon, is one of the grandest scenes in the city, the Church of San Giorgio Maggiore (see page 148). With its four tall columns as the entryway, the church, designed by the late-Renaissance architect Palladio, influenced future government and bank buildings around the world.

Speaking of architects, I will: Sansovino. The Old Library (here in the Piazzetta), the Old Offices (in Piazza San Marco), and the delicate Loggetta (at the base of the Campanile) were all designed by Jacopo Sansovino. From the Piazzetta you can see all three of these at once. More than any single man, he made Piazza San Marco what it is, replacing the city's frilly, pointed-arch Venetian Gothic with round-arch, sober Renaissance.

When Venice floods, the puddles appear first around round, white pavement stones like the one between the Loggetta and the Doge's Palace.

The "Tetrarchs" and the Doge's Palace's "Seventh Column"

Where the basilica meets the Doge's Palace is the traditional entrance to the palace, decorated with four small purple statues of Roman origin. Legend says they're either the scared leaders of a divided Rome during its fall, or four brothers who poisoned each other over stolen treasure, with their loot ending up in Venice's coffers. Whatever the legend, these porphyry statues are very old, having guarded the doge's entrance since the city first rose from the mud.

The Doge's Palace's seventh column (the seventh from the water) tells a story of love, romance, and tragedy in its carved capital:

1) In the first scene (the carving facing the Piazzetta), a woman on a balcony is wooed by her lover, who says "Babe, I want *you*!" 2) She responds, "Why, little old *me*?" 3) They pledge their love. 4) Kiss. 5) Do it in bed. 6) Nine months later, guess what? 7) The baby takes its first steps. 8) The parents suffer through the "terrible twos."

• *At the waterfront in the Piazzetta, turn left and walk (east) along the water. At the top of the first bridge, look inland at . . .*

The Bridge of Sighs

In the Doge's Palace (on your left), the government doled out justice. On your right are the prisons. (Don't let the palatial facade fool you—see the bars on the windows?) Prisoners sentenced in the palace crossed to the prisons by way of the covered bridge in front of you. From this bridge, they got their final view of sunny, joyous Venice before entering the black and dank prisons. They sighed.

Venice has been a major tourist center for four centuries. Anyone who ever came here has stood on this very spot, looking at the Bridge of Sighs. Lean on the railing leaned on by everyone from Casanova to Byron to Hemingway.

> *I stood in Venice, on the Bridge of Sighs,*
> *a palace and a prison on each hand.*
> *I saw, from out the wave, her structures rise,*
> *as from the stroke of the enchanter's wand.*
>
> *A thousand years their cloudy wings expand*
> *around me, and a dying glory smiles*
> *o'er the far times, when many a subject land*
> *looked to the Winged Lion's marble piles,*
> *where Venice sat in state, throned on her hundred isles!*
> —from Lord Byron's
> *Childe Harold's Pilgrimage*

• *Sigh.*

ST. MARK'S BASILICA
TOUR

Basilica di San Marco

Among Europe's churches, St. Mark's is unique. From the outside, it's a riot of domes, columns, and statues, completely unlike the towering Gothic churches of the North. Inside, the decor of mosaics, colored marbles, and oriental treasures is rarely seen elsewhere. Even the Christian symbolism is unfamiliar to Western eyes, done in the style of icons and even Islamic designs. And being older than most of Europe's churches, it feels like a remnant of a lost world.

This is your best chance (outside of Istanbul or Ravenna) to glimpse a forgotten and somewhat mysterious part of the human story—Byzantium.

Orientation

Cost: The church is free. There's a fee to see the Treasury (€2.10, includes informative audioguide—free for the asking), Golden Altarpiece (€2.10), and Museum (€1.60, enter from atrium either before or after you tour church).

Hours: The church is open Mon–Sat 9:30–17:00, Sun 14:00–17:00. The Treasury and Golden Altarpiece are open daily 9:45–17:10, 16:10 in winter. The Museum is open daily 9:45–17:00, 16:00 in winter.

The church is particularly beautiful when lit (unpredictable schedule, maybe middays 11:00–12:00, Sat–Sun 14:00–17:00, plus 18:45 Mass on Sat).

During peak times, the line can be very long, and much of the church interior is roped off for crowd-flow control. You just have to shuffle through on a one-way system. (It's best to read this chapter before you go . . . or while standing in line).

To bypass the line, you can reserve an entry time for free at www.alata.it. (If you have problems with the Web site, try

St. Mark's Basilica

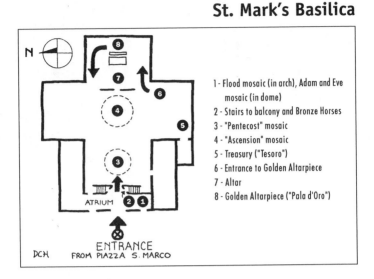

1 - Flood mosaic (in arch), Adam and Eve mosaic (in dome)
2 - Stairs to balcony and Bronze Horses
3 - "Pentecost" mosaic
4 - "Ascension" mosaic
5 - Treasury ("Tesoro")
6 - Entrance to Golden Altarpiece
7 - Altar
8 - Golden Altarpiece ("Pala d'Oro")

ATRIUM

ENTRANCE
FROM PIAZZA S. MARCO

DCH

entering your telephone number without dashes or spaces.)
Just print out your entry time and present it at the church.
Getting There: Signs all over town point to "San Marco"—the
square and the church, located where the Grand Canal spills out
into the lagoon. It's on St. Mark's Square (Piazza San Marco), near
the Grand Canal. Vaporetto stop: San Marco/Vallaresso.
Information: Tel. 041-522-5205. Guidebooks are sold in the
bookstand in the basilica's atrium. There's a public pay WC
just beyond the far end of the square.
Tours: See the schedule board in the atrium listing free English-
language guided tours (schedules vary, but April–Oct there can
be up to 4 per day).
Length of Our Tour: One hour.
Dress Code: The strict dress code applies to everyone, even
kids (no bare shoulders, shorts, or short skirts).
Cuisine Art: Pricier cafés offering live music are on St. Mark's
Square; cheaper bars are just off the square.
Photography: Not allowed.
Starring: St. Mark, Byzantium, mosaics, and ancient bronze horses.

THE EXTERIOR

St. Mark's Basilica is a treasure chest of booty looted during
Venice's glory days. That's only appropriate for a church built on
the bones of a stolen saint.

   The **mosaic over the far left door** shows the theft that put

St. Mark's...
Cathedral, Church, or Basilica?

All three are correct. The church is also a cathedral because it's the home church of the local bishop. It's a basilica because the Roman Catholic Church gives that special designation to certain churches of religious importance. Coincidentally, it's also a basilica in the architectural sense. Its floor plan has a central nave with flanking side aisles, a layout patterned after the ancient Roman law buildings called basilicas.

Venice on the pilgrimage map. Two men (in the center, with crooked staffs) enter the church bearing a coffin with the body of St. Mark, who looks grumpy from the long voyage.

St. Mark was the author of one of the four Bible books telling the story of Jesus' life (Matthew, Mark, Luke, and John). Seven centuries after his death, his holy body was in Muslim-occupied Alexandria, Egypt. In 828, two visiting merchants of Venice "rescued" the body from the infidels, hid it in a pork barrel (which was "unclean" to Muslims) and spirited it away to Venice.

The mosaic shows the merchants presenting the body—not to a pope or bishop—but to the doge (in ermine cape, on the right)

and his wife, the dogaressa (with entourage, on the left), giving instant status to Venice's budding secular state. They built a church here over Mark's bones, and made him the patron saint of the city. You'll see his symbol, the winged lion, all over Venice.

The original church burned down in 976. Today's structure was begun in the 11th century. The mosaic, from 1260, shows that the church hasn't changed much since then—you can even see the famous bronze horses on the balcony.

In subsequent centuries, the church was encrusted with materials looted from buildings throughout the Venetian empire. Their prize booty was the four bronze horses that adorn the balcony (these are copies; the originals are housed inside the church museum). The Venetians stole these horses from their fellow Christians during the looting of Constantinople in 1204. The architecture style of St. Mark's has been called "Early Ransack."

• *Enter the basilica through the central door, past the guard who makes sure all who enter have covered legs and shoulders. The door is a sixth-century, bronze-paneled, Byzantine job. On busy days, crowds are hustled through the church on roped-off pathways, and you'll just have to go with the flow. But this tour will assume a more leisurely visit. Immediately after entering the first door (crowd-flow permitting), stop in the atrium (the entry hall) and drop anchor under the last dome on the right.*

The Atrium Mosaics— Noah's Ark and Adam and Eve

Some of the oldest and finest mosaics of the church are found in the atrium. Medieval mosaics, with their picture symbols, were

easily understood in medieval times, even by illiterate masses. Today's literate masses have trouble reading them, so let's look at two simple examples.

In the arch next to the dome is the story of Noah and the Great Flood. If you face the piazza, you'll see (on top) Noah building the Ark. Below that are three scenes of Noah putting all species of animals into the Ark, two by two. (Who's at the head of the line? Lions.) Turning around and facing the church interior, you'll see the Flood in full force, drowning the wicked. Noah sends out a dove twice to see if there's any dry land to dock at. He finds it, leaves the Ark with a gorgeous rainbow overhead, and offers a sacrifice of thanks to God. Easy, huh?

Now that our medieval literacy rate has risen, let's try the story that rings the bottom of the dome—Adam and Eve in the Garden of Eden. Stand right under the dome facing the church, crane your neck, and read clockwise around the dome:

(1) Adam names the animals; (2) God creates Eve from a spare rib and (3) presents her to Adam;

Mosaics

St. Mark's is famous for its mosaics. Mosaics are designs or pictures made with small cubes of colored stone or glass pressed into wet plaster. Ancient Romans paved floors, walls, and ceilings with them. When Rome "Fell," the art 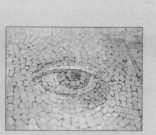 form died out in the West, but was carried on by Byzantine craftsmen. They perfected the gold background effect by baking gold leaf into tiny cubes of glass. The reflecting gold mosaics helped to light thick-walled, small-windowed, lantern-lit Byzantine churches, creating a golden glow that symbolized heaven.

(4) Eve is tempted by the serpent; (5) she picks and gives the forbidden fruit to Adam; (6) they realize that they're naked and, (7) in shame, try to hide from God; (8) God finds them and (9) lectures them; (10) He gives them clothes and (11) pushes them out into the real world, where they have to work for a living.

• *Now enter the church's nave (walking past the museum entrance that leads to the bronze horses upstairs). Take a seat on one of the benches along the back wall (crowd-flow permitting) and let your eyes adjust.*

THE INTERIOR

Greek Cross Floor Plan and Mosaics

The church is laid out with four equal arms, topped with domes, radiating out from the center to form a Greek Cross (+), symbolizing perfection, rather than the more common Latin cross of the crucifixion. In fact, there aren't very many crucifixes at all in the church, giving it an Eastern/Byzantine/Orthodox flavor. While Western Christianity focuses on the death of Jesus, the Orthodox East focuses on His resurrection.

The entire upper part is decorated in mosaic—4,000 square meters (imagine paving a football field with

Byzantium

The Byzantine Empire was the eastern half of the ancient Roman Empire that *didn't* "Fall" in A.D. 500. It remained Christian, Greek-speaking, and enlightened for another thousand years.

In A.D. 330, the emperor Constantine, the first Christian emperor, moved the Roman Empire's capital to the newly built city of Constantinople (modern Istanbul), taking with him Rome's best and brightest. When the city of Rome decayed and fell, plunging western Europe into its "Dark Ages," Constantinople lived on as the greatest city in Europe.

Venice had strong ties with Byzantium from its earliest days. In the sixth century, Byzantine Emperor Justinian invaded northern Italy, briefly reuniting East and West, and making Ravenna his regional capital. In 800, Venetians asked the emperor in Constantinople to protect them from Charlemagne's marauding Franks.

Soon Venetian merchants were granted trading rights to Byzantine ports in the Adriatic and eastern Mediterranean. They traded raw materials from western Europe for luxury goods from the East.

When Muslim Turks threatened Christian Byzantium, the Venetians joined the Crusades, the series of military expeditions designed to "save" Jerusalem and Constantinople. Venetians grew rich renting ships to the Crusaders in exchange for money, favors, and booty. During the Fourth Crusade (1202–1204), which went horribly awry, the Crusaders—led by the Venetian Doge Dandolo—sacked Constantinople, a fellow Christian city. This was, perhaps, the lowest point in Christian history, at least until the advent of TV evangelism. The city of Constantinople finally fell to the Turks in 1453.

Today, we find hints of Byzantium in the Eastern Orthodox Church, in mosaics and icons, and in the looted treasures shipped back to Venice.

contact lenses). These golden mosaics are in the Byzantine style, though many were designed by artists from the Italian Renaissance and later. The often-overlooked lower walls are in beautiful marble. Even the floor is mosaic, mostly geometrical designs and animals. It rolls like the sea. Venice is sinking and shifting, creating these cresting waves of stone.

The initial effect is dark and unimpressive (unless they've got the floodlights on). But as your pupils slowly unclench, the mosaics start to give off a "mystical, golden luminosity," the atmosphere of the Byzantine heaven. The air itself seems almost visible, like a cloud of incense. It's a subtle effect, one that grows on you, especially as the filtered light changes. There are more beautiful, bigger, more overwhelming, and even holier churches, but none are as stately.

• *Find the chandelier near the entrance doorway (in the shape of a Greek Cross cathedral space station), and run your eyes up the support chain to the dome above.*

The Pentecost Mosaic

The scene is the Pentecost. The Holy Spirit, in the form of a dove, sends out a pinwheel of spiritual lasers, igniting tongues of fire on the heads of the 12 apostles below, giving them the ability to speak and understand other languages. You'd think they'd be amazed, but their expressions are as solemn as icons. Their robes have intricate folds, a Byzantine trademark.

This is one the oldest mosaics in the church, from around 1125, and it captures the otherworldliness of Byzantine art that is so different from the literal realism of later Western art. While the mosaics in the atrium were from the Old Testament, we've now entered the new age of the New Testament.

The poet W. B. Yeats stood here and described what he saw: "O sages standing in God's holy fire as in the gold mosaic of a wall, come from the holy fire . . . and be the singing-masters of my soul."

• *Walk up the aisle to the central dome.*

Central Dome Mosaic

Gape upwards. Christ has ascended into the starry sky and takes a seat on a crescent moon. This isn't the dead, crucified, mortal Jesus shown in most churches, but a powerful, resurrected god, the Ruler of the Cosmos (Pantocrator). Below him is Mary (with shiny, golden Greek crosses on each shoulder and looking ready to play patty-cake), flanked by two winged angels and the 12 apostles standing among the trees of earth. The mosaic is a series of perfect circles, the cosmic order, with Christ in the center solemnly blessing us. God's in his heaven, saints are on earth, and all's right with the world.

ST. MARK'S THREE MUSEUMS

Inside the church are three sights, each requiring a separate admission. None are must-sees, but they're your best chance (outside of Istanbul or Ravenna) to experience the glory of the Byzantine civilization. I'd prioritize them in this order: Museum, Golden Altarpiece, and Treasury.

Treasury

• *The Treasury* (Tesoro) *is in the right transept. Admission is €2.10 (includes audioguide—ask for it). It's open daily from 9:45 to 17:10 (until 16:10 in winter). As you wait in line, notice the door under the rose window at the end of the transept. This was the doge's private entrance from the Doge's Palace.*

You'll see Byzantine chalices, silver reliquaries, monstrous monstrances (for displaying the Communion wafer), and icons done in gold, silver, enamels, gems, agate, and so on. This is marvelous handiwork, but all the more marvelous because much of it was done when western Europe was still rooting in the mud. Here are some highlights.

Entryway: The so-called "Throne of St. Mark," just as you enter, is one of the church's oldest Christian objects (around A.D. 550). Carved when Europe was being overrun by pagan hordes, its sheer bulk and Tree of Life offered Christians an image of stability.

Main room: The Cibario di Anastasia, in the far left corner, is a small marble canopy. "Anastasia," the name carved on it in Greek, was a woman in the court of the emperor Justinian (483–565).

The Urn of Artaxerxes I (middle of the right wall) held the ashes of the great Persian king who ruled 2,500 years ago.

The glass case in the center of the room holds the most precious Byzantine objects, including an enamel icon of the Crucifixion, an onyx chalice, and an incense burner shaped like a domed church.

Relics Room: The glass case over the altar contains relics of Jesus' torture and execution (pieces of the sword that pierced him, the crown of thorns, the cross he was crucified on). You may scoff, but of all of Europe's "Pieces of the True Cross," these have at least some claim of authenticity. Legend has it that Christ's possessions were gathered up in the fourth century by Constantine's mother and taken to Constantinople. During the Crusade heist of 1204, Venetians brought them here. They've been paraded through the city every Good Friday for 800 years.

Golden Altarpiece *(Pala d'Oro)*

• *The Golden Altarpiece is located behind the main altar (same fee and hours as Treasury, above).*

The first thing you see after showing your ticket is the high altar itself (under the stone canopy). Beneath this lies the body of Mark, the Gospel writer. (The tomb, through the grate under the altar, says *"Corpus Divi Marce Evangelistae,"* or Body of the Evangelist Mark.) Legend has it that while he was alive he visited

Venice, where an angel
promised him he could
rest his weary bones when
he died. Hmm. Shhh.

Above the altar is
a marble canopy. The
four supporting columns
are wonderful and
mysterious—scholars
don't even know whether they're from fifth-century Byzantium or
13th-century Venice! I spent as much time looking at the funny New
Testament scenes carved in the columns as at the Golden Altarpiece
with its crowds and glaring lights. (On the right-hand pillar closest
to the altarpiece, fourth row from the bottom: Is that a genie escap-
ing from a bottle while someone tries to stuff him back in?)

The Golden Altarpiece is a stunning golden wall made of
80 Byzantine enamels with religious scenes, all set in gold and
studded with hefty rubies, emeralds, sapphires, pearls, amethysts,
and topaz. Byzantine craftsmen made this for the Doge's Palace
over the course of several centuries (976–1345). It's a bit much
to take in all at once, but get up close and find several details you
might recognize:

In the center, Jesus as Ruler of the Cosmos sits on a golden
throne, with a halo of pearls and jewels. He gives us his blessing,
surrounded by Matthew, Mark, Luke, and John.

Along the bottom row, Old Testament prophets show off the
Bible books they've written. With halos, solemn faces, and elabo-
rately creased robes, they epitomize the Byzantine icon style.

The story of Mark is told in the panels along the sides. In
the bottom left panel, Mark meets Peter (seated) at the gates of
Rome. It was Peter (legend has it) that gave Mark his eyewitness
account of Jesus' life that Mark wrote down in his Gospel. Mark's
story ends in the last panel (bottom right) with the two Venetian
merchants carrying his coffin here to be laid to rest.

Once you've looked at some individual scenes, back up as far
as this small room will let you and just let yourself be dazzled by
the "whole picture"—this "mosaic" of Byzantine greatness.

Museum, the Bronze Horses, and View of the Piazza

• *This is the one sight certainly worth the admission price, if only for
the views of the piazza. The staircase up to the museum is in the
atrium near the main entrance. The sign says "Loggia dei Cavalli,
Museo." The museum costs €1.60. It's open daily from 9:45 to
17:00 (16:00 in winter).*

Your ticket gives you admission to:

1. A small museum with fragments of mosaics that you can examine up close.

2. An upstairs gallery with an impressive top-side view of the church interior with its mosaic wallpaper.

3. The Loggia, the balcony overlooking Piazza San Marco, offering a great view with fun pigeon- and people-watching. Stand among statues of water-bearing slaves that serve as drain spouts. Get photographed next to the bronze horses (copies) with their "1978" date on the hoof. Then go inside to a room with the real things.

4. The Bronze Horses. Stepping lively in pairs with smiles on their faces, they exude energy and exuberance. Originally, they pulled a chariot *Ben-Hur* style. They were once gilded, and you can still see some streaks of gold.

These horses have done some traveling in their day. Legend says they were made in the time of Alexander the Great, then taken by Nero to Rome. Constantine brought them to his new capital in Constantinople to adorn the chariot racecourse. The Venetians then stole them from their fellow Christians during the looting of noble Constantinople and brought them to St. Mark's.

What goes around, comes around, and Napoleon came around and took the horses when he conquered Venice in 1797. They stood atop a triumphal arch in Paris until Napoleon's empire was "blown-aparte" and they were returned to their "rightful" home.

The horses were again removed from their spot when attacked by their most dangerous enemy yet—modern man. The threat of oxidation from pollution sent them galloping for cover inside the church.

DOGE'S PALACE TOUR

Palazzo Ducale

Venice is a city of beautiful facades—palaces, churches, carnival masks—that can cover darker interiors of intrigue and decay. The Doge's Palace, with its frilly pink exterior, hides the fact that the "Most Serene Republic" (as it called itself) was far from serene in its heyday.

The Doge's Palace housed the fascinating government of this rich and powerful empire. It also served as the home for the Venetian ruler known as the doge (DOJE-eh), or duke. For four centuries (about 1150–1550), this was the most powerful half acre in Europe. The doges wanted it to reflect the wealth of the Republic, impressing visitors and serving as a reminder that the Venetians were number one in Europe.

Orientation

Cost: Covered by €9.50 Museum Card (valid for 3 months), which includes admission to the Correr Museum (✪ see Tour on page 76) and two lesser museums at the Correr (National Archaeological Museum and the Monumental Rooms of the Marciana National Library). The pricier Museum Pass costs €15.50 and includes the above museums, Ca' Rezzonico, the museums on the neighboring islands, and more (see page 22 for details).

Hours: April–Oct daily 9:00–19:00, Nov–March 9:00–17:00, last entry 90 min before closing. Closed Jan 1, May 1, and Dec 25.

Crowd Control: To avoid the long peak-season line at the Doge's Palace, you have several options (the first is best):

1. Buy your Museum Card at the Correr Museum (at far end of St. Mark's Square); then go directly to the turnstile of the Doge's Palace, skipping the long line at the palace entrance.

2. If your visit falls between April and October, visit the

Doge's Palace Exterior

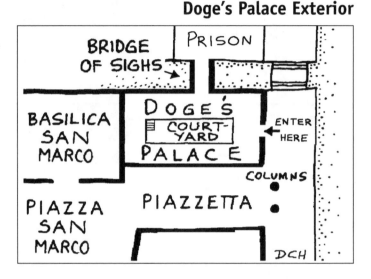

palace around 17:00 when the line disappears (but note that the museum closes at 19:00 and the last entry is 17:30).

3. Book a guided "Secret Itineraries Tour;" see "Tours," below. The only (minor) drawback is that your palace entry fee does not include the Correr Museum.

4. Reserve an Orange Venice Card (which includes admission to Venice's museums) by telephone or Internet (see page 23 for details).

Getting There: The palace is next to St. Mark's Basilica, on the lagoon waterfront, and just off St. Mark's Square. Vaporetto stop: San Marco.

Information: There are no English descriptions. Guidebooks are on sale in the bookshop. Tel. 041-522-4951. WC in courtyard near palace exit.

Tours: Audioguide tours cost €5.50. The fine "Secret Itineraries Tour," which follows the doge's footsteps through rooms not included in the general admission price, must be booked in advance (€12.50, at 10:00 and 11:30 in English, 1.25 hrs, tel. 041-522-4951). As they take only 25 people per tour, call two or three days in advance to confirm times and reserve a spot. The cost includes admission only to the Doge's Palace (and allows you to bypass the long line). While the tour skips the main halls inside, it finishes inside the palace and you're welcome to visit the halls on your own.

Length of Our Tour: 90 minutes.

Cuisine Art: Expensive cafés on St. Mark's Square, cheaper bars/cafés off the square, and a handy canalside gelato shop on the Piazzetta (the small square with two big columns) across from the Doge's Palace.

Photography: Allowed without a flash.

Starring: Tintoretto and the doges.

THE EXTERIOR

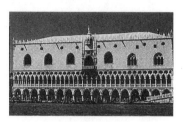

"The Wedding Cake," "The Table Cloth," or "The Pink House" is also sometimes known as the Doge's Palace. The style is called Venetian Gothic, and the arches and windows come to a point like Gothic arches, but the upper half has an Eastern, Islamic flavor with its abstract patterns. The columns originally had bases on the bottoms, but these were covered over as the columns sank. If you compare this delicate, top-heavy structure with the massive fortress palaces of Florence, you realize the wisdom of building a city in the middle of the sea—you have no natural enemies except gravity.

The palace was originally built in the 800s, but most of what we see came after 1300, as it was expanded to meet the needs of the empire. Each doge wanted to leave his mark on history with a new wing. But so much of the city's money was spent on the building that finally a law was passed levying an enormous fine on anyone who even mentioned any new building. That worked for a while, until one brave and wealthy doge proposed a new wing, paid his fine...and started building again.

THE INTERIOR

• *Enter the Doge's Palace from along the waterfront. After you pass through the turnstile, you'll walk through several ground-floor rooms filled with ornately carved column bases from the palace's original facade. Cross the inner courtyard and stand at the base of a big staircase (the one closer to the basilica).*

The Courtyard and the Stairway of Giants *(Scala dei Giganti)*

Imagine yourself as a foreign dignitary on business to meet the doge. In the courtyard, you look up a grand staircase topped with two nearly nude statues of, I think, Moses and Paul Newman (more likely, Neptune and Mars, representing Venice's prowess at sea and at war). The doge and his aides would be waiting for you at the top. No matter who you were—king, pope, or emperor—you'd have to

hoof it up. The powerful doge would descend the stairs for no one.

Many doges were crowned here, between the two statues. The doge was something like an "elected king"—which makes sense only in the "dictatorial republic" that was Venice. Technically, he was just a noble selected by other nobles to carry out their laws and decisions. Many doges tried to extend their powers and rule more like divine-right kings. Many others just put on their funny hats and accepted their role as figure-head and ceremonial ribbon-cutter. Most were geezers, elected in their seventies, committed to preserving the Venetian traditions.

The palace is attached to St. Mark's Cathedral, symbolically welding together church and state. You can see the ugly brick of both structures—the stern inner structure without its painted-lady veneer of marble. On this tour, we'll see the sometimes harsh inner structure of this outwardly serene Republic.

In the courtyard, you'll see a hodgepodge of architecture styles, as the palace was refurbished over the centuries. There are classical statues in Renaissance niches, shaded by Baroque awnings, topped by Flamboyant Gothic spires, and crusted with the Byzantine onion-domes of St. Mark's Basilica.

• *Go up the tourists' staircase to the first-floor balcony where you can look back down on the courtyard (and the backside of Paul Newman). From here on, it's hard to get lost (though I've managed). It's a one-way system, so just follow the arrows.*

Midway along the balcony, you'll find a face in the wall, the . . .

Mouth of Truth

This fierce-looking androgyne opens his/her mouth, ready to swallow a piece of paper. Letter-boxes like this (some with lions' heads) were scattered throughout the palace. Anyone who had a complaint or suspicion about anyone else could accuse him anonymously (*Denontie Secrete*) by simply dropping a slip of paper

in the mouth. This set the blades of justice turning inside the palace.

• *Near Paul Newman is the entrance to the . . .*

Golden Staircase *(Scala D'Oro)*

The palace was propaganda, designed to impress visitors. This gilded-ceiling staircase was something for them to write home about.
• *Head up the Golden Staircase to the first landing (the* Primo Piano Nobile), *and turn right, which takes you up into the . . .*

Doge's Apartments *(Appartamenti Ducale)*

The dozen or so rooms on the first floor are where the doge actually lived. Wander around this once sumptuous, now sparse suite, admiring coffered wood ceilings, chandeliers, and very little furniture, since doges were expected to bring their own. Despite his high office, the doge had to obey several rules that bound him to the city. He couldn't leave the palace unescorted, couldn't open official mail in private, and he and his family had to leave their own home and live in the Doge's Palace. Poor guy.

In the large Map (or "Shield") Room, work clockwise around the room to trace local boy Marco Polo's (c. 1254–c. 1325) eye-opening trip across Asia—from Italy to Greece (quite accurate maps) to Palestine, Arabia, and "Irac." Finally, he arrived at the other side of the world. This last map (shown upside-down, with south on top) gives a glimpse at the Venetian worldview circa 1550. There's China, Taiwan ("Formosa"), and Japan ("Giapan"), while America is a nearby island with "California" and lots of "Terre Incognite."
• *After browsing the dozen or so private rooms, you'll arrive at the second floor, which was the "public" part of the palace. The first room at the top of the stairs is the . . .*

Square Room *(Atrio Quadrato)*

The ceiling painting, *Justice Presenting the Sword and Scales to Doge Girolano,* by Tintoretto, is a late-Renaissance masterpiece. So what? As you'll soon see, this place is virtually wallpapered with Titians, Tintorettos, and Veroneses. Many have a similar theme: the doge, in his ermine cape and funny one-horned hat with earflaps, kneeling in the presence of saints, gods, or mythological figures.
• *Enter the next room.*

Room of the Four Doors
(Sala delle Quattro Porte)

This was the central clearinghouse for all the goings-on in the palace. Visitors presented themselves here and were directed to their destination—the executive, legislative, or judicial branch of government.

The room was designed by Palladio, the architect who did the impressive Church of San Giorgio Maggiore, across the Grand Canal from St. Mark's Square. On the intricate stucco ceiling, notice the feet of the women dangling down below the edge (above the windows), a typical Baroque illusion, blending 2-D painting with 3-D sculpture.

On the wall is a painting by (ho-hum) Titian, showing a doge kneeling with great piety before a woman embodying Faith holding the Cross of Jesus. Notice old Venice in the misty distance under the cross. This is one of many paintings you'll see of doges in uncharacteristically humble poses—paid for, of course, by the doges themselves.

G. B. Tiepolo's well-known *Venice Receiving Neptune* (now displayed on an easel but originally on the wall above the windows; you'll get closer to the painting as you progress through the museum) shows Venice as a woman—Venice is always a woman

to artists—reclining in luxury, dressed in the ermine cape and pearl necklace of a doge's wife (dogaressa). Crude Neptune, enthralled by the First Lady's beauty, arrives bearing a seashell bulging with gold ducats. A bored Venice points and says, "Put it over there with the other stuff."

• *Enter the small room with the big fireplace and several paintings.*

Antecollegio

It took a big title or bribe to get in to see the doge. Once accepted for a visit, you would wait here before you entered, combing your hair, adjusting your robe, popping a breath mint, and preparing the gifts you'd brought. While you cooled your heels and warmed your hands at the elaborate fireplace, you might look at some of the paintings—among the finest in the palace, worthy of any museum in the world.

The Rape of Europa, by Paolo Veronese (on the wall opposite the fireplace), most likely shocked many small-town visitors with its risqué subject matter. Here Zeus, the king of the Greek gods, appears in the form of a bull with a foot fetish, seducing a beautiful earthling, while cupids spin playfully overhead. The Venetian Renaissance looked back to pagan Greek and Roman art, a big change from the saints and crucifixions of the Middle Ages. This painting doesn't

portray the abduction as a medieval condemnation of sex and violence, but rather as a celebration in cheery pastel colors of the earthy, optimistic spirit of the Renaissance.

Tintoretto's ***Bacchus and Ariadne*** (to the left of the exit door) is another colorful display of Venice's sensual tastes. The god of wine offers a ring to the mortal Ariadne, who's being crowned with stars by Venus who turns slowly in zero gravity. The ring is the center of a spinning wheel of flesh, with the three arms like spokes.

But wait, the doge is ready for us. Let's go in.

• *Enter the next room.*

Executive Branch *(Collegio)*

Surrounded by his cabinet of six advisers, one for each Venetian neighborhood, the doge would sit on the platform at the far end to receive ambassadors, who laid their gifts at his feet and pleaded their country's case. The gifts were often essentially tributes from lands conquered by Venetian generals. All official ceremonies, such as the ratification of treaties, were held here.

At other times, it was the private meeting room of the doge and his cabinet to discuss secrets of state, proposals to give the legislature, or negotiations with the pope. The wooden benches around the sides (where they sat) are original. The clock on the wall is a backward-running 24-hour clock with Roman numerals and a sword for hands.

The ceiling is 24-karat gold, with paintings by Veronese. These are not frescoes (painting on wet plaster), like in the Sistine Chapel,

but actual canvases painted here on earth and then placed on the ceiling. Venice's humidity would have melted frescoes like so much mascara within years. The T-shaped painting of the woman with the spider web (on the ceiling, opposite the big window) was the Venetian symbol of ***Discussion.*** You can imagine the many intricate webs of truth and lies woven in this room by the doge's sinister nest of advisers. In ***Mars and Neptune with Campanile and Lion*** (the ceiling painting near the entrance), Veronese presents four symbols of the

Executive and Legislative Rooms

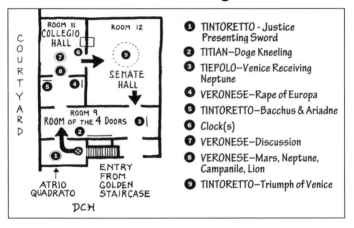

❶ TINTORETTO - Justice Presenting Sword

❷ TITIAN—Doge Kneeling

❸ TIEPOLO—Venice Receiving Neptune

❹ VERONESE—Rape of Europa

❺ TINTORETTO—Bacchus & Ariadne

❻ Clock(s)

❼ VERONESE—Discussion

❽ VERONESE—Mars, Neptune, Campanile, Lion

❾ TINTORETTO—Triumph of Venice

Republic's strength—military, sea trade, city, and government (plus a cherub about to be circumcised by the Campanile).

• *Enter the large Senate Room.*

Senate Chamber—
Legislative Branch *(Sala del Senato)*

This was the center of the Venetian government. This body of 60 annually elected senators, chaired by the doge, debated and passed laws, and made declarations of war in this room. Senators would speak from the podium between the windows.

Venice was technically a republic ruled by the elected Senate that met here, though its power was gradually overshadowed by the doge and, later, the Council of Ten. Which branch of government really ruled? All of them. It was an elaborate system of checks and balances to make sure no one rocked the boat, and the ship of state sailed smoothly ahead.

Tintoretto's *Triumph of Venice* on the ceiling (center) shows the city in all its glory. Lady Venice is up in heaven with the Greek gods, while barbaric lesser nations swirl up to give her gifts and tribute. Do you get the feeling the Venetian aristocracy was proud of its city?

On the wall are two large clocks with the signs of the zodiac and phases of the moon. And there's one final oddity in this room, in case you hadn't noticed

Judicial Rooms

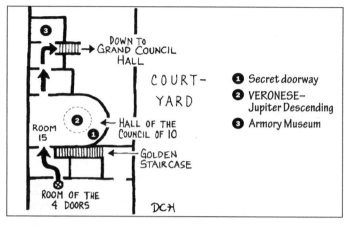

COURT-YARD

DOWN TO GRAND COUNCIL HALL

❶ Secret doorway
❷ VERONESE—Jupiter Descending
❸ Armory Museum

ROOM 15

HALL OF THE COUNCIL OF 10

GOLDEN STAIRCASE

ROOM OF THE 4 DOORS

DCH

it yet. In one of the wall paintings (above the entry door), there's actually a doge...not kneeling.

• *Pass again through the Room of the Four Doors, then around the corner into the large hall with a semicircular platform at the far end.*

Room of the Council of Ten— Judicial Branch *(Sala del Consiglio dei Dieci)*

By the 1700s, Venice had a worldwide reputation for swift, harsh, and secret justice. The dreaded Council of Ten, consisting of 10 judges, the doge, and his six advisers (note the 17 wood panels where they presided), dealt out justice for traitors, murderers, and "morals" violators.

Slowly, they developed into a CIA-type unit with their own force of police officers, guards, spies, informers, and even assassins. They had their own budget and were accountable to no one, soon making them the de facto ruling body of the "Republic." No one was safe from the spying eye of the "Terrible Ten." You could be accused anonymously by a letter dropped into a "Mouth of Truth," swept off the streets, tried, judged, and thrown into the dark dungeons in the palace for the rest of your life without so much as a Miranda warning.

It was in this room that the Council met to decide punishments—who lived, died, was decapitated, tortured, or merely thrown in jail. The small, hard-to-find door leading off the platform (the fifth panel to the right of center) leads through secret passages to the prisons and torture chambers.

The large, central, oval ceiling painting by Veronese (a copy of the original stolen by Napoleon and still in the Louvre) shows *Jupiter Descending from Heaven to Strike Down the Vices*, redundantly informing the accused that justice in Venice was swift and harsh.

The dreaded Council of Ten was, of course, eventually disbanded. Today, their descendants enforce the dress code for tourists entering St. Mark's.

• *Pass through the next room, then up the stairs to the Armory Museum.*

Armory Museum

The aesthetic of killing is beyond me, but I must admit I've never seen a better collection of halberds, falchions, ranseurs, mulchers, targes, morions, and brigandines in my life. (One of those words is a fake.) The stock of weapons in these three rooms makes you realize the important role the military played in keeping open the East–West trade lines.

Room 1: In the glass case on the right, you'll see the suit of armor worn by the great Venetian mercenary general, Gattamelata (far right, on horseback), as well as "baby's first armor" (how soon they grow up). A full suit of armor could weigh 30 kilos (66 pounds). Before gunpowder, crossbows were made still more lethal by attaching a crank on the end to draw the bow with extra force.

Room 2: In the thick of battle, even horses needed a helmet. The hefty broadswords were brandished two-handed by the strongest and bravest soldiers who waded into enemy lines. Suspended from the ceiling is a large banner captured from the Turks at the Battle of Lepanto (1571).

Room 3: At the far end is a very, very early (17th-century) attempt at a 20-barrel machine gun. On the walls and weapons, the "C-X" insignia means this was the private stash of the "Council of Ten."

Room 4: Squint out the window to see Palladio's San Giorgio Maggiore and Venice's Lido (beach) in the distance. To the right of the window, the glass case contains a tiny crossbow, some torture devices (including an effective-looking thumbscrew), "the devil's box" (a clever item that could fire in four directions at once), and a nasty, two-holed chastity belt. These "iron breeches" were worn by the devoted wife of the Lord of Padua.

• *Exit the Armory Museum. Go downstairs, turn left, and pass through the long hall with a wood-beam ceiling. Now turn right and open your eyes as wide as you can . . .*

Hall of the Grand Council

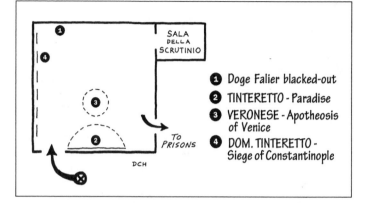

1. Doge Falier blacked-out
2. TINTERETTO - Paradise
3. VERONESE - Apotheosis of Venice
4. DOM. TINTERETTO - Siege of Constantinople

Hall of the Grand Council
(Sala del Maggiore Consiglio)

It took a room this size to contain the grandeur of the Most Serene Republic. This huge room (53 by 25 meters) could accommodate up to 2,000 people at one time. The doge sat on the raised dais, while the nobles, the backbone of the empire, lined the long walls. Nobles were generally wealthy men over 25, but the title had less to do with money than with long bloodlines. In theory, the doge, the Senate, and the Council of Ten were all subordinate to the Grand Council of nobles that elected them.

A newly elected doge was presented to the people of Venice from the balcony of the nearby "Sala dello Scrutinio" room that overlooks the Piazzetta. A noble would announce, "Here is your doge, if it pleases you." That was fine, until one time when the people weren't pleased. From then on they just said, "Here is your doge."

Ringing the hall are portraits, in chronological order, of the first 76 doges. The one at the far end that's blacked out is the notorious Doge Marin Falier, who opposed the will of the Grand Council in 1355. He was tried for treason and beheaded. Two panels to the right is one of the few doge-and-dogaressa couples who were elected co-rulers.

On the wall over the doge's throne is Tintoretto's monster-piece, *Paradise*, the largest oil painting in the world. At 160 square meters (190 square yards), it could be sliced up to wallpaper my entire apartment with enough left over for placemats.

Christ and Mary are at the top of heaven, surrounded by 500 saints who ripple out in concentric rings. Tintoretto worked

on this in the last years of his long life. On the day it was finished, his daughter died. He got his brush out again and painted her as saint #501. She's dead center with the blue skirt, hands clasped, getting sucked up to heaven. (At least that's what an Italian tour guide told me.)

Veronese's *The Apotheosis of Venice* (on the ceiling at the Tintoretto end) is a typically unsubtle work showing Lady Venice being crowned a goddess by an angel.

Along the wall to the right of Paradise, **battle scenes** (by Tintoretto's son, Domenico) show Venice's greatest military—if not moral—victory, the con-

quest of the fellow-Christian city of Constantinople during the Fourth Crusade (1204). The mighty walls of Constantinople repelled every attack for nearly a thousand years. But the sneaky Venetians (in the **fifth painting**) circled around back and attacked where the walls rose straight up from the water's edge. Skillful Venetian oarsmen cozied their galleys right up to the dock, allowing soldiers to scoot along crossbeams attached to the masts, to the top of the city walls. In the foreground, an archer cranks up his crossbow. The gates were opened, the Byzantine emperor parades out to surrender, and tiny Doge Dandolo says, "Let's go in and steal some bronze horses."

But soon, Venice would begin its long slide to historical oblivion. One by one the Turks gobbled up Venice's trading outposts. In the West the rest of Europe ganged up on Venice to reduce her power. To top it off, by 1500, Portugal had broken Venice's East–West trade monopoly by finding a sea route to the East around Africa. For the next three centuries, Venice remained a glorious city, but not the great world power she once was. Finally, in 1797, the French general Napoleon marched into town shouting *"Liberté, Egalité, Fraternité."* The Most Serene Republic was finally conquered and the last doge was deposed in the name of modern democracy.

Out the windows is a fine view of the domes of the basilica, the palace courtyard below, and Paul Newman.

• *Read the intro to the prisons here in the Grand Council Hall, where there are more benches and fewer rats.*

Prisons

The palace had its own dungeons. In the privacy of his own home, a doge could sentence, torture, and jail political opponents. The most notorious cells were "the Wells" in the basement, so-called because they were deep, wet, and cramped.

By the 1500s, the Wells were full of political prisoners. New prisons were built across the canal to the east of the palace and connected with a covered bridge—covered so that opponents could be imprisoned without public knowledge.

• *Exit the Grand Hall (through the door to the left of Tintoretto's monsterpiece) and pass through a series of rooms and once-secret passages, following signs for* "Ponte dei Sospiri/Prigioni," *through the covered Bridge of Sighs over the canal to the "new" prisons.*

Medieval justice was harsh. The cells consisted of cold stone with heavily barred windows, a wooden plank for a bed, a shelf, and a bucket. (My question—what did they put on the shelf?) You can feel the cold dampness.

Circle the cells. Notice the carvings made by prisoners—from olden days up until 1930—on some of the stone windowsills of the cells, especially in the far corner of the building.

The Bridge of Sighs

Criminals were tried and sentenced in the palace, then marched across the canal here to the dark prisons. On this bridge, they got their one last look at Venice. They gazed out at the sky, the water, and the beautiful buildings.

• *Cross back over the Bridge of Sighs, pausing to look through the marble-trellised windows at all of the tourists and the dreamy Church of San Giorgio Maggiore. Heave one last sigh.*

CORRER
MUSEUM
TOUR

Museo Civico Correr

A doge's hat, gleaming statues by Canova, and paintings by the illustrious Bellini family—for some people, that's a major museum; for others, it's a historical bore. But the Correr Museum has one more thing to offer, and that's a quiet refuge—a place to rise above St. Mark's Square when it's too hot, too rainy, or too overrun with tourists. Those who enter are rewarded with an easy-to-manage overview of Venice's art and history.

Orientation

Cost: Covered by €9.50 Museum Card (valid for 3 months), which includes two lesser museums within the Correr (National Archaeological Museum and the Monumental Rooms of the Marciana National Library) and the crowded Doge's Palace. Avoid ticket lines at the Doge's Palace by buying your Museum Card at the Correr Museum. For details on the Museum Card and pricier Museum Pass, see page 22.

Hours: Daily April–Oct 9:00–19:00, Nov–March 9:00–17:00, last entry 90 minutes before closing.

Getting There: The entrance is on St. Mark's Square in Napoleon's Wing—the building at the far end of the square, opposite the basilica. Climb the staircase to the first-floor ticket office and bookstore.

Information: English descriptions are provided throughout. Tel. 041-522-5625.

Length of Our Tour: One hour.

Cuisine Art: The museum café has tables with a fine view of St. Mark's Square.

Starring: Canova statues, doges' hats, three Bellinis, and a Carpaccio.

Overview

The Correr Museum gives you admission and access to three connected museums—the Correr proper (which we'll see), the National Archaeological Museum, and the Marciana Library.

The Correr itself is on three long, skinny floors that parallel St. Mark's Square. This tour covers the first two floors: The first floor contains Canova statues and Venetian history; the second floor displays a chronological overview of Venetian paintings. The third floor, which presents the history of Italy's *Risorgimento* (national unification), is undergoing renovation and may reopen in 2003 (ask at the ticket booth).

FIRST FLOOR

• *Buy your ticket and wander through the first few rooms (which are typically used for temporary exhibits). At the entrance to the permanent collection, see:*

Room 3:
Canova—*Paris*

The guy with black measles is not a marble statue of Paris; it's a plaster of Paris, a life-size model that Antonio Canova used to carve the real one in stone. The dots are sculptor's "points," to tell the sculptor how far into the block he should chisel to establish the figure's rough outline. On the base is Canova's key to translate the measurements.

Antonio Canova (1757–1822)

Son of a Venetian stonemason, Canova grew up with a chisel in his hand in a studio along the Grand Canal, precociously mastering the sentimental, elegant Rococo style of the late 1700s. At 23, he went to Rome and beyond, where he studied ancient statues at recently discovered Pompeii. These new archaeological finds inspired a new Renaissance-style revival of the classical style. Canova's pure, understated elegance and "neo"-classical style soon became the rage all over Europe.

Called to Paris, Canova became Napoleon's court sculptor and carved perhaps his best-known work: Napoleon's sister as Venus, reclining on a couch (now in the Borghese Gallery, Rome). Canova combined Rococo sentiment and elegance with the cool, minimal lines of classicism.

Correr Museum—First Floor

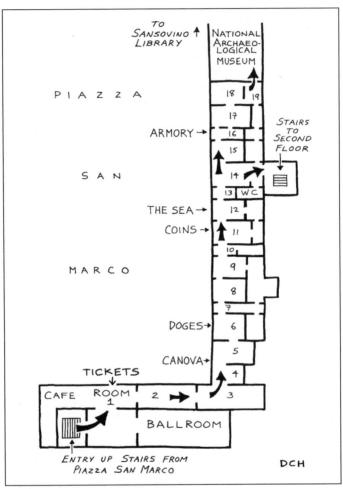

TO
SANSOVINO ↑
LIBRARY

NATIONAL
ARCHAEO-
LOGICAL
MUSEUM

PIAZZA

18   19

17

ARMORY →   16

15

STAIRS
TO
SECOND
FLOOR

SAN

14

13   WC

THE SEA →   12

COINS →   11

10

MARCO

9

8

7

DOGES→   6

CANOVA→   5

4

TICKETS

ROOM 1

CAFE   2

3

BALLROOM

ENTRY UP STAIRS FROM
PIAZZA SAN MARCO

DCH

Room 4:
Canova—*Daedalus and Icarus (Dedalo e Icaro)* 1778–1779
Serious Daedalus straps wings that he's just invented onto his son's shoulders. The boy looks thrilled with the new toy, not knowing what we do—that they will soon melt in the sun, plunging him to his death. Daedalus' middle-aged, sagging skin contrasts with Icarus' supple form. Canova, a stonemason's son, displays the tools of the family trade on the base.

Antonio Canova was only 20 when Venice's Procurator commissioned this work from the hometown prodigy. It was so realistic, it caused a stir—skeptics accused Canova of not really sculpting it, but making it from plaster casts of live humans.

Room 5:
Canova—*Orpheus and Eurydice*
(*Orfeo*, 1775–1776; *Euridize*, 1775)

Orpheus is leading his beloved back from Hell when she's tugged from behind by the cloudy darkness. She calls for help. Orpheus

looks back, smacks his forehead in horror . . . but he can do nothing to help, and has to hurry on. In this youthful work, Canova already shows elements of his later style: high-polished, slender, beautiful figures; an ensemble piece, with more than one figure; open space between the figures that's almost as compelling as the figures themselves; and a statue group that's interesting from many angles.

Carved by a teenage Canova, this piece captures the Rococo spirit of Venice in the late 1700s—elegant and beautiful, but tinged with bittersweet loss. Even Canova's later works—which were more sober, minimalist, and emotionally restrained—always retained the elegance and romantic sentiment of the last days of the Venetian Republic.

Canova—*Amor and Psyche*

Though not a great painting, this is Canova's version of a famous work he set in stone (now in the Louvre). The two lovers spiral around each other in the never-ending circle of desire. The two bodies and Cupid's two wings form an X. But enough X's and O's—the center of the composition is the empty space that separates their hungry lips.

Other Canovas

The other large statues are either lesser works or more plaster studies for works later executed in marble. You'll also see small clay models, where Canova worked out ideas rather than risk ruining an expensive block of marble.

The pyramid-shaped model of the ***Tomb of Maria Christina of Austria (Monumento a Tiziano)*** shows Canova's design (based on the pyramid of Gaius Cestius in Rome) for a tomb he intended for the painter Titian. The design was not used for Titian, but instead for a tomb for an Austrian princess in Vienna, as well as for Canova's own memorial in the Frari Church (see page 116).

• *Enter the world of Venice's doges. On an easel in room 6, find . . .*

Room 6:
Lazzaro Bastiani—*Portrait of Doge Francesco Foscari*

Doge Foscari, dressed in the traditional brocaded robe and cap with cloth earflaps, introduces us to the powerful, regal world of these

"elected princes," who served as the cere-monial symbol of the glorious Republic.

Foscari (1373–1457, buried in the Frari Church) inherited Venice at its his-torical peak as a prosperous sea-trading empire with peaceful ties to both eastern Turks and mainland Europeans. He has a serene look of total confidence . . . that would slowly melt as he led Venice on a 31-year war of expansion that devastated northern Italy and drained Venice's coffers.

Meanwhile, the Turks attacked the unprotected eastern front, cap-turing Constantinople. By the time the Venetian Senate "impeached" Foscari, forcing his resignation, Venice was sapped, soon to be sur-passed by the new sea-trading powers of Spain and Portugal.

In the glass case, find doge memorabilia, including the funny **doge cap** with earflaps and a single horn at the back.

• *High on the wall opposite the room's entrance, find the large painting by . . .*

Andre Michieli—*Arrival of Dogess Grimani (Sbarco a San Marco della Dogaressa Morosina Grimani)*

Although doges were men, several wives were elected as co-rulers. This painting shows coronation ceremonies (1597) along the water by the Piazzetta. The lagoon is jammed with boats. Notice the Doge's Palace on the right, the Marciana Library on the left (designed by Jacopo Sansovino), and the Campanile and clock tower in the distance. The dogess (left of center, in yellow, wearing her doge cap tilted back) arrives to receive the front-door key to the Doge's Palace.

The doge's private boat, the *Bucintoro*, (docked at lower left, with red roof) has brought the First Lady and her entourage of red-robed officials, court dwarves, musicians, dancers, and ladies in formal wear. She walks toward the World Theater (on the right, in the water), a floating pavilion used for public ceremonies.

• *Find more doge memorabilia in room 7, in the glass case immediately to the right.*

Room 7:
Manino and Procedural Chart
(Schemi per L'elezione del Doge)

Not a doge backscratcher, the *manino* is a ceremonial hand that counted votes in doge elections.

The elaborate procedural chart established the intricate rules for electing a doge: 30 nobles were chosen by casting lots. Then 21 of the 30 were eliminated by lots. The remaining nine elected 40 nobles, whose number was whittled down to 25 by lots... and so on through several more steps until finally, 41 electors—chosen by their peers and by chance—selected the next doge.

Some doges were powerful dictators, but in general, their power was severely restricted by the Venetian constitution and powerful senators. Doges were largely ceremonial figures, expected to show up in their funny hats for ribbon-cutting ceremonies and state funerals. Doges even needed permission to leave the city.

• *Along the walls of room 7 are two depictions of big parades.*

Processions of the Doge in St. Mark's Square (a woodcut by Matteo Pagan, and a painting by Cesare Vecellio)

The woodcut shows the doge and his court parading around St. Mark's Square in the kind of traditional festivities that Venetians enjoy even today. At the head of the parade (to the right) come the flag bearers and the trumpets sounding the fanfare. Next are the bigwigs, the bishop, the bearer of the doge cap, the doge's chair, and finally "Il Serenissimo" himself, under an umbrella. The ladies look on from the windows above.

In the painting, locate the very same windows of the room you're standing in (at far right of the painting). The square looks much like it does today.

• *The Correr Museum once housed offices, which you'll see in . . .*

Rooms 8–10: Government Offices

Some of the rich furnishings on display in these rooms—rare books in walnut bookcases, a Murano chandelier, wood-beamed ceiling, and paintings—are reminders that this wing once housed the administrative offices of a wealthy, sophisticated Republic.

• *Move to the next room to view Venetian coins. The collection runs chronologically clockwise around the room.*

Room 11: Coins

The Venetian ducat weighed a bit more than a U.S. penny, but was mostly gold. First minted around 1280 (find Giovanni Dandolo's *zecchino*, or "sequin," in the first glass case), it soon became the strongest currency in all Europe.

Also in room 11, find **Tintoretto's** painting of three red-robed, fur-lined treasury officials, the kind of high-level bureaucrats who inhabited these offices. The richness of their robes suggests the almost religious devotion officials were expected to have when care-taking the state business.

Room 12: Venice and the Sea

Venice's wealth came from its sea trade. Raw materials from Europe were exchanged for luxury goods from eastern lands controlled by Muslim Turks.

Models of Galleys *(Modello di Galera)*

These fast, oar- and wind-powered warships rode shotgun for Venice's commercial fleets plying the Mediterranean. With up to four men per oar (some prisoners, some proud professionals) and three horizontal sails, they could cruise from here to Constan-tinople in mere days rather than weeks. In battle, their specialty was turning on a dime to aim cannons, or quickly building up speed to ram and board other ships with their formidable prows.

• *Find two similar paintings depicting . . .*

The Battle of Lepanto (Battaglia di Lepanto, 1571)

The two paintings capture the confusion of a turning-point battle fought in 1571 between Muslim Turks and a coalition of Christ-ians off the coast of Greece. Sort it out by their flags. The turbaned Turks fought under the crescent moon. As for the Christian coali-tion, Venetians had the winged lion, the pope's troops flew the cross, and Spain was marked with the Hapsburg eagle.

The fighting was fierce and hand-to-hand as they boarded each other's ships and cannons blasted away point-blank. Miguel de Cervantes lost his hand, and had to pen *Don Quixote* one-handed.

The Christians won, sinking 240 Turkish ships and killing up to 30,000. It was a major psychological victory, as it finally put to rest the Muslim threat to Europe.

But for Venice, it marked the end of an era. The city lost 4,000 men and many ships, and never fully recovered its trading empire in Turkish lands. Moreover, Spain's cannon-laden sailing ships proved to be masters of the waves, making it a true seagoing power. Venice's shallow-hulled galleys, so swift in the placid Mediterranean, were no match on the high seas.

• *Breeze through room 13, the Arsenale, which depicts a large ship-building factory from Venice's heyday. Next, you'll come to . . .*

Room 14: The Map Room (*Venezia Forma Urbis*)

Old maps show a city relatively unchanged over the centuries, hemmed in by water. Find your hotel on Ughi's map from 1729.

Rooms 15–18: Armory

You'll find weapons from medieval times to the advent of gun powder—maces, armor, swords, Turkish pikes, rifles, cannons, shields, and a teeny-tiny pistol hidden in a book (in a glass case in room 17).

• *Those interested in visiting the National Archaeological Museum (Greek and Roman statues) and the impressive Marciana Library can gain access to them through room 19 (included with Correr admission).*

Otherwise, backtrack to room 14, then head upstairs to the second floor, following signs to the Art Gallery (Pinacoteca). Enter room 25.

SECOND FLOOR
Venetian Painting

The painting highlights (the Bellinis) are located at the far end of this wing, and you have permission to hurry there. But along the way, trace the development of Venetian painting from golden Byzantine icons to Florentine-inspired 3-D to the natural beauty of Bellini and Carpaccio.

Correr Museum—Second Floor

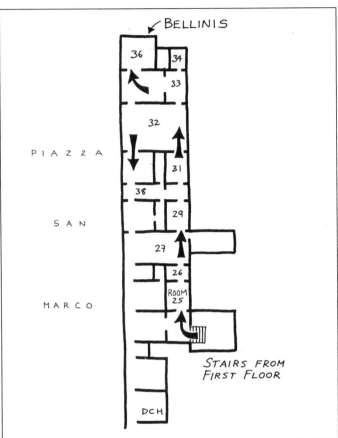

BELLINIS

36   34
33
32
PIAZZA
31
38
SAN
29
27
26
ROOM 25
MARCO

STAIRS FROM FIRST FLOOR

DCH

Room 25:
Paolo Veneziano—*Six Saints* (c. 1310–1358)

Gold-backed saints combine traits from Venice's two cultural sources: Byzantine (serene, somber, and iconic, with gold background, like St. Mark's mosaics) and the Gothic of mainland Europe (curvy, expressive bodies posed at 3/4 angle, and individualized faces).

Room 26:

Lorenzo Veneziano—
Figures and Episodes of Saints
(Figure e Storia di Santi,
c. 1356–1370)*

Influence from the mainland puts
icons in motion, adding drama to
the telling of saints' lives (in the
small figures above the 3 saints).
St. Nicolas grabs the executioner's
sword and lifts him right off the ground before he even knows
what's happening.

Room 27: Ornate (Flamboyant) Gothic

Architectural fragments of Gothic buildings remind us that
Venice's distinctive architecture is French Gothic filtered through
Eastern exoticism.

Room 29.2: International Gothic

Two Painted Lids of Hope Chest
(Storie di Alatiel, c. 1425)*

As humanism spread,
so did art that was not
exclusively religious.
These scenes depict a
story from Boccaccio's
bawdy *Decameron.*
Done in the so-called
International Gothic style, the painted lids emphasize decorative
curves—curvy filigree patterns in clothes, curvy boats, curvy
sails, curvy waves, curvy horses' rumps—all enjoyed as a
decorative pattern.

Room 31.1:

Ferrarese Painters—*Portrait*
of a Young Man (Ritratto di
Gentiluomo, c. 1442–1564)*

The young man in red is not a saint,
king, or pope, but an ordinary citizen
painted, literally, wart and all. On the
window ledge is a strongly foreshortened book. And behind the young
man, the curtain opens to reveal a
new world—a spacious 3-D vista
courtesy of the Tuscan Renaissance.

Room 32:
Jacopo de Barbari—*Venetie MD* (1500)

How little Venice has changed in 500 years! Barbari's large, intricately detailed woodcut of the city put his contemporaries in a unique position—a mile up in the air, looking down on the rooftops. He chronicles nearly every church, alleyway, and gondola. Both the final product and the reverse-image woodcut are on display, a tribute to all of Barbari's painstaking labor.

Room 33: 15th-Century Flemish Artists

Pieter Breughel the Younger—*Adoration (Adorazione dei Magi)*

Venetian artists were strongly influenced by the detailed everyday landscapes of Northern masters. Lost in this snowy scene of the secular work world is baby Jesus in a stable (lower left), worshiped by the Magi. Venetians learned that landscape creates its own mood, and that humans don't have to be the center of every painting.

Room 34:
Antonello da Messina— *Christ with Three Angels (Pieta con Tre Angeli,* c. 1475)

This Sicilian painter wowed Venice with this work when he visited in 1475, bringing a Renaissance style and new painting techniques. After a thousand years of standing rigidly on medieval crucifixes, Christ can finally let his body relax into a natural human posture.

Remember this work; I'll refer to it later in this tour.

Room 36: The Bellini Family (I Bellini)

One family brought Venetian painting into the Renaissance—
the Bellinis.

Jacopo Bellini—*Crucifixion (La Crocifissione)*

Father Jacopo (c. 1400–1470) had studied in Florence when Donatello and Brunelleschi were pioneering 3-D naturalism.

Daughter Cecilia (not a painter) married the painter Mantegna, whose precise lines and statuesque figures influenced his brothers-in-law.

Gentile Bellini—
Portrait of Doge Mocenigo

Elder son Gentile (c. 1429–1507) took over the family business and established a reputation for documenting Venice's rulers and official ceremonies. His straight-forward style and attention to detail captures the ordinary essence of this doge.

Giovanni Bellini—
Crucifixion (La Crocifissione)

Younger son Giovanni (c. 1430) became the most famous Bellini,

the man who pioneered new techniques and subject matter, trained Titian and Giorgione, and almost single-handedly invented the Venetian High Renaissance.

Compare this early *Crucifixion* (young Giovanni's earliest documented work) with his father's version. Young Giovanni weeds out all the crowded, medieval mourners, leaving only Mary and John. Behind, he paints a spacious (Mantegnesque) landscape, with a lake and mountains in the distance. Our eyes follow the winding road from Christ to the airy horizon, ascending like a soul to heaven.

Giovanni Bellini—*Christ Supported by Two Angels*
(Cristo Morto Sorreto da Due Angeli, 1453–1455)

In another early work, Giovanni explores human anatomy, with exaggerated veins, a heaving diaphragm, and even a hint of pubic

hair. Mentally compare this stiff, static work with Antonello da Messina's far more natural *Christ with Three Angels* done 20 years later to see how far Giovanni still had to go. In fact, Giovanni was greatly influenced by Antonello, learning above all about the new invention of oil-based paint. Armed with this more transparent paint, he could add subtler shades of color and rely less on the sharply outlined forms we see here.

Giovanni Bellini—*Madonna and Child* (*Madonna Frizzoni*)

Though the canvas is a bit wrinkled, it reminds us of the subject Giovanni would paint again and again—lovely, forever young Mary (often shown from the waist up) holding rosy-cheeked baby Jesus. He portrayed their holiness with a natural-looking, pastel-colored, soft-focus beauty.

Room 38:
Vittore Carpaccio—*Two Venetian Ladies* (*a.k.a. The Courtesans*, c. 1500–1510)

Two well-dressed Venetians look totally bored, despite being surrounded by a wealth of exotic pets and amusements. One lady absentmindedly plays with a dog, while the other stares into space. Romantics imagined them to be kept ladies awaiting lovers, but the recent discovery of the missing companion painting tells us they're waiting for their menfolk to return from hunting.

The colorful details and love of luxury are elements that would dominate the Venetian High Renaissance. Fascinating stuff, but my eyes are starting to glaze like theirs . . . .

ACCADEMIA
TOUR
Galleria dell'Accademia

The Accademia (ack-ah-DAY-mee-ah) is the greatest museum anywhere for Venetian Renaissance art, and a good overview of painters whose works you'll see all over town. Venetian art is underrated and, I think, misunderstood. It's nowhere near as famous today as the work of the florescent Florentines, but it's livelier, more colorful, and simply more fun.

Orientation
Cost: €6.20.

Hours: Mon 8:15–14:00, Tue–Sun 8:15–19:15 (shorter hours off-season). Visit early or late to miss crowds.

Getting There: The museum faces the Grand Canal, just over the Accademia Bridge (15-min walk from St. Mark's Square—follow signs to "Accademia"). Vaporetto stop: Accademia.

While you're in the Accademia neighorhood, consider visiting the Peggy Guggenheim Museum's excellent collection of modern art, a five-minute walk east along the Grand Canal (🟊 see Tour on page 130); and the historic La Salute Church (🟊 see Tour on page 143), just beyond the Guggenheim.

Information: Precious little. Some rooms have sheets of infor mation in English. Guidebooks are sold for €7.75 in the book-shop. Tel. 041-522-2247.

Tours: An audioguide tour costs €3.60 (€5.20 with 2 ear-phones, or €6 for palm pilot). You can't fast forward through the dull parts.

Length of Our Tour: One hour.

Cuisine Art: Bar Accademia Foscarini is a simple pizzeria at the base of the Accademia Bridge.

Photography: Not allowed.

Starring: Titian, Veronese, Giorgione, Bellini, and Tintoretto.

Accademia Overview

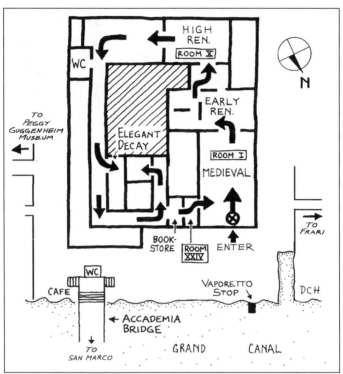

VENICE—SWIMMING IN LUXURY

The Venetian love of luxury shines through in Venetian painting.
We'll see grand canvases of colorful, spacious settings peopled
with happy Venetians in luxurious clothes having a great time.
Even in solemn religious works, the Venetian love of color and
beauty is obvious.

We'll work chronologically from medieval days to the 1700s.
But before we start at the medieval beginning, let's sneak a peek
at a work by the greatest Venetian Renaissance master, Titian.

• *Buy your ticket, check your bag, and head upstairs to a large hall
filled with gold-leaf altarpieces. Immediately past the turnstile, turn
left, enter the small room XXIV, and take a seat.*

Titian (Tiziano Vecellio)—*Presentation of the Virgin*

This work is typical of Venetian Renaissance art. Here and
throughout this museum, you will find: 1) bright, rich color;

2) big canvases; 3) Renaissance architectural backgrounds; 4) slice-of-life scenes of Venice (notice the market woman in the foreground selling eggs); and 5) 3-D realism.

The scene is the popular story of the child Mary, later to be the mother of Jesus, being presented to the high priest in Jerusalem's temple. But here the religious scene is more an excuse for a grand display of Renaissance architecture and colorful robes.

The painting is a parade of colors. Titian (TEESH-un) leads you from color to color. First, the deep blue sky and mountains in the background. Then down to the bright red robe of one of the elders. Then you notice the figures turning and pointing at something. Your eye follows up the stairs to the magnificent jeweled robes of the priests.

But wait! What's that along the way? In a pale blue dress that sets her apart from all the other colored robes, dwarfed by the enormous staircase and columns, is the tiny, shiny figure of the child Mary, almost floating up to the astonished priest. She is unnaturally small, towered over by the priests, and easily overlooked at first glance. When we finally notice her, we realize all the more how delicate she is, a fragile flower amid the hustle, bustle, and epic grandeur. Venetians love this painting and call it, appropriately enough, "the Little Mary."

Now that we've gotten a taste of Renaissance Venice at its peak, let's backtrack and see some of Titian's predecessors.

• *Return to room I, stopping at a work (near the turnstile) of Mary and baby Jesus.*

MEDIEVAL ART—PRE-3-D

Medieval painting, such as the work you see in this hall, was religious. The point was to teach Bible stories and doctrines to the illiterate masses by using symbolism. This art, then, is less realistic, less colorful, and less dramatic than later Renaissance art. Look around the hall, and you'll see a lot of gold in the paintings. Medieval Venetians, with their close ties to the East, borrowed techniques such as gold-leafing from Byzantine (modern Istanbul) religious icons.

Medieval Art

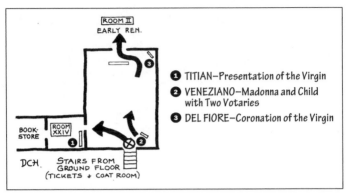

1 TITIAN—Presentation of the Virgin
2 VENEZIANO—Madonna and Child with Two Votaries
3 DEL FIORE—Coronation of the Virgin

Veneziano—*Madonna and Child with Two Votaries (Madonna e Bambino con Due Votari)*

There's a golden Byzantine background of heaven, and the golden

haloes let the masses know that these folks are holy. The child Jesus is a baby in a bubble, an iconographical symbol of his "aura" of holiness.

Notice how two-dimensional and unrealistic this painting is. The size of the figures reflects their religious importance, not their actual size—

Mary is huge, being both the mother of Christ as well as "Holy Mother Church." Jesus is next, then the two angels crowning Mary. Finally, in the corner, are two mere mortals kneeling in devotion.

• *In the far right corner of the room, you'll find . . .*

Jacobello del Fiore—*Coronation of the Virgin*

This swarming beehive of saints and angels is an attempt to cram as much information as possible into one space. The architectural setting is a clumsy attempt at three-dimensionality (the railings of the wedding-cake structure are literally glued on). The saints are simply stacked one on top of the other, rather than receding into the distance as they would in real life.

• *Enter room II at the far end of this hall.*

Early Renaissance

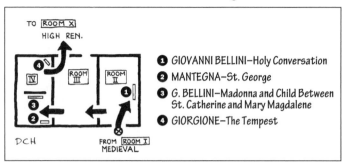

● GIOVANNI BELLINI–Holy Conversation

② MANTEGNA–St. George

❸ G. BELLINI–Madonna and Child Between St. Catherine and Mary Magdalene

④ GIORGIONE–The Tempest

EARLY RENAISSANCE (1450–1500)

Only a few decades later, artists rediscovered the natural world and how to capture it on canvas. With this Renaissance, or "rebirth," of the arts and attitudes of ancient Greece and Rome, painters took a giant leap forward. They weeded out the jumble of symbols, fleshed out cardboard characters into real people, and placed them in spacious 3-D settings.

Giovanni Bellini—*Holy Conversation* (*Pala di San Giobbe*)

Giovanni Bellini (bell-EE-nee) takes only a few figures, places them in a spacious architectural setting, and balances them half on one side of Mary and half on the other. Left to right, you'll find Francis (founder of an order of medieval monks), John the Baptist, Job, Dominic (founder of another order of monks), Sebastian, and Louis. The overall effect is one of calm and serenity, rather than the hubbub of the "Coronation" we just saw. Look at St. Sebastian—even arrows can't disturb the serenity.

This is one of Bellini's lifelong series of paintings in the *Sacra Conversazione* formula: Mary and Child surrounded by saints "conversing" informally about holy matters. The formula, developed largely by Fra Angelico (1400–1455), became a common Renaissance theme—compare this painting with other *Sacras* by Bellini that can be seen in the Frari Church (on page 115) and the Church of San Zaccaria (on page 166).

This religious scene—a mythical meeting of Mary and the baby Jesus with saints—is set underneath an arched half dome. In its original church setting, the painting's pillars and arches matched the real ones in the church, as though Bellini had blown a hole in the wall and built another chapel, allowing us mortals to mingle with holies.

The painting has three descending arches. The top one is the Roman arch. Below it is a pyramid-shaped "arch" formed by the figures themselves, with Mary's head at the peak. Still lower is a smaller arch formed by the three musician angels. Subconsciously, this creates a mood of spaciousness, order, and balance.

Bellini was the teacher of two more Venetian greats, Titian and Giorgione. His gift to the Venetian Renaissance was the "haze" he put over his scenes, giving them an idealized, glowing, serene—and much copied—atmosphere. (You can see more of Bellini's work at the Correr Museum, page tk; Frari Church, page tk; and the Church of San Zaccaria, page tk.)

• *Climb the small staircase and pass through room III and into the small room IV.*

Mantegna—*St. George (San Giorgio)*
This Christian warrior is essentially a Greek nude sculpture with armor painted on. Notice his stance with the weight resting on one leg (*contrapposto*), the same as a classical sculpture, Michelangelo's *David*, or an Italian guy trying to look cool on the street corner. Also, Mantegna (mahn-TAYN-yah) has placed him in a doorway that's like an architectural niche for a classical statue.

The Renaissance began in Florence among sculptors and architects. Even the painters were sculptors, "carving" out figures (like this) with sharp outlines, filling them in with color, and setting them in front of distant backdrops. *St. George* is different from other works in the museum. It has a harder Florentine edge to it, compared with the hazy Venetian outlines of Bellini. But when Mantegna married Bellini's sister, he brought Florentine realism and draftsmanship to his in-laws.

St. George typifies Renaissance balance—a combination of stability and movement, alertness and relaxation, humility and

proud confidence. With the broken lance in his hand and the dragon at his feet, George is the strong Renaissance Man slaying the medieval dragon of superstition and oppression.
• *Find three women and a baby on a black background.*

Giovanni Bellini—*Madonna and Child Between St. Catherine and Mary Magdalene*

In contrast to Mantegna's sharp three-dimensionality, this is just three heads on a flat plane with a black backdrop. Their features are soft, hazy, and atmospheric, glowing out of the darkness as though lit by the soft light of a candle. It's not sculptural line that's important here, but color—warm, golden, glowing flesh tones.

Bellini painted dozens of Madonna and Childs in his day. (Others are nearby.) This Virgin Mary's pretty, but she can't compare with the sheer idealized beauty of Mary Magdalene (on the right). With her hair down like the prostitute that legend says she was, yet with a childlike face, thoughtful and repentant, this is the perfect image of the innocent woman who sinned by loving too much.
• *Around the partition, you'll find . . .*

Giorgione—*The Tempest*

It's the calm before the storm. The atmosphere is heavy, luminous but ominous. There's a sense of mystery. Who is the woman nursing her baby in the middle of the countryside? And the soldier—is he spying on her or protecting her? Will lightning strike? Do

they know that the serenity of this beautiful landscape is about to be shattered by an approaching storm?

The mystery is heightened by contrasting elements. The armed soldier contrasts with the naked lady with her baby. The austere ruined columns contrast with the lusciousness of Nature. And, most important, the stillness of the foreground scene is in direct opposition to the threatening storm in the background.

Giorgione (jor-JONE-ee) was as mysterious as his few paintings, yet he left a lasting impression. A student of Bellini, he learned to use haziness to create a melancholy mood of beauty in his work. But nothing beautiful lasts. Flowers fade, Mary Magdalenes grow old, and, in *The Tempest*, the fleeting stillness of a rare moment of peace is about to be shattered by the slash of lightning—the true center of the composition.

• *Exit and pass through several rooms, then continue up the steps to the large room X.*

VENETIAN HIGH RENAISSANCE— TITIAN, VERONESE, AND TINTORETTO (1500–1600)

Veronese—*Feast of the House of Levi*

Parrrrty!! Stand about 10 meters away from this enormous canvas, to where it just fills your field of vision . . . and hey, you're invited. Venice loves the good life, and the party's in full swing. You're in a huge room with a great view of Venice. Everyone's dressed to kill in brightly colored silks. Conversation roars and the servants bring on the food and drink.

This captures the Venetian attitude (more love, less attitude) as well as the style of Venetian Renaissance painting. Remember: (1) bright colors, (2) big canvases, (3) Renaissance architectural settings, (4) scenes of Venetian life, and (5) 3-D realism. Painters had mastered realism and now gloried in it.

The *Feast of the House of Levi* is, believe it or not, a religious work painted for a monastery. The original title was *The Last Supper*. In the center of all the wild goings-on, there's Jesus, flanked by his disciples, sharing a final meal before his crucifixion.

This festive feast shows the optimistic spirit of pagan Greece and Rome that was reborn in the Renaissance. Life was a good thing, beauty was to be enjoyed, and man was a strong, good creature capable of making his own decisions and planning his own life. Yet, to Renaissance men and women, this didn't exclude religion. To them, the divine was seen in the beauties of Nature, God was glorified by glorifying man, and humanism was an expression of devotion.

Uh-uh, said the Church. In its eyes, the new humanism was the same as the old atheism. The false spring of the Renaissance

High Renaissance

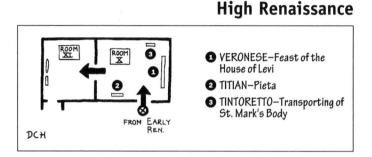

0 VERONESE–Feast of the House of Levi

2 TITIAN–Pieta

3 TINTORETTO–Transporting of St. Mark's Body

FROM EARLY REN.

DCH

froze quickly after the Reformation, when half of Europe left the Catholic Church and became Protestant.

Veronese (vayr-oh-NAY-zee) was hauled before the Inquisition. What did he mean by painting such a bawdy Last Supper? With dwarf jesters? And apostles picking their teeth? And half-dressed ladies? And dogs? And a black man, God forbid? And worst of all, some German soldiers—that is, Protestants (gasp!)— at the far right!

Veronese argued that it was just artistic license, so they asked to see his—it had expired. But the solution was simple. Rather than change the painting, just fine-tune the title. *Si, no problema. The Last Supper* became the *Feast of the House of Levi.* (See the new title written in Latin on the railing to the left: *"FECIT D. COVI...,"* etc.)

Titian (Tiziano Vecellio)—*Pietà*

The Counter-Reformation affected even the great Titian in his last years. Titian was perhaps the most famous painter of his day— even more famous than Michelangelo. He was a great portrait painter and a friend of the dukes, kings, and popes he painted. He was cultured, witty, a fine musician, and businessman—an all-around Renaissance kind of guy.

Titian was old when he painted this. He had seen the rise and decline of the Renaissance. Remember "Little Mary," the colorful, exuberant Titian painting we saw at the beginning, done at the height of the Renaissance? Now the canvas is darker, the mood more somber. Jesus has just been executed, and his followers have removed his body from the cross. They grieve over it before burying it. Titian painted this to hang over his own tomb.

There are some Renaissance elements, but they create a whole different mood—the optimism is gone. Jesus is framed by a sculpture niche like Bellini's *Holy Conversation*, but here the massive Roman architecture overpowers the figures, making them look puny and helpless. The lion statues are downright fierce and

threatening. Instead of the clear realism of Renaissance paintings, Titian has used rough, messy brush strokes, a technique that would be picked up by the Impressionists three centuries later. Instead of simple Renaissance balance, Titian has added a dramatic compositional element—starting with the lion at lower right, a line sweeps up diagonally along the figures, culminating in the grief-stricken Mary Magdalene, who turns away, flinging her arm in despair.

Finally, the kneeling figure of old, bald Nicodemus is a self-portrait of the aging Titian himself, tending to the corpse of Jesus, who symbolizes the once powerful, now dead Renaissance Man. In the lower right, a painting-within-the-painting shows Titian and his son kneeling, asking the Virgin to spare them from the plague of 1576. Unfortunately, Titian's son died from it, and a heartbroken Titian died shortly after.

(To see more Titians, visit the Frari Church, which houses the painter's tomb, on page 112, and the Doge's Palace, on page 63.)
• *On the opposite wall, find . . .*

Tintoretto (Jacopo Robusto)—
The Transporting of St. Mark's Body
(Trafugamento del Corpo di San Marco)
This portrays the event that put Venice on the map, painted in the dramatic, emotional style that developed after the Renaissance. Tintoretto has caught the scene at its most dramatic moment. The Muslims in Alexandria are about to burn Mark's body

(there's the smoke from the fire in the center) when suddenly a hurricane appears miraculously, sending them running for cover. (See the wisps of baby-angel faces in the storm, blowing on the infidels? Look hard, on the left-hand side.) Meanwhile, the Venetian merchants whisk the body away.

Tintoretto makes us part of the action. The square tiles in the courtyard run straight away from us, an extension of our reality, as though we could step right into the scene—or the merchants could carry Mark into ours.

Tintoretto would have made a great black-velvet painter. His colors burn with a metallic sheen, and he does everything possible to make his subject popular with common people.

In fact, Tintoretto was a common man himself, self-taught, who took only a few classes from Titian before striking out on his own. He sold paintings in the marketplace in his youth and insisted on living in the poor part of town even after he became famous.

Tintorettos abound here, in the next room, and throughout Venice. Look for these characteristics, some of which became standard features of Baroque art that followed the Renaissance: 1) heightened drama, violent scenes, strong emotions; 2) elongated bodies in twisting poses; 3) strong contrasts between dark and light; 4) vibrant colors; and 5) diagonal compositions.

(Tintoretto fans will want to visit the Scuola San Rocco, Tintoretto's "Sistine Chapel"; see page 102.)

• *Spend some time in this room, the peak of Venice and the climax of the museum. After browsing, enter the next large room (room XI) and find a large round painting.*

ELEGANT DECAY (1600–1800)

G. B. Tiepolo—*Discovery of the True Cross (La Scopera della Vera Croce)*

Tiepolo was the last of the great colorful, theatrical Venetian painters. He took the colors of Titian, the grand settings of Veronese, and the dramatic angles of Tintoretto and plastered them on the ceilings of Europe. His works decorate the ceilings of Baroque palaces such as the Royal Palace in Madrid, Spain; the Residenz in Würzburg, Germany; and the Ca' Rezzonico in Venice (✪ see Ca' Rezzonico Tour on page 118). This one is from a church ceiling.

Tiepolo blasts open a sunroof as though the church opens up into heaven. He places us viewers down in the hole where they've just dug up Christ's cross. We look up dresses and nostrils as saints and angels cavort overhead. His strongly "foreshortened" figures are masterpieces of technical skill, making us feel like the heavenly vision is taking place right overhead. Think back on those clumsy attempts at three-dimensionality we saw in the medieval room, and realize how far painting has come.

• *Works of the later Venetians are in rooms branching off the long corridor to your left. Walking down the corridor, the first right leads to the WC. Stop in room XVII, the first door on the left.*

Elegant Decay

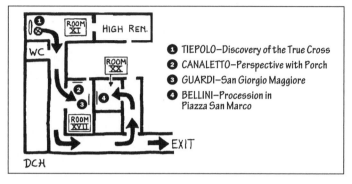

① TIEPOLO—Discovery of the True Cross
② CANALETTO—Perspective with Porch
③ GUARDI—San Giorgio Maggiore
④ BELLINI—Procession in Piazza San Marco

Canaletto and Guardi: Views of Venice

By the 1700s, Venice had retired as a world power and become Europe's #1 tourist attraction. Wealthy offspring of the nobility traveled here to soak up its art and culture. They wanted souvenirs, and what better memento than a picture of the city itself?

Guardi and Canaletto painted "postcards" for visitors who lost their heart to the romance of Venice. The city produced less art... but *was* art. Here are some familiar views of a city that has aged gracefully.

Canaletto (Antonio Canal, detto Canaletto)—
Perspective with Porch (Prospettiva con Portico)

Canaletto gives us a sharp-focus, wide-lens, camera's-eye perspective on the city. Although this view of a porch looks totally realistic, Canaletto has compressed the whole scene to allow us to see more than the human eye could realistically take in. We see the porch as though we were standing underneath it, yet we also see the whole porch at one glance. The pavement blocks, the lines of columns, and the slanting roof direct our eye to the far end, which looks very far away, indeed. Canaletto even shows a coat of arms (at right) at a very odd angle, demonstrating his mastery of 3-D perspective.

Guardi—*San Giorgio Maggiore (Il Bacino di San Marco con San Giorgio Maggiore e Giudecca)*

Unlike Canaletto, with his sharp-focus detail, Guardi sweetens

Venice up with a haze of messy brushwork. In this familiar view across the water from St. Mark's Square, he builds a boat-man with a few sloppy smudges of paint. Guardi catches the play of light at twilight, the shadows on the buildings, the green of the water and sky, the pink light off the distant buildings, the Venice that exists in the hearts of lovers—an Impressionist work a century ahead of its time.

• *Follow the corridor, turn left at the end, then take another left, and then left again. Are you in room XX?*

Gentile Bellini—*Procession in Piazza San Marco (Processione in Piazza San Marco)*

A fitting end to our tour is a look back at Venice in its heyday. This wide-angle view by Giovanni's big brother—more than any

human eye could take in at once—reminds us how little Venice has changed over the centuries. There is St. Mark's gleaming gold with mosaics, the three flagpoles out front, the old Campanile on the right, and the Doge's Palace. There's the guy selling 10 postcards for a dollar. (But there's no clock tower with the two bronze Moors yet.) Every detail is in perfect focus regard-less of its distance from us, presented for our inspection. Take some time to linger over this and the other views of old Venice in this room. Then get outta here and enjoy the real thing.

• *To exit, backtrack to the main corridor and turn left past the book-store. Say* ciao *to Titian's* Little Mary *on the way out.*

SCUOLA SAN ROCCO TOUR

Scuola Grande di San Rocco

The 50-plus paintings in the Scuola Grande di San Rocco—often called Tintoretto's "Sistine Chapel"—present one man's very personal vision of Christian history. Tintoretto (1518–1594) spent the last 20 years of his life working virtually for free, driven by the spirit of Christian charity the Scuola promoted. For Tintoretto fans, this is the ultimate. But even for the art-weary, his large, colorful canvases, framed in gold on the walls and ceilings of a grand upper hall, are an impressive sight.

Orientation

Cost: €5.20. (If you see an evening concert here, you can enjoy the art as a bonus; see page 236.)

Hours: Daily 9:00–17:00.

Getting There: It's next to the Frari Church (✪ see Tour on page 112). Vaporetto: San Tomá. To walk here from the Rialto Bridge, take my recommended Rialto to Frari Church Walk, page 159.

Comfort Tip: Use the mirrors scattered about the museum (some are set in rolling tables, others are handheld), because much of this art is on the ceiling and a literal pain in the neck.

Length of Our Tour: One hour.

Starring: Tintoretto, Tintoretto, and Tintoretto.

Overview

The art of the "Scuola" is contained in three rooms—the ground-floor entry hall and two rooms upstairs. We'll start upstairs, seeing the art roughly in the order Tintoretto painted it:

1. Albergo Hall (a small room on the upper floor), with Passion scenes.
2. Great Upper Floor Hall, with the biggest canvases.
3. Ground Floor, with the life of Mary.

Scuola San Rocco

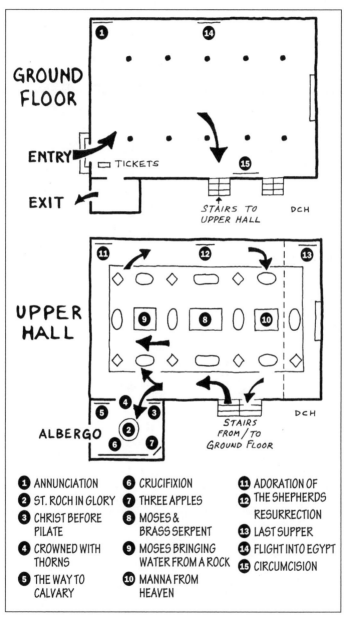

GROUND FLOOR

ENTRY

TICKETS

EXIT

STAIRS TO UPPER HALL

DCH

UPPER HALL

STAIRS FROM / TO GROUND FLOOR

DCH

ALBERGO

1. ANNUNCIATION
2. ST. ROCH IN GLORY
3. CHRIST BEFORE PILATE
4. CROWNED WITH THORNS
5. THE WAY TO CALVARY
6. CRUCIFIXION
7. THREE APPLES
8. MOSES & BRASS SERPENT
9. MOSES BRINGING WATER FROM A ROCK
10. MANNA FROM HEAVEN
11. ADORATION OF THE SHEPHERDS
12. RESURRECTION
13. LAST SUPPER
14. FLIGHT INTO EGYPT
15. CIRCUMCISION

• *Enter on the ground floor. When you buy your ticket, you find yourself in the Ground Floor Hall, which is lined with big, colorful Tintoretto canvases. Before heading upstairs, begin in the left corner with . . .*

The Annunciation

An angel swoops through the doorway, dragging a trail of naked baby angels with him, to tell a startled Mary she'll give birth to Jesus.

This canvas illustrates many of Tintoretto's typical characteristics:
• **The miraculous and the everyday mingle side by side**. Glorious angels are in a broken-down house with stacks of lumber and a frayed chair.
• **Bright light and dark shadows**. A bright light strikes the brick column, highlighting Mary's face and the angel's shoulder, but casting dark shadows across the room.
• **Strong 3-D sucks you into the scene**. Tintoretto literally tears down Mary's wall to let us in. The floor tiles recede sharply into the distance, making Mary's room an extension of our real space.
• **Colors that are bright, almost harsh**, with a metallic "black-velvet" sheen, especially when contrasted with the soft-focus haze of Bellini, Giorgione, Veronese, and some Titian.
• **Twisting, muscular poses**. The angel turns one way, Mary turns the other, and the baby angels turn every which way.
• **Diagonal composition**. Shadows run diagonally on the floor as Mary leans back diagonally.
• **Rough brushwork**. The sketchy pattern on Mary's ceiling contrasts with the precise photo-realism of the brick column.

And finally, *The Annunciation* exemplifies the general theme of the San Rocco paintings—God intervenes miraculously into our everyday lives in order to save us.

• *We'll return to the ground floor later, but let's start where Tintoretto did. Climb the staircase (admiring plague scenes that are not by Tintoretto) and enter the impressive Great Hall.*

The Albergo Hall is a small room in the left corner of the Great Hall. On the ceiling of the Albergo Hall is an oval painting of St. Roch, best viewed from the doorway.

Jacopo Tintoretto (1518–1594)

The son of a silk dyer ("Tintoretto" is a nickname meaning "little dyer"), Tintoretto applied a blue-collar work ethic to painting, becoming one of the most prolific artists ever. He trained briefly under Titian, but their egos clashed. He was more influenced by Michelangelo's recently completed *Last Judgment*, with its muscular, twisting, hovering nudes and epic scale.

By age 30, Tintoretto was famous, astounding Venice with the innovative *St. Mark Freeing the Slave* (now in the Accademia). He married, had eight children (3 of whom became his assistants), and dedicated himself to work and family, shunning publicity and living his whole life in his old Venice neighborhood.

The last 20 years of his life were spent decorating the Scuola di San Rocco. It was a labor of love, showing his religious faith, his compassion for the poor, and his passion for art.

ALBERGO HALL *(SALA D'ALBERGO)* — Christ's Passion

St. Roch in Glory (1564)

This is the first of Tintoretto's 50-plus paintings in the Scuola. It's also the one that got him the job, beating entries by Veronese and others.

Tintoretto amazed the judges by showing the saint from beneath, as though he hovered above in a circle of glory. At the time, this was an almost unheard-of feat of painterly illusion, though it would later become standard in Baroque ceilings. Tintoretto trained by dangling wax models from the ceiling and lighting them from odd angles.

St. Roch (San Rocco) was a French med student in the 1300s who dedicated his short life to treating plague victims. The "Scuola" of San Rocco was a kind of Venetian "Elk's Club" whose favorite charity was poor plague victims.

• *On the walls are scenes of Christ's trial, torture, and execution. Work counterclockwise around the room, starting by the door with . . .*

Christ Before Pilate (Ecce Homo)

Jesus has been arrested and brought before the Roman authorities in a cavernous hall. Though he says nothing in his own defense, he stands head and shoulders above the crowd, literally "rising above" the slanders. Tintoretto shines a bright light on his white robe, making Christ radiate innocence.

At Christ's feet, an old bearded man in white stoops over to record the events on paper—it's Tintoretto himself.

Christ Crowned with Thorns

Jesus was beaten, whipped, then mocked by the soldiers who dressed him as a king "crowned" with thorns. Seeing the bloodstains on the cloth must have touched the hearts of Scuola members, generating compassion for those who suffer.

The Way to Calvary

Silhouetted against a stormy sky, Jesus and two other prisoners trudge up a steep hill, carrying their own crosses to the execution site. The cycle culminates with . . .

The Crucifixion

The crucified Christ is the calm center of this huge and chaotic scene that fills the wall. Workers struggle to hoist crosses, mourners swoon, riffraff gamble for Christ's clothes, and soldiers

mill about aimlessly. Scarcely anyone pays any attention to the Son of God . . . except us, because Tintoretto directs our eye there.

All the lines of sight point to Christ at the center: the ladder on the ground, the cross being raised, the cross still on the ground, the horses on the right, and the hillsides that slope in. In a trick of multiple perspectives, the cross being raised seems to suck us in toward the center, while the cross still on the ground seems to cause the figures to be sucked toward us.

Above the chaos stands Christ, high above the horizon, higher than everyone, glowing against the dark sky. Tintoretto lets us appreciate the quiet irony lost on the frenetic participants—that this minor criminal suffering such apparent degradation is, in fact, triumphant.

• *Displayed on an easel to the left of and beneath* The Crucifixion *is a small fragment of . . .*

Three Apples

This fragment, from the frieze around the upper reaches of the Albergo Hall, was discovered folded under the frieze in 1905. Because it was never exposed to light, it still has Tintoretto's original (bright)

colors. All his paintings are darker today, despite cleaning, due to the irretrievable chemical alteration of the pigments.

• *Now step back out into the Great Upper Hall . . .*

GREAT UPPER HALL—
Old Testament and New Testament

Thirty-four enormous oil canvases, set into gold frames on the ceiling and along the walls of this impressive room, tell the biblical history from Adam and Eve to the Ascension of Christ. Tintoretto's storytelling style is straightforward, and anyone with Bible knowledge can quickly get the gist.

Tintoretto's success in the Albergo Hall won him the job of the enormous Great Upper Hall. He dutifully delivered three canvases a year on St. Roch's feast day, refusing payment beyond expenses.

Understanding What You're Standing Under

The ceiling has Old Testament scenes; the walls have New Testament scenes. The three large rectangles on the ceiling are stories of Moses.

Beyond that, it's difficult to say what overall program Tintoretto had in mind. It's not chronological. There's no consistent symbolism. Theologically, a few panels seem to belong together, matching, say, the *Fall of Man* with Christ's redemption. And some clusters of panels have similar motifs, such as water (at the Albergo end of the hall), plagues and death (middle of the hall), and nourishment (altar end).

But ultimately, Tintoretto's vision is a very personal one, open to many interpretations. The art was inspired by the charitable spirit of the Scuola—just as God has helped those who suffer, so should we.
• *Start with the large, central rectangle on the ceiling. View it from the top (the Albergo end), not directly underneath.*

Moses and the Brass Serpent

The tangle of half-naked bodies (at the bottom of the painting) is the children of Israel, wrestling with poisonous snakes and writhing in pain. At the top of the pile, a young woman gestures toward Moses (in pink), who points to a pole carrying a brass serpent sent by God. Those that looked at the statue were miraculously healed. His work all done, God (above in the clouds) high-fives an angel.

This was the first of the Great Hall panels, and no sooner had Tintoretto begun than Venice was hit by its worst plague (1576). One in four died. Four hundred a day were buried. (They say Tintoretto's colleague, Titian, died of heartbreak soon after his son died of the plague.) Like today's Red Cross, the Scuola sprang into action, raising funds, sending doctors, and giving beds to the sick and aid to their families. Tintoretto saw the dead and dying firsthand. He captures their suffering while giving a ray of hope that help is on the way.

There are dozens of figures in the painting, shown from every conceivable angle. Tintoretto was well aware of where it would hang and how it would be viewed. Walk around beneath it, and see the different angles come alive. The painting becomes a movie, and the children of Israel writhe like snakes.
• *The rectangular panel at the Albergo end of the hall is . . .*

Moses Bringing Water from a Rock

Moses (in pink, in the center) hits a rock in the desert with his staff, and it miraculously spouts water, which the thirsty Israelites catch in jars. The water spurts like a ray of light. Moses is a strong, calm center to a spinning wheel of activity.

Tintoretto worked fast, and if nothing else, his art is exuberant. He'd trained in fresco painting, where you have to finish before the plaster dries. With these, he sketched an outline right onto the canvas, then improvised details as he went.

The sheer magnitude of the San Rocco project is staggering.

This canvas alone is 28 square meters (300 square feet)—like painting a bathroom with an artist's tiny brush. The whole project, counting the Albergo Hall, Great Upper Hall, and the Ground Floor Hall together, totals some 800 square meters (8,500 square feet)—more than enough to cover a typical house, inside and out. (The Sistine Chapel ceiling, by comparison, is 530 square meters, or 5,700 square feet.)

• *The rectangular panel at the altar end of the hall is . . .*

Manna from Heaven

It's snowing bread, as God feeds the hungry Israelites with a miraculous storm. They stretch a blanket to catch it, and gather it up in baskets. Up in the center of the dark cloud is a radiant, almost transparent God painted with sketchy brush strokes that suggest he's an unseen presence.

Tintoretto tells these Bible stories with a literalness that was very popular with the poor, uneducated sick who sought help from the Scuola. He was the Spielberg of his day, with the technical know-how to bring imagination to life, to make the miraculous tangible.

• *You could grow old studying all the art here, so we'll select just a couple of the New Testament paintings on the walls. Start at the Albergo end with . . .*

The Adoration of the Shepherds

Christ's glorious life begins in a straw-filled stable with cows,

chickens, and peasants who pass plates of food up to the new parents. It's night, with just a few details lit by phosphorescent moonlight: the kneeling shepherd's forehead and leggings, the serving girl's shoulders, the faces of Mary and Joseph . . . and little baby Jesus, a smudge of light.

Notice the different points of view. Tintoretto clearly has placed us on the lower floor, about eye level with the cow, and looking up through the roof beams at the night sky. But we also see Mary and Joseph in the loft above as though they were at eye level. By using multiple perspectives (and ignoring the laws of physics), Tintoretto could portray every detail at its perfect angle.

• *In the middle of the long wall, find . . .*

The Resurrection

Angels lift the sepulchre lid, and Jesus springs forth in a blaze of light. The contrast between dark and light is extreme, with great dramatic effect.

• *At the altar end of the wall, find . . .*

The Last Supper

A dog, a beggar, and a serving girl dominate the foreground of Christ's final Passover meal with his followers. More servants work in the background. The disciples themselves are dining in the dark, some with their backs to us, with only a few stray highlights to show us what's going on. Tintoretto emphasizes the human, everyday element of that gathering, in contrast to, say, Leonardo da Vinci's more stately

version. And he sets the scene at a diagonal for dramatic effect.

The table stretches across a tiled floor, a commonly used device to create 3-D space. But Tintoretto makes the more distant tiles unnaturally small to exaggerate the distance. Similarly, the table and the people get proportionally smaller and lower until, at the far end of the table, tiny Jesus (with glowing head) is only half the size of the disciple at the near end.

Theatrically, Tintoretto leaves it to us to piece together the familiar narrative. The disciples are asking each other, "Is it I that will betray the Lord?" Jesus, meanwhile, unconcerned, hands out Communion bread.

• *Browse the Great Upper Hall, noticing the various easel paintings by other artists. Contrast Titian's placid, evenly lit, aristocratic Annunciation with the blue-collar Tintoretto version downstairs. After you've gotten your fill of the Great Upper Hall, head back downstairs for Tintoretto's last works.*

GROUND FLOOR HALL—
The Life of Mary

The Flight into Egypt

There's Mary, Joseph, and the baby, but they're dwarfed by palm trees. Tintoretto, in his old age, returned to composing a Venetian specialty—landscapes—after years as champion of the Michelangelesque style of painting beefy, twisting nudes. The leafy greenery, the still water, the supernatural sunset, and the hut whose inhabitants go about their work, tell us better than any human action that the holy family has found a safe haven.

The Circumcision

This painting, bringing the circumcision of the baby Jesus into sharp focus, is the final canvas Tintoretto did for the Scuola. He collaborated on this work with his son Domenico, who carried on the family business.

In his long and prolific career, Tintoretto saw fame and many high-paying jobs. But at the Scuola, the commission became an obsession. It stands as one man's very personal contribution to the poor, to the Christian faith, and to art.

FRARI CHURCH TOUR

Chiesa dei Frari

The spirit of St. Francis of Assisi warms both the church of his "brothers" (*frari*) and the art that decorates it. Francis' love of Nature and Man later inspired Renaissance painters to capture the beauty of the physical world and human emotions, showing worshipers the glory of God in human terms.

Orientation

Cost: €2.

Hours: Mon–Sat 9:00–18:00, Sun 13:00–18:00 (closed Sun in Aug), last entry 15 minutes before closing, no visits during services.

Getting There: It's on the Campo dei Frari, near the San Tomá vaporetto and *traghetto* stops.

Tips: If you're walking to Frari Church from the Rialto Bridge, take my recommended Rialto to Frari Church Walk (see page 159). For efficient sightseeing, combine your visit with the Scuola San Rocco (see page 102), located behind the Frari Church. The Ca' Rezzonico (page 118) is a seven-minute walk away (from the back end of Frari Church, go through alleyway Sotoportego S. Rocco, at the first T intersection, turn left, then right. The rest is easy. Along the way, you'll pass by the university).

Information: Audioguides are available (€1.60/person, €2.60/ double set). The church often hosts evening concerts (tel. 041-523-4864); check for fliers.

Length of Our Tour: One hour.

Dress Code: Modest dress recommended.

Starring: Titian, Giovanni Bellini, and Donatello.

THE TOUR BEGINS

• *Enter the church through the tourist's entry, on the north side. Start at the altar and go roughly clockwise around the church.*

Frari Church

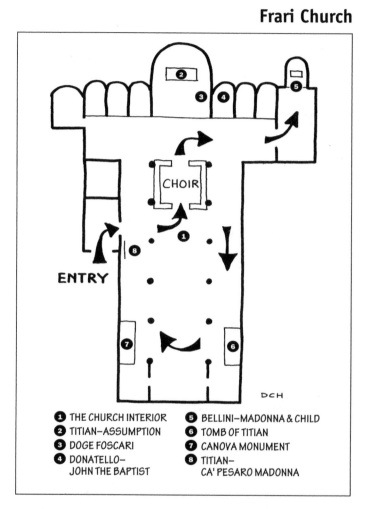

❶ THE CHURCH INTERIOR
❷ TITIAN–ASSUMPTION
❸ DOGE FOSCARI
❹ DONATELLO–
    JOHN THE BAPTIST
❺ BELLINI–MADONNA & CHILD
❻ TOMB OF TITIAN
❼ CANOVA MONUMENT
❽ TITIAN–
    CA' PESARO MADONNA

1. Church Interior (1250–1443)

The simple, spacious (102 meters/110 yards long), well-lit church, with rough wood crossbeams and a red-and-white color scheme, is truly a remarkable sight in a city otherwise crammed with exotic froufrou. The wooden choir area in the center of the nave allowed monks to hold smaller, more intimate services. Imagine entering the church from the main door (at the far end) and looking down the long nave to the altar. The first thing you'd see over the main altar is...

2. Titian—*The Assumption of Mary*

Glowing red and gold like a stained-glass window, this altarpiece sets the tone of exuberant beauty found in the otherwise sparse church. Mary, at the end of her life (though looking 17), was spared the pain of death, being miraculously "assumed" into heaven. As cherubs lift her up to meet a Jupiter-like God, the stunned apostles on earth reach up to touch the floating bubble of light.

Unveiled in 1518, the work also stunned a Venice used to simpler, more subdued church art. The sheer size (7 meters/22 feet tall inside its original marble frame), the rich colors, twisting poses, and the mix of saccharine angels with blue-collar apostles were unheard of.

Titian (1488–1576), in a burst of youthful innovation, rewrote the formula for church art, signaling the Mannerist and Baroque styles. His complex composition overlaps a circle (Mary's bubble) and a triangle (draw a line from the apostle reaching up to Mary's face and down the other side) on three horizontal levels (God in heaven, Man on earth, Mary in between). Together, these elements draw our eyes from the swirl of arms and legs to the painting's focus—the radiant face of the once dying, now triumphant Mary.

• *Also in the apse (behind the main altar) are marble tombs lining the walls. On the wall to the right of the altar . . .*

3. Tomb of Doge Foscari

In contrast with the poverty of the Franciscans, this heavy, ornate tomb marks the peak of Venice's worldly power. Doge Francesco Foscari (1373–1457) assumed control of Venice's powerful seafar-

ing empire, then tried to expand it farther onto the mainland, plunging the Republic into a 31-year war of attrition with Milan that devastated northern Italy. Meanwhile, on the unprotected eastern front, the Turks took Constantinople (1453) and scuttled Venice's trade. Venice's long slide into historical oblivion had begun. Drained city fathers forced Foscari to resign, turn in his funny hat, and hand over the keys to the Doge's Palace. He died eight days later . . . but *did* get his damage deposit refunded.

• *In the first chapel to the right of the altar, you'll find . . .*

4. Donatello—Wooden Statue of John the Baptist

Anorexic from his breakfast of bugs 'n honey, and dressed in animal skins, the cockeyed prophet of the desert freezes in the

middle of his rant when he spies something in the distance. His jaw goes slack, he twists his face and raises his hand to announce the coming of . . . the Renaissance.

The Renaissance began in Florence of the 1400s, where Donatello (1386–1466) created realistic statues with the full range of human emotions. This warts-and-all John the Baptist contrasts greatly with, say, Titian's sweet Mary. Florentine art (including painting) was sculptural, strongly outlined, and harshly realistic, with muted colors. Venetian art was painterly, soft-focus, and beautiful, with bright colors.

Donatello's statue must have made Florentine expatriate "brothers" feel at home when they worshiped at the Frari.

• *Enter the sacristy, through the door at the far end of the right transept, where you'll find . . .*

5. Giovanni Bellini—*Madonna and Child with Saints and Angels* (1488)

Mary sits on a throne under a half dome, propping up baby Jesus (who's just learning to stand), flanked by saints and serenaded by musician angels. Giovanni Bellini (c. 1430–1516), the father of the Venetian Renaissance, painted fake columns and a dome to match

the real ones in the gold frame, making the painting seem to be an extension. He completes the illusion with glimpses of open sky in the background. Next, he fills the artificial niches with symmetrically posed, thoughtful saints—left to right, find Saints Nicholas, Peter, Mark, and Sean Connery (Benedict).

Bellini pioneered painting in oil (pigments dissolved in vegetable oil) rather than medieval tempera (egg yolk–based). More transparent, it allowed subtler colors, made with successive layers of paint. Notice how Jesus' body is "built"

with different shades, as a patchwork of brightly lit mountains (his chest) and dark-shadowed valleys (his armpit).

Bellini virtually invented the formula for Venetian altarpieces (that would later be broken by his precocious pupil, Titian). This type of "holy conversation" (*sacra conversazione*) between saints and Mary can also be seen in Venice's Accademia (page 89), and Church of San Zaccaria (page 166).

Renaissance humanism demanded Madonnas and saints that were accessible and human. Bellini delivers, but places them in a physical setting so beautiful it creates its own mood of serene holiness. The scene is lit from the left, but no one casts a harsh shadow— Mary and the babe are enveloped in a glowing aura of reflected light from the golden dome. The beauty is in the details, from the writing in the dome to the red brocade backdrop to the swirls in the marble steps to the angels' dimpled legs to Bellini's signature in the base of the throne: IOANNES.BELLINVS.

• *Return to the nave and head toward the far end. Turn around and face the altar, and the Tomb of Titian will be in the second bay on your right.*

6. Tomb of Titian (Titiano Ferdinandus MDCCCLII)

The tomb celebrates both the man (see a carved relief of Titian in the center with beard and crown of laurels) and his famous paintings (depicted in relief).

Titian (1488–1576) was the greatest Venetian painter, excelling equally in inspirational altarpieces, realistic portraits, joyous mythological scenes, and erotic female nudes.

He moved to Venice as a child, studied under Giovanni Bellini, and soon established his own bold style starring teenage Madonnas (see a relief of *The Assumption* behind Titian). He became wealthy and famous, traveling Europe to paint stately portraits of kings and nobles, or colorful erotic works for their bedrooms. But Titian always returned to his beloved Venice (see winged lion on top)...and favorite Frari Church.

In old age, he painted dark, tragic masterpieces, including the *Pietà* (see relief in upper left) that was intended for his tomb but ended up in the Accademia (see page 89). Nearing 90, he labored to finish the *Pietà* as the plague enveloped Venice. One in four people died, including Titian's son and assistant, Orazio. Heartbroken, Titian died soon after, of natural causes.

• *On the opposite side of the nave is the pyramid-shaped...*

7. Canova Monument

Antonio Canova (1757–1822, see his portrait above the door) was Venice's greatest sculptor, creating gleaming, white, high-polished statues of beautiful Greek gods and goddesses in the neoclassical style. (See several of his works at the Correr Museum, page 76.)

The pyramid shape is timeless, suggesting pharaohs' tombs and the Christian Trinity. Mourners, bent over with grief, shuffle up to pay homage to the master artist. Even the winged lion is choked up.

Follow me here. Canova himself designed this pyramid-shaped tomb, not for his own use but as the tomb of an artist he greatly admired . . . Titian. But the Frari Church used another design for Titian's tomb, so Canova used the pyramid for an Austrian princess . . . in Vienna. After his death, Canova's pupils reused the design here to honor their master. But Canova isn't buried here; instead, he lies in southern Italy. But inside the tomb's open door, you can (barely) see an urn, which contains his heart.

• *Head back toward the altar. Halfway up the left wall is . . .*

8. Titian—*Madonna of Ca' Pesaro* (1526)

Titian's second altarpiece for the Frari Church displays all of his many skills. Following his teacher, Bellini, he puts Mary (seated) and baby (standing) on a throne, surrounded by saints having a "holy conversation" (*sacra conversazione*). And, like Bellini, he paints fake columns that echo the church's real ones.

But Mary is off-center, Titian's idealized saints mingle with Venetians sporting five o'clock shadows, and the stairs run diagonally away from us. These things upset traditional Renaissance symmetry, but turn a group of figures into a true scene. St. Peter

(center, in blue and gold, with book) looks down at Jacopo Pesaro, who kneels to thank the Virgin for his recent naval victory over the Turks (1503). A flag-carrying lieutenant drags in a turbaned captive. Meanwhile, St. Francis talks to baby Jesus while gesturing down to more members of the Pesaro family.

Titian combines opposites—a soft-focus Madonna with photo-realist portraits, chubby winged angels with the real-life child looking out (lower right), and a Christian cross with a battle flag. In the true spirit of St. Francis' humanism, Titian lets ordinary Joes mingle with saints.

CA' REZZONICO
TOUR

Museum of 18th-Century Venice

> *"Endowed by nature with a pleasing physical appearance, a confirmed gambler, a great talker, far from modest, always running after pretty women . . . I was certain to be disliked. But, as I was always willing to take responsibility for my actions, I decided I had a right to do anything I pleased."*
> —from *The Memoirs of Giacomo Casanova* (1725–1798)

Venice in the 1700s was the playground for Europe's aristocrats. The Ca' Rezzonico palace, once owned by the wealthy Rezzonico family, is decorated with furniture and artwork from the period. This grand home on the Grand Canal is the best place in town to capture the luxurious, decadent spirit of Venice in the Settecento (1700s).

Orientation

Cost: €6.70.

Hours: April–Oct Wed–Mon 10:00–18:00, Nov–March Wed–Mon 10:00–17:00, closed Tue. Last entry 60 minutes before closing.

Getting There: The museum is located on the west bank of the Grand Canal, right where the canal makes its hairpin turn. It's a 10-minute walk northwest from the Accademia (or a €1.55 traghetto ride). Or a 20-minute walk southwest from the Rialto Bridge (en route, you could visit the Frari Church and the neighboring Scuola San Rocco). Or you can use vaporetto #1 and get off at the Ca' Rezzonico stop (between Rialto and Accademia). Another way to arrive is by taking a quick *traghetto* ride across the Grand Canal from San Samuele (near entrance to Palazzo Grassi).

Information: The Ca' Rezzonico—pronounced "red-ZON-ico"—is also known as the Museo del Settecento Veneziano. Audioguides cost €5.50. On the ground floor, there's a baggage check, a bookstore, and WCs. Tel. 041-520-4036.

Length of Our Tour: 90 minutes.

Cuisine Art: The museum's café has a few scenic tables facing the Grand Canal.

Starring: A beautiful palace with 18th-century furnishings and paintings by G. B. Tiepolo, Canaletto, and Guardi.

Overview

Our Ca' Rezzonico tour covers two floors. The first floor has rooms decorated with period furniture and ceiling frescoes by G. B. Tiepolo. The second floor displays paintings by Canaletto, Guardi, G. D. Tiepolo, Longhi, and others. (The third floor painting gallery—which we won't visit—shows lots of flesh in lots of rooms.)

FIRST FLOOR

• *Buy tickets on the ground floor, admire the old gondola, then ascend the grand staircase to the first floor, entering the...*

Ballroom

A great place for a wedding reception. At 520 square meters (5,600 square feet), it's the biggest private venue in the city. Stand in the center, and the room gets even bigger, with a ceiling painting that opens up to the heavens and painted, trompe l'oeil

(optical illusion) columns and arches that open onto fake alcoves.

Imagine dancing under candlelit chandeliers to Vivaldi's *Four Seasons*. Servants glide by with drinks and finger foods. The gentlemen wear powdered wigs, silk shirts with lacy sleeves, tight velvet coats and breeches, striped stockings, and shoes with big buckles. They carry snuffboxes with dirty pictures inside the lid. The ladies powder their own hair, pile it high, and weave stuff in—pictures of their children or locks of a lover's hair. And everyone carries a mask on a stick to change identity in a second.

The chandeliers of gold-covered wood are original. But most of the furniture we'll see, while it's from the 1700s, is not from the Rezzonico family collection.

• *Promenade across squeaky floors into the next room.*

Room 2: Nuptial Allegory Room

In fact, there *was* a wedding here—see the happy couple on the

First Floor

```
G R A N D    C A N A L

        6                      5

STAIRS →    STAIRS
UP TO       7
SECOND      8                  4
FLOOR
                    12

        9                      3

                          ROOM
        10                 2

        B A L L R O O M

        DCH
            STAIRS FROM
            GROUND FLOOR
```

ceiling, riding in a chariot pulled by four white horses and serenaded by angels, cupids, and Virtues. In 1757, Ludovico Rezzonico exchanged vows with Faustina Savorgnan in this room, under the bellies of the horses painted for the occasion by Giovanni Battista ("John the Baptist") Tiepolo. Tiepolo (1696–1770), the best-known decorator of Europe's palaces, was at the height of his fame and technique. He knocked this off in 12 days. His bright colors, mastery of painting figures from every possible angle, wide knowledge of classical literary subjects, and sheer unbridled imagination made his frescoes blend seamlessly with ornate Baroque and Rococo furniture.

The Rezzonicos were a family of nouveaux riches who bought their way into the exclusive club of Venetian patrician families. The *Portrait of Clement XIII*, pink-cheeked and well-fed, shows the most famous Rezzonico. As pope (elected 1758), Clement spent his reign defending the Jesuit society from anti-Catholic European nobles. A well-used prayer kneeler (in the adjoining chapel) suggests that luxury and religion went hand-in-hand in Settecento Venice.

Room 3: Pastel Room

Europe's most celebrated painter of portraits in pastels was a Venetian, Rosalba Carriera (1675–1757). Wealthy French and English tourists on holiday wanted a souvenir of Venice, and Carriera obliged, with miniature portraits on ivory rather than the traditional vellum (soft animal skin). She progressed to portraits in pastel, a medium that caught the luminous, pale-skin, white-haired, heavy-makeup  look that was considered so desirable. Still, her *Portrait (Ritratto) of Sister Maria Caterina* has a warts-and-all realism that doesn't hide the nun's heavy eyebrows, long nose, and forehead vein—only intensifying the spirituality she radiates.

At age 45, Carriera was invited by tourists she'd befriended to visit them in Paris. There, she became the toast of the town. Returning triumphant to Venice, she settled into her home on the Grand Canal, painting until her eyesight failed.

Also in the room is the portrait of Cecilia Guardi Tiepolo: wife of famous painter G. B. Tiepolo, sister of famous painter Francesco Guardi, and mother of not-very-famous painter Lorenzo Tiepolo, who painted this when he was 21.

Room 4: Tapestry Room

Tapestries, furniture, a mirror, and an oriental-style door showing an opium smoker on his own little island paradise (lower panel) give a sense of the Rococo luxury of the wealthy. In a century dominated by the French court at Versailles, Venice was one of the few cities that could hold its own. The furniture ensemble of gilded wood chairs, tables, and chests hints at the Louis XV style, but the pieces were made in a Venetian workshop.

Despite Venice's mask of gaiety, in the 1700s it was a poor, politically bankrupt, dirty city. Garbage floated in the canals, the streets were either unpaved or slippery with slime, and tourists could hardly stand visiting St. Mark's Basilica or the Doge's Palace because of the stench of mildew. But its reputation for decay and sleaze was actually romanticized into a metaphor for adventures into shady morality. With licensed casinos and a reputed "20,000 courtesans" (prostitutes), it was a fun city for foreigners freed from hometown blinders.

Room 5: Throne Room

"Nowhere in Europe are there so many and such splendid fêtes, ceremonies, and public entertainments of all kinds as there are in Venice," wrote a visitor from France. As you check out the view of the Grand Canal, imagine once again that you're attending a party here. You could watch the *Forze d'Ercole* (Force of Hercules) acrobats, who stood in boats and kept building a human pyramid until they tumbled joyously into the Grand Canal. At midnight, the

hosts would dim the mirrored candleholders on the walls, so you could look out on a fireworks display over the water.

Carnevale, Venice's prime party time, stretched from the day after Christmas to Lent. Everyone wore masks. Frenchmen, dressed as turbaned Turks, mingled with Turkish traders dressed as harlequins. Fake Barbary pirates fought playfully with skin-blackened "Moors." And long-nosed Pulcinella clowns were everywhere, reveling in the time when all

18th-Century Venetians and Their Contemporaries

Venetians	Famous People Elsewhere in the World
Antonio Canaletto (painter of Venice views)	Louis XV (king of Europe's #1 power, France)
Antonio Vivaldi (composer of Four Seasons)	J. S. Bach (composer, organist)
Carlo Goldoni (playwright, realistic comedies)	Voltaire (intellectual wit proposing new ideas)
G. B. Tiepolo (painter of Rococo ceilings)	James Watt (turning brain power into steam power)
Francesco Guardi (painter of romantic Venice views)	Peter the Great (Russian czar with Enlightened ideas)
Giacomo Casanova (gambler, womanizer, adventurer)	Ben Franklin (inventor, womanizer, revolutionary)
G. D. Tiepolo (painter son of famous Tiepolo)	Louis XVI (head of state destined to lose his head)
Baldassare Longhena (architect of La Salute Church and Ca' Rezzonico)	Robespierre ("architect" of French Revolution)
Antonio Canova (neoclassical sculptor)	Napoleon (conqueror of Europe in name of democracy)

social classes partied as one because, "the mask levels all distinctions." (For information on this year's Carnevale celebration, see page 256).

The **ceiling fresco** (previous page), again by G. B. Tiepolo, certainly trompes my oeil. Tiepolo opens the room's sunroof, allowing angels to descend to earth to pick up the Rezzonico clan's patriarch. The old, bald, bearded fellow is crowned with laurels and begins to rise on a cloud up to the translucent temple of glory.

Giacomo Casanova (1725–1798)

"I began to lead a life of complete freedom, caring for nothing except what pleased me."
              —from *The Memoirs of Giacomo Casanova*

Casanova, a real person who wrote an exaggerated autobiography, typifies the Venice that so entranced the rest of Europe. In his life, he adopted many personae, worked in a number of professions, and always took the adventurous path.

The son of an actor, Casanova trained to be a priest, but was expelled for seducing nuns. To Venetians, he was first known as a fiery violinist at fancy parties in palaces such as the Ca' Rezzonico. He would later serve time in the Doge's Palace prison, accused of being a "magician."

As a professional gambler and charmer, he roamed Europe's capitals seducing noblewomen, dueling with fellow men of honor, and impressing nobles with his knowledge of Greek literature, religion, politics, and the female sex. His *Memoirs*, published after his death, cemented his reputation as a genial but cunning rake, rogue, and rapscallion.

Tiepolo captures the moment just as the gang is exiting out the "hole" in the ceiling. The leg of the lady in blue hangs over the "edge" of the fake oval. Tiepolo creates a zero-gravity universe that must have astounded visitors. Walk in circles under the fresco and watch the bugle baby spin.

• *Pass through the large next room and into . . .*

Room 6: Tiepolo Room

The ceiling fresco by G. B. Tiepolo depicts Nobility and Virtue as a kind of bare-breasted Xena and Gabriela defeating Perfidy, who tumbles down.

Portraits around the room are by Tiepolo and his sons, Lorenzo and Gian Domenico. The paintings are sober and down-to-earth, demonstrating the artistic range of this exceptional family. Giovanni Battista was known for

his flamboyance, but he passed to his sons his penchant for painting wrinkled, wizened old men in the Rembrandt style. In later years, G. B. had the pleasure of traveling with his sons to distant capitals, meeting royalty, and working on palace ceilings. Gian Domenico ("G. D.") contributed some of the minor figures in the Ca' Rezzonico ceilings and went on to carve his own niche (we'll see his work upstairs).

Room 7: Passage

This narrow corridor displays vessels for serving three foreign beverages that became popular in the 1700s—coffee, tea, and hot chocolate.

Room 8: Library

In the 1880s, Ca' Rezzonico was the home of the English poet Robert Browning (1812–1889) in his later years. Imagine him here in this study, in a melancholy mood after a long winter, reading a book and thinking of words from a poem of his: *"Oh to be in England, now that April's there...."*

Room 9: Lazzarini Room

The big, colorful paintings are by Gregorio Lazzarini, Tiepolo's teacher. Tiepolo took Lazzarini's color, motion, and twisted poses and suspended them overhead.

Room 10: Brustolon Room

Andrea Brustolon (1662–1732) carved Baroque fantasies into the custom-made tables, chairs, and vase-stands he crafted in his Venice workshop. In black ebony, reddish boxwood, and brown walnut, they overwhelm with the sheer number of figures, yet each carving is a gem worth admiring. The big vase-stand is a harmony of different colors: white vases supported by politically incorrect ebony slaves in chains and a brown box-wood Hercules.

• *Backtrack to Room 9, then turn right into the large, sparsely decorated room called the...*

Room 11: Portego

That funny little cabin in the room is a sedan chair, a servant-powered taxi for Venice's nobles. Four strong-shouldered men ran poles through the iron brackets on either side, then carried it on their shoulders, while the rich rode in red-velvet luxury above the slimy streets.

• *The staircase to the second floor is here in Room 11 in the middle of the long wall. On the second floor, you emerge into Room 12.*

SECOND FLOOR

The first floor showed the rooms and furniture of the 1700s. The second-floor paintings depict the people that sat in those chairs.

Room 12: Painting Portego

Rich tourists wanting to remember their stay in Venice sought out Antonio Canaletto (1697–1768) for a "postcard" view. The ***Grand Canal from Ca' Foscari to Rialto*** (by Antonio Canal detto il Canaletto) captures the view you'd see from the palazzo two doors down. With photographic clarity, Canaletto depicts buildings, boats, and shadows on the water, leading the eye to the tiny, half-hidden Rialto Bridge on the distant horizon.

The ***View of Rio dei Mendicante*** chronicles every chimney, every open shutter, every pair of underwear hanging out to dry.

Canaletto was a young theater-set painter working in Rome on Scarlatti operas when he decided his true calling was painting reality, not Baroque fantasy. He moved home to Venice, set up his easel outside, and painted scenes like these two, directly from nature. It was considered a very odd thing to do in his day.

Despite the seeming photo-realism and crystal clarity, these wide-angle views are more than any human eye could take in without turning side to side. Canaletto, who meticulously studied the mathematics of perspective, was

Second Floor

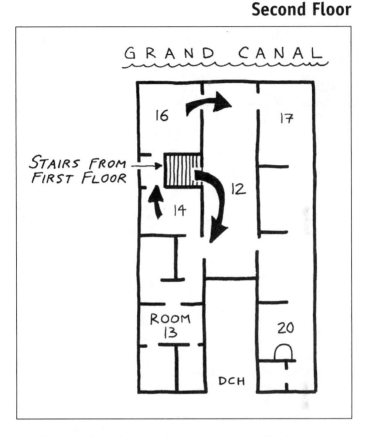

not above tweaking those rules to compress more Venice into the frame. His paintings still have a theater set look to them, but here, the Venice backdrop is the star.

To meet the demand for postcard scenes of Venice, Canaletto resorted in later years to painting from engravings or following formulas. But these two early works reflect his pure vision to paint accurately the city he loved.

• *From here, we'll move roughly clockwise around the second floor. "Room 13" is actually a maze of several rooms displaying...*

Room 13: Gian Domenico Tiepolo's Frescoes from the Villa in Zianigo

The son of G. B. Tiepolo decorated the family villa with frescoes for his own enjoyment. They're far more down-to-earth

than G. B.'s high-flying fantasies. *New World* features butts, as ordinary folk crowd around a building with a peepshow window. At the far right, the two men in profile are G. D. Tiepolo (with eyeglass) and his father, G. B. Tiepolo (arms folded). The **Pulcinella Room** (far corner) has several scenes (including one overhead) of the hook-nosed,

white-clothed, hunchbacked clown who, at Carnevale time, represented the lovable country bumpkin. But here, he and his similarly dressed companions seem tired, lecherous, and stupid. The decadent gaiety of Settecento Venice was at odds with the *Liberté*, *Egalité*, and *Fraternité* erupting in France.

• *Traveling through the maze of Room 13, wind your way into a room with a harpsichord, cleverly named the* ...

Room 14: Harpsichord Room

The 1700s saw the development of new keyboard instruments that would culminate by century's end in the modern piano. This particular specimen has strings that are not hammered (like a piano) but plucked (like a mechanical guitar). The spacing of "white" keys and "black" keys is chromatic like a modern piano. This newly invented "tempered" scale of evenly spaced notes let you play in all keys without retuning.

Room 16: Parlor Room

Francesco Guardi (1712–1793), like Canaletto, supplied foreigners with Venice scenes. But Guardi uses rougher brushwork that casts a romantic haze over the decaying city.

The Parlor (Il Parlatorio delle Monache di S. Zaccaria) is an interior landscape featuring visiting day at a convent school. The girls, secluded behind grills, chat and have tea with family

members, friends, ladies with their pets, and potential suitors.
Convents were more like finishing schools for aristocratic
girls, where they got an education and learned manners before
reentering the world. Note the puppet show (starring spouse-
abusing Pulcinella).

Guardi's ***Il Ridotto di Palazzo Dandolo*** shows party-goers in
masks at one of the palaces licensed for gambling. Casanova and
others claimed that these casino houses had back rooms for the
private use of patrons and courtesans.

• *Continuing along, you'll pass back through the Painting Portego
and into . . .*

Room 17: Longhi Room

There is no better look at 1700s Venice than these genre scenes by Pietro
Longhi (1702–1785), depicting everyday life among the upper classes. See

ladies and gen-
tlemen going to
the hairdresser
or to the dentist,
dressed in the finery that was standard in
every public situation.

Contrast these straightforward scenes
with G. B. Tiepolo's sumptuous ceiling
fresco of nude gods and goddesses. The
Rococo fantasy world of aristocrats was
slipping increasingly into the more prosaic
era of the bourgeoisie.

• *Pass through several rooms to the far corner.*

Room 20: The Alcove

Casanova daydreamed of fancy boudoirs like this one, complete
with a large bed (topped with a Carriera Madonna), a walnut
dresser, neoclassical wallpaper, and silver toiletries. Even the
presence of the baby cradle would not have dimmed his ardor.

PEGGY GUGGENHEIM MUSEUM TOUR

Peggy Guggenheim (1898–1979)—an American-born heiress to the Guggenheim fortune and niece of Solomon Guggenheim (who built New York's modern art museum)—made her mark as a friend, lover, and patron of modern artists.

As a gallery owner, she introduced Europe's avant-garde to a skeptical America. As a collector, she gave instant status to modern art too radical for serious museums. As a patron, she fed starving artists such as Jackson Pollock. And as a person, she lived larger than life, unconventional and original, with a succession of lovers that enhanced her reputation as a female Casanova.

In 1948, Peggy "retired" to Venice, moving into a small, unfinished palazzo on the Grand Canal. Today, it's a museum, decorated much as it was in her life, with one of the best collections anywhere of 20th-century art. It's the only museum I can think of where the owner is buried in the garden.

Orientation

Cost: €8.

Hours: Wed–Mon 10:00–18:00, Sat until 22:00 April–Oct, closed Tue.

Getting There: The museum, overlooking the Grand Canal, is at #701 Dorsoduro, a five-minute walk from the Accademia Bridge (vaporetto: Accademia) or from La Salute Church (vaporetto: Salute).

Information: The museum shop sells guidebooks (€18). Tel. 041-240-5411, www.guggenheim-venice.it.

Tours: Audioguide tours cost €4. Guided 45–60 minute tours, which cost €60, can be booked by calling the museum. Free 15–minute tours on Peggy's life and collection are given daily at 12:00 and 16:00. Student interns guarding the works are happy to tell you about particular pieces if you ask.

Peggy Guggenheim Museum

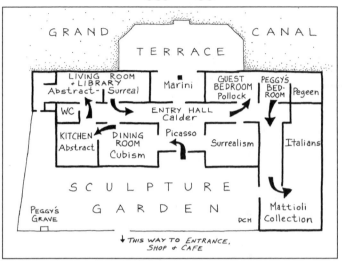

Length of Our Tour: One hour.
Baggage Check: Free.
Cuisine Art: Pricey café on site.
Photography: Allowed only in garden and terrace.
Starring: Picasso, Kandinsky, Mondrian, Dalí, Pollock...
and everyone else who made a mark on modern art.

Overview

After passing through a café and a garden, you enter the palazzo. There's a wing to the left and a wing to the right, plus a modern annex. The collection is (very) roughly chronological, starting to the left with Cubism and ending to the right with young, postwar artists.

The collection is strongest on Abstract, Surrealist, and Abstract-Surrealist art. The order of paintings changes often, so use this chapter as an overview, not a painting-by-painting tour.
• *Let's walk through Peggy's collection...and through her life, which is mirrored in the art on the walls. From the sculpture garden, you walk into the...*

Entry Hall: Meet Peggy Guggenheim

Picture Peggy Guggenheim greeting guests here—standing under the trembling-leaf **mobile by Alexander Calder**, surrounded by her yapping dogs and wearing her

Peggy G.

Calder-designed earrings, Mondrian-print dress, and "Catwoman" sunglasses.

During the '50s and '60s, this old palazzo on the Grand Canal was a mecca for "Moderns," from composer Igor Stravinsky to actor Marlon Brando, from painter Mark Rothko to writer Truman Capote, from choreographer George Balanchine to Beatle John Lennon and performance artist Yoko Ono. They came to sip cocktails, tour the great art, talk about ideas, and meet the woman who had become a living legend.

Pablo Picasso—*On the Beach* (1937)

Curious, balloon-animal women play with a sailboat while their friend across the water looks on. Of all Peggy's many paintings, this was her favorite.

By the time Peggy Guggenheim first became serious about modern art (about the time this was painted),

Pablo Picasso—the most famous and versatile modern artist—had already been through his Blue, Rose, Fauve, Cubist, Synthetic Cubist, Classical, Abstract, and Surrealist phases, finally arriving at a synthesis of these styles. Peggy had some catching up to do.

• *Enter the first room to the left, and you'll see a dining-room table in the center.*

1900–1920: Cubists in the Dining Room

Peggy's dining-room table reminds us that this museum was, indeed, Peggy's home for the last 30 years of her life. Most of the furniture is now gone, but the walls are decorated much as they were when she lived here, with paintings and statues by her friends, colleagues, and mentors. Here, she entertained countless artists and celebrities (more name-dropping), from actor Paul Newman to poet Allen Ginsberg, from sculptor Henry Moore to playwright Tennessee Williams, from James Bond creator Ian Fleming to glass sculptor Dale Chihuly.

The art in the Dining Room dates from Peggy's childhood, when she was raised in the lap of luxury in New York, oblivious to the artistic upheavals going on in Europe.

In 1912, the *Titanic* went down, taking Peggy's playboy

tycoon father with it...and leaving his 14-year-old daughter with a small but comfortable trust fund and a man-sized hole in her life.

Approaching adulthood, Peggy rejected her traditional American upbringing, hanging out at a radical bookstore, getting a nose job (a botched operation, leaving her with a rather bulbous schnozz)...and planning a trip to Europe.

In 1920, 21-year-old Peggy arrived in Paris, where a revolution in art was taking place.

• *Find the following art in the dining room and adjoining hallway.*

Pablo Picasso—*The Poet* (1911)

Picasso, a Spaniard living in Paris, shattered the Old World into brown shards ("cubes") and reassembled it in Cubist style. It's a vaguely recognizable portrait of a man from the waist up—tapering to a head at the top, smoking a pipe (?), and cradling the traditional lyre of a poet. While the newfangled motion-picture camera could capture a moving image, Picasso suggests motion with a collage of stills.

Marc Chagall—*Rain*

The rain clouds are gathering over a farmhouse, the wind blows the trees and people, and everyone prepares for the storm. Quick, put the horse in the barn, grab an umbrella, take a leak, and round up the goats in the clouds.

Marc Chagall, a Russian living in France, found the romantic, weightless, childlike joy of topsy-turvy Paris.

Marcel Duchamp—*Nude (Study), Sad Young Man on a Train* (1911–1912)

In a self-portrait, Duchamp poses gracefully with a cane, but the moving train jiggles the image into a blur of brown. Duchamp, who is perhaps best known for his outrageous urinal-as-statue and moustache-on-the-*Mona Lisa*, would later become Peggy's friend and mentor in modernism, steering her to buy these early-modern "classics."

Abstract Art

Abstract art simplifies. A man becomes a stick figure. A squiggle is a wave. A streak of red expresses anger. Arches make you want a cheeseburger. These are universal symbols that everyone from a caveman to a banker understands. Abstract artists capture the essence of reality in a few lines and colors, even things a camera can't—emotions, abstract concepts, musical rhythms, and spiritual states of mind.

Most 20th-century paintings are a mix of the real world ("representation") and the colorful patterns of "abstract" art. Artists purposely distort camera-eye reality to make the resulting canvas more decorative.

Umberto Boccioni—*Dynamism of a Speeding Horse + Houses* (assemblage, 1915)

This statue captures the blurred motion of the modern world—accelerated by technology, then shattered by World War I, which left nine million Europeans dead and everyone's moral compass scattered.

(In fact, this statue was shattered by the destructive force of Boccioni's own kids, who scattered the cardboard "houses" while using it as a rocking horse.)

Constantin Brancusi—*Maiastra* (bronze statue)

For the generation born before air travel, flying was magical. This high-polished bird is the first of many by Brancusi, who dreamed of flight. But this bird just sits there. For centuries, a good sculptor was one who could capture movement in stone. But Brancusi reverts to the style of "primitive" African art, where even the simplest statues radiate mojo.

• *Browse through the next few rooms. You'll find the following art scattered through the west wing of the palazzo.*

1920s: Abstraction in the Kitchen, "-Isms" in the Living Room

Peggy spent her twenties in the Roaring Twenties, right in the center of avant-garde craziness: Paris. For the rest of her life, Europe—not America—would be her permanent address.

In Paris, trust-funded Peggy lived the bohemian life. Post–World War I Paris was cheap and, after the bitter war years, ready to party. Days were spent drinking coffee in cafés, talking ideas with the likes of feminist Emma Goldman, writer Djuna ("Nightwood") Barnes, and photographer Man Ray. Nights were spent abusing the drug forbidden in America (alcohol), dancing to jazz music into the wee hours, and talking about Freud and s-e-x.

One night, on top of the Eiffel Tower, a dashing artist and intellectual nicknamed "The King of Bohemia" popped the question. Peggy and Laurence Vail soon married and had two children, but the partying only slowed somewhat. This thoroughly modern couple dug the wild life and the wild art it produced.

Wassily Kandinsky— *White Cross*

I see white, I see crosses, but where's the "white cross"? Oh, there it is on the right, camouflaged among black squares.

Like a jazz musician improvising from a set scale, Kandinsky plays with new patterns of related colors and lines, creating something that's simply beautiful, even if it doesn't "mean" anything. As Kandinsky himself would say, his art was like "visual music—just open your eyes and look."

Piet Mondrian (1872–1944)— *Composition*

Like a blueprint for modernism, Mondrian's T-square style boils painting down to its basic building blocks—black lines, white canvas, and the three primary colors (red, yellow, and blue) arranged in orderly patterns. This stripped-down canvas even omits yellow and blue.

Mondrian started out painting realistic landscapes of the orderly fields in his native Holland. Increasingly, he simplified it into horizontal and vertical patterns, creating rectangles of different proportions. This one has horizontal lines to the left, vertical ones to the right. The horizontals appear to dominate, until we see that they're "balanced" by the tiny patch of red.

For Mondrian, heavy into Eastern mysticism, "up vs. down" and "left vs. right" were metaphors for life's ever-shifting dualities—"good vs. evil," "man vs. woman," "fascism vs. communism." The canvas is a bird's-eye view of Mondrian's personal landscape.

1930s: Abstract Surrealists in the Living Room and Library

In 1928, Peggy's marriage to Laurence Vail ended, and she entered into a series of romantic attachments—some loving and stable, others sexual and impersonal. Though not stunningly attractive, she was easy to be with, and she truly admired artistic men.

In 1937, she began an on-again, off-again (so to speak) sexual relationship with playwright Samuel *(Waiting for Godot)* Beckett. Beckett steered her toward modern painting and sculpture—something she'd never paid much attention to.

She started hanging out with the French Surrealists, from artist Marcel Duchamp to writer André Breton to filmmaker/artist Jean *(Beauty and the Beast)* Cocteau. Duchamp, in particular, mentored her in modern art, encouraging her to use her money to collect and promote it. Nearing 40, she moved to London and launched a new career.

Yves Tanguy—*The Sun in Its Jewel Case*

In May 1938, this painting was featured at "Guggenheim Jeune," the art gallery Peggy opened in London. Tanguy's painting sums up the outrageous art that shocked a sleepy London during that first season.

Weird, phallic, tissue-and-bone protuberances cast long shadows across a moody, dream-like landscape—the landscape of the

mind. (Peggy said the picture "frightened" her, but "I got over my fear . . . and now I own it.") The figures are Abstract (unrecognizable) and the mood is Surreal, producing the style cleverly dubbed Abstract Surrealism.

Peggy was drawn to Yves Tanguy and had a short but intense affair with the married man. Tanguy, like his art, was wacky and spontaneous, occasionally shocking friends by suddenly catching and gobbling up a spider, washing it down with white wine. The Surrealists saw

themselves as spokesmen for Freud's "id," the untamed part of your personality that thinks dirty thoughts when your ego goes to sleep.

The Guggenheim Jeune gallery exhibited many of the artists we see in this museum, including Kandinsky, Mondrian, and Calder. Guggenheim Jeune closed after just two years as a financial failure, but the outrageous art certainly created a buzz in the art world, and over the years, the gallery's failure gained a rosy glow of success.

1939–1940: Peggy's Shopping Spree in Paris

Peggy moved back to Paris, renting an apartment on the Ile St. Louis. In September, Nazi Germany invaded Poland, sparking World War II. All of France waited ... and waited ... and waited for the inevitable Nazi attack on Paris.

Meanwhile, Peggy spent her days shopping for masterpieces. Using a list compiled by Duchamp and others, she personally visited artists in their studios—from Brancusi to Dalí to Giacometti—often negotiating directly with them. (Picasso initially turned Peggy down, thinking of her as a gauche, bargain-hunting housewife. When she entered his studio he said, "Madame, you'll find the lingerie department on the second floor.") In a few short months, she bought 37 of the paintings now in the collection, perhaps saving them from a Nazi regime that labeled such art "decadent."

In 1941, with the Nazis occupying Paris and most of Europe, Peggy fled her adopted homeland. With her stash of paintings and a new companion—Max Ernst—she sailed from Lisbon to safety in New York.

• *Pass back through the Entry Hall—where Peggy welcomed celebrity guests, from writer Somerset Maugham to actor Rex Harrison to painter Marc Chagall—and into the east wing. The large room you first enter is filled with Surrealist canvases.*

1941–1945: Surrealists Invade New York

Trees become women, women become horses, and day becomes night. Balls dangle, caves melt, and things cast long shadows across film-noir landscapes—Surrealism. The world was moving fast, and Surrealists caught the jumble of images. They scatter seemingly unrelated things on the canvas, leaving us to trace the connections in a kind of connect-the-dots game without numbers.

Peggy spent the war years in America. She married the painter Max Ernst, and their house in New York City became a gathering place for exiled French Surrealists and young American artists.

In 1942, she opened a gallery/museum in New York called "Art of This Century" that featured, well, essentially the collection we see here in Venice. But patriotic, gung-ho America was not quite ready for the nonconformist, intellectual art of Europe.

Max Ernst (1891–1976)—*The Antipope*

The horse-headed nude in red is a portrait of Peggy—at least, that's what she thought when she saw it. She loved the painting and insisted that Max give it to her as a wedding present, renamed *The Mystic Marriage*.

Others read more into it. Is the horse-headed warrior (at right) Ernst himself? Is he being wooed by one of his art students?

Is that Peggy's daughter, Pegeen (center), watching the scene, sadly, from a distance? And is Peggy turning toward her beloved Max, subconsciously suspicious of the young student...who would (in fact) soon steal Max from her? Ernst uses his considerable painting skill to bring to light the tangle of hidden urges, desires, and fears—hidden like the grotesque animal faces in the reef they stand on.

Paul Delvaux (1897–1944)— *The Break of Day*

Full-breasted ladies with roots cast long shadows and awaken to a mysterious dawn. If you're counting boobs, don't forget the one reflected in the night-stand mirror.

René Magritte (1898–1967)— *Empire of Light*

Magritte immigrated to America and found that, even under a sunny blue sky, suburbia has its dark side.

Salvador Dalí (1904–1989)— *The Birth of Liquid Desires*

Salvador Dalí could draw exceptionally well. He painted "unreal" scenes with photographic realism, making us believe they could really happen. This creates an air of mystery—the feeling that anything can happen—that's both exciting and unsettling. His men explore the caves of the dreamworld and morph into something else before our eyes.

Personally, Peggy didn't like Dalí or his work, but she dutifully bought this canvas (through his wife, Gala) to complete her collection.

• *Across the hall is a room with a fireplace and works of Pollock.*

1945–1948, The Postwar Years: Pollock in the Guest Bedroom

Certain young American painters—from Mark Rothko to Robert Motherwell to Robert De Niro, Sr. (the actor's father)—were strongly influenced by Peggy's collection. Adopting the Abstract style of Kandinsky and Mondrian, they practiced Surrealist spontaneity to "express" their personal insights. The resulting style (duh)—Abstract Expressionism.

Jackson Pollock (1912–1956)—*Enchanted Forest*

"Jack the Dripper" attacked America's postwar conformity with a can of paint, dripping and splashing a dense web onto the canvas. Picture Pollock in his studio, jiving to the hi-fi, bouncing off the walls, throwing paint in a moment of alcohol-fueled enlightenment.

Peggy helped make Pollock a celebrity. She bought his earliest works (which show Abstract-Surreal roots), exhibited him at her gallery, and even paid him a monthly stipend to keep experimenting.

By the way, if you haven't yet tried the Venetian specialty *spaghetti al nero di seppia* (squid in its own ink), it looks something like this.

In 1946, Peggy published her memoirs, titled *Out of This Century: The Informal Memoirs of Peggy Guggenheim*. The front cover was designed by Max Ernst, the back by Pollock. Peggy herself was now a celebrity.

• *The room in the northeast corner was Peggy's bedroom.*

1950s: Peggy in the Bedroom

As America's postwar factories turned swords into kitchen appliances, Peggy longed to return "home" to Europe. The one place that kept calling to her was Venice, ever since a visit with Laurence Vail in the '20s. "I decided Venice would be my future home," she wrote. "I felt I would be happy alone there."

In 1947, after a grand finale exhibition by Pollock, she closed the "Art of This Century" gallery, crated up her collection, and moved to Venice. In 1948, she bought this palazzo and moved in.

This was Peggy's bedroom. She painted it turquoise. She commissioned the **silver headboard by Alexander Calder** for her canopy bed, using its silver frame to hang her collection of earrings, handmade by the likes of Calder and Tanguy. Venetian mirrors hung on the walls, along with a sentimental portrait of herself and her sister as children. Ex-husband Laurence Vail's collage-decorated bottles sat on the nightstand.

In 1951, Peggy met the last great love of her life, an easy-going, blue-collar Italian with absolutely no interest in art. She was 53, Raoul was 30, and their relationship, though rather odd, was tender and mutually satisfying. Raoul died in 1954 in a car accident, and Peggy comforted herself with her pets.

• *The tiny room adjoining the bedroom displays paintings by Pegeen.*

Pegeen

Peggy's daughter, named Pegeen, inherited some of Laurence Vail's artistic talent, painting childlike scenes of Venice, populated by skinny Barbie dolls with antennae.

The guest bedroom (where the Pollocks are) was a busy place. Pegeen and her brother, Sinbad, visited their mother, as did Peggy's ex-husbands and their new loves. Other overnight guests ranged from sculptor Alberto Giacometti (who honeymooned here) to cultural-explorer Paul Bowles to artist Jean Arp.

• *Cross the hall and go down a few steps into the wing perpendicular to the palazzo, the Annex.*

Italians in the Annex

You'll find a few paintings by famous Italians (**Modigliani, Boccioni**) and a lot by the postwar generation of young Italians who were strongly influenced by Peggy's collection. In 1948, Peggy showed her collection in its own pavilion at the Biennale, Venice's semiannual "world's fair of art," and it was the hit of the show. Europeans were astounded and a bit shocked, finally seeing the kind of "degenerate" art forbidden during the fascist years, plus the radical new stuff coming out of New York City.

Peggy sponsored young artists, including **Tancredi**—just one name, back when that was odd—who was given a studio in the palazzo's basement. Tancredi had a relationship with daughter Pegeen, with her mother's blessing. (Pegeen died in 1967 of an overdose of barbiturates.)

• *Return to the Entry Hall, then go out onto the Terrace, overlooking the Grand Canal.*

Exhibitionists on the Terrace

"You fall in love with the city itself. There is nothing left over in your heart for anyone else."

—Peggy Guggenheim

Marino Marini's equestrian statue, *The Angel of the City,* faces the Grand Canal, spreads his arms wide, and tosses his head back in sheer joy, with an eternal hard-on for the city of Venice. Every morning, Peggy must have felt a similar exhilaration as she sipped coffee with this unbelievable view.

Marini originally designed his bronze rider with a screw-off penis (which sounds dirtier than it is) that could be removed for prudish guests or by curious ones. Someone stole it for some unknown purpose, so the current organ is permanently welded on.

The palazzo—called Palazzo Venier dei Leoni—looks modern but is old. Begun in 1748, only its ground floor was built before construction was halted. Legend has it that the rival family across the canal in Palazzo Corner squelched the plans for the upper stories to prevent being upstaged. The palazzo remained unfinished until Peggy bought it in 1948 and spruced it up. She added the annex in 1958. The **lions** (*leoni*) of the original palace still guard the water entrance.

Peggy's outlandish and rather foreign presence in Venice— drinking, dressing up outrageously, or sunbathing on her rooftop for all to see—was not immediately embraced by the Venetians. But for artists in the '50s and '60s, Peggy's palazzo was *the* place to be, especially when the Biennale brought the jet set. Everyone from actor Alec Guinness to columnist Art Buchwald to costume designer Hedda Hopper signed her guest book. Picture Peggy and guests, decked out in evening clothes, hopping into Peggy's custom-built gondola (called *La Barchessa*, after the doge's private boat) to ride slowly down the canal for a martini and a Bellini at Harry's Bar.

• *Pass back through the Entry Hall, then outside to the ...*

Sculpture Garden

Peggy opened her impressive collection of sculpture to the Venetian public for free. It features first-rate works by all the greats, from Brancusi to Moore to Giacometti. After so much art already, you may find the trees—so rare in urban Venice—more interesting.

If, after your visit here, you still don't like modern art, think of what Peggy used to tell puzzled visitors: "Come back again in fifty years."

• *In the southwest corner of the garden, find ...*

Peggy's Grave and Her Dogs' Grave

"Here Lie my Beloved Babies," marks the grave of her many dogs that were her steady companions as she grew old. Note the names of some of these small, long-haired Lhasa apsos. Along with "Cappuccino" and "Baby," you'll see "Pegeen" (after her daughter) and "Sir Herbert" for Herbert Read, the art critic who helped Peggy select her collection.

Peggy's ashes are buried alongside, marked with a simple plaque. In the nonconformist 1960s, Peggy's once shocking art and unconventional lifestyle became more acceptable, even commonplace. By the 1970s, she was universally recognized as a major force in early modern art, and was finally even honored by the Venetians with a nickname—"The Last Dogess" *(La Ultima Dogaressa)*. When she died in a Padua hospital in 1979, she was mourned by the art world, from sculptor Henry Moore to composer Virgil Thomson, from choreographer Jerome Robbins to writer George Plimpton, from composer John Cage to...

LA SALUTE CHURCH
TOUR

Santa Maria della Salute

Where the Grand Canal opens up into the lagoon stands one of Venice's most distinctive landmarks—the church dedicated to Santa Maria della Salute (Our Lady of Health). The architect, Baldassare Longhena, who also did St. Mark's Square's "New" Wing and the Ca' Rezzonico, remade Venice in the Baroque style. Crown-shaped La Salute was his crowning achievement, and the last grand Venetian building built before Venice's slide into poverty.

Orientation

Cost: Free (minimal charge for sacristy, if it's open).
Hours: Daily 9:00–12:00 & 15:00–17:30 (tel. 041-522-5558 to confirm).
Getting There: On the Grand Canal, near the point where the canal spills into the lagoon. It's a 10-minute walk from the Accademia Bridge (past the Peggy Guggenheim Museum). Vaporetto stop "Salute" drops you off at the doorstep. Or take a cheap *traghetto* from near St. Mark's Square (at Harry's Bar). If it's November 21 (see below), you can walk directly to the church across the Grand Canal on a floating, pontoon-like bridge.
Length of Our Tour: 30 minutes.
Starring: Baldassare Longhena's church and works by Titian and Giordano.

EXTERIOR

The white stone church has a steep dome rising above a circular structure crusted with Baroque scrolls, leafy Corinthian columns, and 125 statues, including the lovely ladies lounging over the central doorway. The architect conceived of the church "in the shape of a crown."

La Salute Church

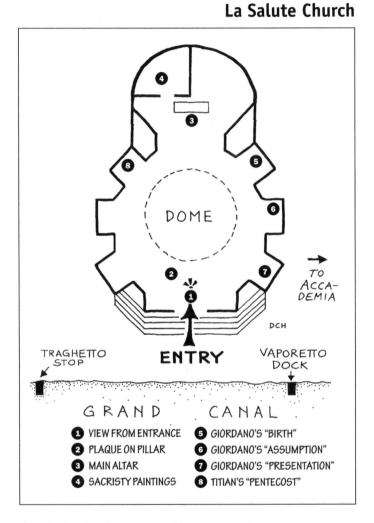

GRAND CANAL

1 VIEW FROM ENTRANCE
2 PLAQUE ON PILLAR
3 MAIN ALTAR
4 SACRISTY PAINTINGS
5 GIORDANO'S "BIRTH"
6 GIORDANO'S "ASSUMPTION"
7 GIORDANO'S "PRESENTATION"
8 TITIAN'S "PENTECOST"

During the bitter plague of 1630, the Virgin Mary took pity on the city of Venice, miraculously allowing only one in three Venetians (46,000 souls) to die. The grateful survivors spent the next 50 years building this church in honor of Our Lady of Health, whose statue tops the lantern.

Even today, Mary's intercession is celebrated every November 21, when a floating bridge is erected across the Grand Canal, the *traghetto* driver takes a day off, and Venetians can walk from San Marco across the water and right up the seaweed-covered steps to the front door.

At age 32, architect Baldassare Longhena (1598–1682) sank a million-plus pilings into the sandy soil for a foundation. When the dome still proved too heavy, he improvised, supporting it with the 12 Baroque scrolls at the base.

INTERIOR

1. View from the Entrance

The church has a bright, healthy glow, with white-gray stone lit by filtered light from the windows of the dome. The church is circular, surrounded by chapels. In contrast with the ornate Baroque exterior, the inside is sparse, with only some Corinthian columns and two useless balcony railings up in the dome. The red, white, and yellow marble of the floor adds a cheerful note.

Longhena focuses our immediate attention on the main altar. Every other view is blocked by heavy pillars. Longhena, a master of "theatrical architecture," only reveals the side chapels one by one as we walk around and explore.

The church is an octagon surrounding a circular nave that's topped by the dome. Viewed from the center of the church, the altar and side chapels are framed by arches.

The church is glorious but low-budget, having been finished during Venice's slow fade. Some of the "marble" is brick covered with marble dust, and the windows are cheap roundlets, the simple shape a drop of molten glass makes.

2. Bronze Plaque (on a pillar near the entrance)

The church is dedicated not just to physical health but to spiritual health as well. The plaque tells us that on September 16, 1972, the future Pope John Paul I—the predecessor of John Paul II—visited here and paid homage to the Virgin of Health . . . (then fell sick and died after only 100 days in office).

3. Main Altar

The marble statues on the top tell the church's story: Mary and Child (center) are approached for help by a kneeling, humble Lady Venice (left). Mary takes compassion and sends an angel baby (right) to drive away Old Lady Plague.

The icon of a black, sad-eyed Madonna with a black baby (12th-century Byzantine) is not meant to be racially accurate. Here, a "black" Madonna means an otherworldly one.

• *Through the door to the left of the altar . . .*

4. Sacristy

If it's open, you'll see several famous paintings in the sacristy, including three Titians, and Tintoretto's *Wedding at Cana* (1561).

• *Back in the circular nave, there are six side chapels—three to the left, three to the right. Start near the altar, on the right side (to your right as you face the altar).*

Side Chapel Paintings

Luca Giordano (1632–1705) celebrates the Virgin in three paintings with a similar composition—heaven and angels above, dark earth below.

Giordano, a prolific artist from Naples, was known as "Luca *fa presto*" (Fast Luke) for his ambidextrous painting abilities.

• *In the chapel to the right of the altar is . . .*

5. Giordano—*Birth of the Virgin* (1674)

Little baby Mary in her mom's arms seems like nothing special. But God the Father looks down from above and sends the dove of the Spirit.

• *In the middle chapel . . .*

6. Giordano—*The Assumption*

Mary, at the end of her life, is being taken gloriously by winged babies, up from the dark earth to the golden light of heaven. The apostles cringe in amazement. A later artist thought his statue was better, and planted it right in our way.

• *In the chapel closest to the entrance . . .*

7. Giordano—*Presentation of the Virgin*

The child Mary (in blue, with wispy halo) ascends a staircase that goes diagonally "into" the canvas. (If you've seen Titian's *Little Mary* in the Accademia, you'll see where Giordano got his inspiration.) Giordano places us viewers at the foot of the stairs. The lady in the lower left tells her kids, "Why can't you be more like her?!"

• *From here, look kitty-corner across to the other side of the nave, to the chapel closest to the main altar. At this distance and angle, Titian's painting looks its best.*

8. Titian (Tiziano)— *Pentecost* (1546)

The dove of the Holy Spirit sends spiritual rays that fan out to the apostles below, giving them tongues of fire above their heads. They gyrate in amazement, each one in a different direction.

Using floor tiles and ceiling panels, Titian has created the 3-D illusion of a barrel-arched chapel, with the dove coming right into the church through a fake window. But the painting was not designed for this location and, really, the whole fake niche looks...fake.

SAN GIORGIO MAGGIORE TOUR

The best view in all of Venice is from the bell tower of San Giorgio Maggiore, a five-minute vaporetto ride away from St. Mark's Square. Even if you're not interested in Palladio's influential architecture, Tintoretto's famous *Last Supper*, or even the stunning view back at the city skyline, it's worth a trip just to escape from tourist-mobbed St. Mark's Square.

Orientation

Cost: Admission to the church is free; the bell-tower lift costs €3.

Hours: Daily 9:30–12:30 & 15:30–18:30, closed Sun afternoon and Mon. The lift up the bell tower stops 30 minutes before closing times. The bells ring (very loudly!) at 12:00. A Gregorian Mass is sung at 8:00 Mon–Sat and at 11:00 on Sunday.

Getting There: San Giorgio Maggiore is the impressive church you see across the lagoon from St. Mark's Square. Catch vaporetto #82 from the "San Marco (M.V.E.)" stop, located 200 meters east of St. Mark's Square, at the third bridge along the waterfront. (Note: This is not the same vaporetto stop as "San Marco.")

Length of Our Tour: One hour.

Starring: Palladio, Tintoretto, and views.

EXTERIOR

The facade looks like a Greek temple, a style so common today only because the architect Palladio was so influential. In fact, the facade is like two temple fronts overlapping. The four tall columns topped by a triangular pediment resemble a Greek porch, marking the entryway to the tall, central nave. This is superimposed over the facade of the lower side aisles. Behind the facade rises a dome topped with a statue of St. George (the Christian slayer of medieval

San Giorgio Maggiore

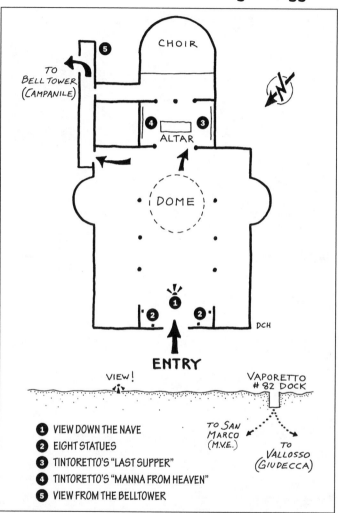

1 VIEW DOWN THE NAVE
2 EIGHT STATUES
3 TINTORETTO'S "LAST SUPPER"
4 TINTORETTO'S "MANNA FROM HEAVEN"
5 VIEW FROM THE BELLTOWER

dragons) holding a flag. The whole complex is completed by the bell tower, which echoes St. Mark's Campanile across the water.

Andrea Palladio (1508–1580) influenced centuries of architects in England and America with his revival of Greco-Roman styles. His churches, palaces, and villas were popularized by a famous treatise he wrote on architecture.

INTERIOR

1. View Down the Nave

The interior matches the
outer facade, with a high nave
flanked by lower side aisles.
The walls are white, the windows have clear, rather than
stained, glass, and the well-
lit church has a clarity and
mathematical perfection that
exudes the classical world.

• *Above the entrance door are eight statues . . .*

2. Evangelists and Doctors of the Church

The four Evangelists in the upper niches and four Doctors of the
Church below are all as pure white as the rest of the church. But
the Evangelists are white stucco, the Doctors are whitewashed
wood . . . and the rest of the church is a mix of white Istrian stone
(the columns) with white-painted cheaper materials (the pilasters).

In the transepts are works by Gian Domenico Tiepolo, the
son and assistant of his more famous father.

Main Altar and Tintoretto

The altar is topped with a bronze globe of the world. The monks
who once lived on this island congregated in the choir area behind
the main altar.

• *On the wall to the right of the altar is . . .*

3. Tintoretto—*Last Supper*

This is the last of several versions of the *Last Supper* by Tintoretto
that decorate Venice, each one different and inventive. Here, the
table stretches diagonally away from us on a tiled floor, with such
a convincing 3-D effect that the tiny diners at the far end look a
mile away. The scene is crowded—servants and cats mingle with
wispy, unseen angels. A blazing lamp radiating supernatural light

illuminates the otherwise
dark interior. Dark sha-
dows are cast on the table.
In the foreground, a lady
offers a man a breath mint.

Tintoretto's jumble
of the spiritual with the
mundane proclaims his
common theme that God

works miraculously with us on an everyday level. Almost lost in the hubbub is Jesus (middle of the table in red and blue), serving the bread and wine.
• *On the wall to the left of the altar is...*

4. Tintoretto— Manna from Heaven

This shows the sunny morning after the storm when God rained bread down on the hungry Israelites. They luxuriate on the ground, gathering the heavenly meal in baskets, basking in the glow of the miracle.
• *The lift up the bell tower (campanile) is in the far left corner of the church.*

VIEW FROM THE BELL TOWER

Facing north (toward the city): This is the famous view of Venice's skyline, with St. Mark's Campanile dominating. The big, long brick church is San Giovanni e Paolo. Farther to the right (east) is the artificial bay of the Arsenale, and farther still is the green parkland where the Biennale International Art Exhibition is held (scheduled for summer of 2003; see page 257). North of Venice, in the hazy distance, you may catch a glimpse of several islands: tiny San Michele (with trees and cemetery), Murano (the next-closest), Burano (leaning bell tower), and Torcello (see page 36).

Facing east: At your feet are the green gardens of the Isle of San Giorgio. Farther out is the tail of Venice. In the far distance is the lo-o-o-ng island called the Lido (with beaches, casinos, modern hotels, and cars), which serves as a natural breakwater against the Adriatic tides. This creates the placid waters of the lagoon, which surrounds you. (Engineers plan to erect tide barriers between the Lido and its neighboring islands to, hopefully, keep Venice from sinking.) The green dome on the island marks the Lido's main town.

Facing south: At your feet are the cloisters of the convent of San Giorgio Maggiore.

Facing west: At your feet is the church, with its dome topped

View from the Bell Tower

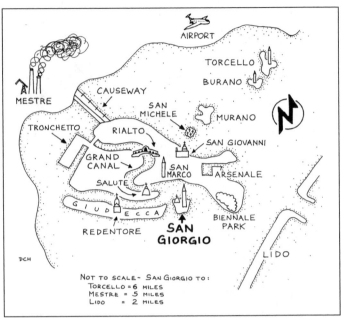

by a green St. George carrying a flag. You can see the back of Palladio's false-front facade. Stretching to the left is the island of Giudecca, which is oh-so-close to the isle of San Giorgio Maggiore but must be reached by a short swim or vaporetto #82. On Giudecca is Palladio's other masterpiece in Venice, the domed Redentore Church. To the right, across the water on the point at the opening of the Grand Canal, sits the golden globe of the old Customs House and the nearby dome of La Salute Church. And in the far distance, through the smog, are the burning smokestacks and cranes of lovely Mestre on the mainland.

ST. MARK'S TO RIALTO
WALK

Two rights and a left (simple!) can get you from St. Mark's Square to the Rialto Bridge via a completely different route than most tourists take. Along the way, take in some lesser sights in the area west of St. Mark's Square, including an often photographed but rarely found architectural gem, the spiral staircase of Scala Contarini del Bovolo.

The Route

The route takes about 30 minutes.

- From the waterfront at St. Mark's Square, head 100 meters west along the water, jogging inland at Harry's Bar, then continuing west on Calle Larga XXII Marzo.
- Turn right on Calle del Sartor da Veste; head north 200 meters.
- Turn right at the T intersection on Calle de la Mandola; head east 100 meters.
- Turn left on Calle del Forno and work your way north to the Grand Canal.

There are actually three easy routes from St. Mark's Square to Rialto: 1. Along the crowded Mercerie (follow the tourists underneath the clock tower), 2. A straight shot on Calle dei Fabbri (exit St. Mark's Square next to the Quadri Café), and 3. The slightly longer route in this chapter.

Orientation

Church of San Moisé: Free. Open daily 15:30–18:30 (may also be accessible at other times through door along left side of church).

Scala Contarini del Bovolo: €2.50 to enter and climb it (daily 10:00–17:30), but it's viewable for free any time from the outside.

St. Mark's to Rialto Walk

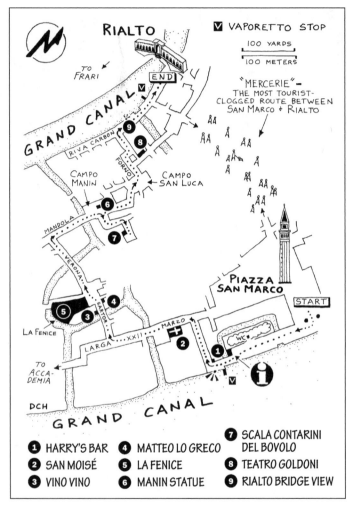

V VAPORETTO STOP

RIALTO

TO FRARI

END

GRAND CANAL

RIVA CARBON

FORNO

CAMPO MANIN

CAMPO SAN LUCA

MANDOLA

VERONA

RIALTO

"MERCERIE" – THE MOST TOURIST-CLOGGED ROUTE BETWEEN SAN MARCO + RIALTO

PIAZZA SAN MARCO

START

LA FENICE

SARTOR

LARGA XXII MARZO

WC

TO ACCADEMIA

DCH

GRAND CANAL

❶ HARRY'S BAR ❹ MATTEO LO GRECO ❼ SCALA CONTARINI DEL BOVOLO
❷ SAN MOISÉ ❺ LA FENICE ❽ TEATRO GOLDONI
❸ VINO VINO ❻ MANIN STATUE ❾ RIALTO BRIDGE VIEW

Start at St. Mark's Square

• *From the square, walk to the waterfront and turn right, walking along the water until you must turn right again at Harry's Bar and the San Marco/Vallaresso vaporetto stop.*

Along the waterfront, you'll see the various boats that ply Venice's waters. The gondolas here are often more expensive than elsewhere. Water taxis, in classic wooden motorboats, are pricey

(about €50 from here to the train station), but a classy splurge if you can split the fare with others. Hotel shuttle boats bring guests here from distant, $700-dollar-a-night hotels. Huge building-sized cruise boats kiss right up to the quay to disgorge day-trippers. The vaporetto stop up ahead is next to a *traghetto* that ferries locals across to La Salute Church.

The Giardinetti Reali Park offers some precious greenery in a city built of stone on mud. There are WCs, a TI in the nearby pavilion, and public pay phones where you can call home and just tell everyone where you are right now. From the top of the little bridge at the TI, look across the mouth of the Grand Canal to view the big dome of La Salute Church, and the guy balancing a bronze ball on one foot—the old Customs House. Twelve steps down and 20 meters ahead, on the right, is Harry's Bar.

1. Harry's American Bar

If Dennis Hopper or Henry Winkler are in town (I've seen both), this is where they'll be. If they're not, you'll see plenty of dressed-up Americans looking around for celebrities that rarely show. The food is expensive, but if you wear something a bit fancy, you can sit at the tiny bar by the entrance and enjoy a decent martini or a Bellini (*prosecco* and peach juice), their house girly-drink—invented here in Venice.

• *Head inland on Calle Vallaresso, one of Venice's most exclusive streets, past fancy boutiques like Gucci and Bruno Magli. At the T intersection, turn left and head west on (what becomes) Calle Larga XXII Marzo. You'll pass American Express, continuing to the first bridge and a square dominated by the ornate facade of the...*

2. Church of San Moisé

This is one of Venice's oldest churches, dating from the 10th century. Inside, the impressive main altar is dedicated to Moses (Moisé). God and his angels stand on top of Mount Sinai, giving Moses the Ten Commandments. Moses is often portrayed with horns because someone mistranslated a biblical phrase meaning "became radiant" as "sprouted horns."

Tintoretto's *Christ Washing the Disciples' Feet* (in the chapel to the left of the altar) is a dark, dirty, and often overlooked late work. The disciples lounge around. We barely notice Christ (in the upper right on a platform) bending to wash Peter's feet. In the lower left are portraits of Tintoretto's patrons. One disciple raises his hands as if to tell them, "Get out of here. You don't belong in this picture."

• *Continue west halfway to the end of the street and turn right on tiny Calle del Sartor da Veste. (If you pass the "La Caravella Restaurant," you've overshot the turn.) Head north on Calle Sartor 75 meters, crossing a bridge, where on the left you'll find . . .*

3. Vino Vino

Here you can taste wines and enjoy a reasonably priced meal in a casual setting (closed Tue, at #2007-A Calle Sartor).

• *A few doors farther ahead, on the right . . .*

4. Matteo Lo Greco Studio

This sculptor makes balloon-shaped people in bronze, celebrating the lighter-than-air joy of being fat (#1998 Calle Sartor).

• *Just ahead (on the left), the scaffolding and cranes belong to . . .*

5. La Fenice

Venice's famed opera house (built in 1792) is now in ruins after a disastrous fire in 1996 that left it a hollowed-out shell. Peeking through the scaffolding, you can follow the rebuilding progress. Is there a roof on yet? Hopefully, "The Phoenix" will be true to its name and rise again from the ashes.

Venice is one of the cradles of the art form known as opera. Opera is a sung play, a multimedia event, blending music, words, story, costume, and set design. Some of the great operas were first performed here in this luxurious setting. Verdi's *Rigoletto* (1851) and *La Traviata* (1853) were actually commissioned by La Fenice. Mozart's librettist was a Venetian who drew inspiration from the city's libertine ways and joie de vivre. In recent years, La Fenice's musical reputation was overshadowed by its reputation as a place for the wealthy to parade in furs and jewels.

The small square nearby, Campo San Fantin, has several nice cafés that cater to theater patrons.

• *Continue north along the same street (though its name is now Calle de La Verona), crossing a bridge over a quiet canal that will tempt photographers to catch reflections in the water. After 100 meters, at the T intersection, turn right on Calle de la Mandola. You'll cross over a bridge and into a spacious square dominated by an ugly modern building.*

6. Campo Manin

The centerpiece of the square is a statue of Daniele Manin (1804–1857), Venice's fiery leader in the battle for democracy and a

united Italy (the Risorgimento). The
statue faces the red house he lived in.
Chafing under Austrian rule, the Venetians rose up. The Austrians laid siege to
the city (1849), bombing it into surrender.
Manin was banished and spent his final
years in Paris, still proudly drumming
up support for modern Italy.

• *The Scala Contarini del Bovolo is well-
signposted a block south of here. Facing the
Manin statue, turn right, exiting the square
down an alley. Follow yellow signs to the left,
then right, into a courtyard with one of
Venice's hidden treasures...*

7. Scala Contarini del Bovolo

Sometimes called Venice's Non-Leaning Tower
of Pisa, the Scala is a cylindrical brick tower
with five floors of spiral staircase faced
with white marble banisters. Built in 1499,
it was the external staircase of a palace
(external stairs saved interior space for
rooms). Architecture buffs admire the
successful blend of Gothic, Byzantine,
and Renaissance styles.

Wind your way up (*bovolo* means "snail
shell" in the local dialect) 113 steps to the top, where you're
rewarded with views of the sublime Venetian skyline. There are

the onion domes of St. Mark's,
the Campanile, the dome of
La Salute, and the roofline
(is it done yet?) of La Fenice.
You'll also see plenty of red-
tiled rooftops, underwear on
clotheslines, and a curious relic
of a bygone era—TV antennas.

• *Unwind and return to the Manin statue. Continue east, circling
around the big modern Cassa di Risparmio bank, into Campo San Luca.
At Campo San Luca, turn left (north) on Calle del Forno. Heading
north, glance down the street to the right at the...*

8. Teatro Goldoni

Though this theater looks modern, it dates from the 1500s,
when Venice was at the forefront of secular entertainment.
Many of Carlo Goldoni's (1707–93) groundbreaking comedies

got their first performance here, and the theater was renamed in his honor. It's still a working theater (mainly Italian productions).
• *Continue north on Calle del Forno. You're very close to the Grand Canal. Keep going—veering to the right of the Matteo Lo Greco statue—then down a teeny-tiny alleyway. Pop! You'll soon emerge on the Grand Canal, about 150 meters "downstream" from the . . .*

9. Rialto Bridge

Of Venice's 408 bridges, only three cross the Grand Canal. Of these three bridges, the Rialto was the first.

The original Rialto Bridge, dating from 1180, was a platform supported by boats tied together. It linked the political side (Palazzo Ducale) of Venice with the economic center (Rialto). Rialto, which takes its name from *rivo alto* (high bank), was one of the earliest Venetian settlements. When Venice was Europe's economic superpower, it was the city's commercial center, where bankers, brokers, and merchants conducted their daily business.

Rialto Bridge II was a 13th-century wooden drawbridge. This was replaced in 1588 by the current structure, with its bold single arch spanning 49 meters (158 feet) and arcades on top designed to strengthen the stone structure. Its immense foundations stretch 200 meters (650 feet) on either side. Heavy buildings were then built atop the foundations to hold everything in place. The Rialto remained the only bridge crossing the Grand Canal until 1854.

Reliefs of the Venetian Republic's main mascots, St. Mark and St. Theodore, crown the arch as barges and vaporetti run the busy waterways below and merchants vie for tourists' attention topside.

The Rialto has long been a symbol of Venice. Aristocratic inhabitants built magnificent palaces just to be near it. The poetic Lord Byron swam to it. And thousands of proposals have been sealed with a kiss as the moon rose over *La Serenissima*.

RIALTO TO FRARI CHURCH
WALK

The area west of the Grand Canal is less touristy—the place where "real" Venetians live. This walk is the most direct route from the Rialto Bridge to the Frari Church and Scuola San Rocco, but along the way you'll see lively produce and stinky fish markets, local pubs, squares, and churches that are at least a bit off the tourist path.

The Route
- Head west from the Rialto Bridge one long block, through the busy market.
- After 100 meters, turn left and head down Ruga Vecchia San Giovanni. Walk southwest along the Ruga (paralleling the Grand Canal) about half a kilometer (quarter mile) to spacious Campo San Polo.
- From San Polo, continue southwest another 200 meters, then jog left, then right, where you'll soon see signs directing you to the Scuola Grande di San Rocco.

Orientation
Rialto Market: The souvenir stalls are open daily; the produce market is closed on Sunday; and the fish market is closed on Sunday and Monday.

Church of San Polo: €2.50. Mon–Sat 10:00–17:00, Sun 10:00–13:00, last entry 15 minutes before closing.

Casa Goldoni: €2.50, covered by €15.50 Museum Pass. Mon–Sat 10:00–17:00, until 16:00 Nov–March, closed Sun.

Frari Church: €2, audioguides available (€1.60/person, €2.60/double set). Mon–Sat 9:00–18:00, Sun 13:00–18:00, last entry 15 minutes before closing.

Scuola San Rocco: €5.20, good audioguide included. Daily 9:00–17:00.

Rialto to Frari Church Walk

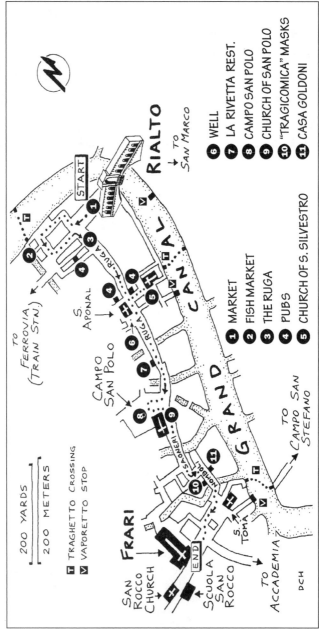

200 YARDS
200 METERS

- ▪ TRAGHETTO CROSSING
- ▾ VAPORETTO STOP

1 MARKET
2 FISH MARKET
3 THE RUGA
4 PUBS
5 CHURCH OF S. SILVESTRO
6 WELL
7 LA RIVETTA REST.
8 CAMPO SAN POLO
9 CHURCH OF SAN POLO
10 "TRAGICOMICA" MASKS
11 CASA GOLDONI

1. Market *(Erberia)*

The street west of the
Rialto Bridge is lined
with stalls selling cheese,
arugula, dripping coconut
slices, glass beads, postcards, masks, leather purses,
and T-shirts. Beyond that,
along the canal, is a thriving
produce market offering a
good peek at work-a-day Venice. The area is busy with colorful
cafés, fragrant with cheese and meat shops, and slimy with a
colonnaded fish market (which is closed Sun–Mon).

• *At the end of the market stalls, look left down the busy street, the Ruga
Vecchia San Giovanni, which we'll follow in a moment. But first, jog to
the right and follow your nose to the . . .*

2. Fish Market

The open-air stalls have the catch of the day—Venice's cuisine
specialty. Find eels, scallops, and crustaceans with five-inch antennae. This is the Venice that has existed for centuries: workers toss
boxes of fish from delivery boats while shoppers step from the
traghetto (gondola shuttle) into the action.

• *Return to the Ruga Vecchia San Giovanni and head southwest,
roughly paralleling the Grand Canal.*

3. The Street Called the "Ruga"

The busy street is lined with shops that get increasingly less
touristy. You'll see fewer trinkets and more clothes, bread, shoes,
watches, shampoo, and underwear.

• *About a hundred meters along the Ruga—just past a Chinese
restaurant—is a pub on the left-hand side.*

4. Pubs: Ostaria Ruga Rialto Pub

This bar/café, with a wine barrel out front, paintings of old
Venice on the walls, and outdoor tables, is one of several pubs
in the area that cater to tourists by day and locals by night. Even
teetotaling Venetians hang out in pubs, grabbing a sandwich on
their feet, nibbling finger-food appetizers *(cicchetti)*, or ordering
a small tumbler of cheap wine (an *ombra*). Other atmospheric
places nearby include the teensy **Ruga Rialto** (at #1045, about
100 meters farther along) and the **Cantina Do Mori** (back near
the head of the Ruga, see map on page 160).

• *A block or so farther along the Ruga, a detour to the left on Rio
Tera S. Silvestro leads to a big white church.*

5. Church of San Silvestro

True Tintoretto gourmets on their way to the Scuola may want a Tintoretto appetizer. His *Baptism of Christ* (first chapel on right) shows a twisted, unbalanced John the Baptist as Jesus gingerly tests the waters of the Jordan River.
• *Continue southwest along the Ruga to Campo S. Aponal, with a . . .*

6. Well

Wells like this were the center of village Venice, back before drinking water was piped in from the mainland starting in 1886. The well (now capped) sits in a square that slopes into drains that caught rainwater, which filtered down through sand into a cistern (roughly the size of the outline in the paving stones).
• *Continue southwest along Calle di Mezzo, past the recommended . . .*

7. La Rivetta Ristorante

Stop in for their inexpensive Venetian specialties, such as *spaghetti al nero di seppie* (sqid ink) or *fegato alla Veneziana* (calf liver and onions); see page 225.
• *Beyond the restaurant, Calle di Mezzo opens up into . . .*

8. Campo San Polo

One of the largest squares in Venice, Campo San Polo is shaped like an amphitheater, with its church tucked away in the corner (just ahead of you). There are a few rare trees with rare benches with grateful locals on them. In the summer, bleachers and a screen are erected for open-air movies, a true *Cinema Paradiso* experience.
• *On the square is the . . .*

9. Church of San Polo (S. Paolo Apostoli)

The church is one of the oldest in Venice, from the ninth century (€2.50 entry fee). The wooden boat-shaped ceiling recalls the earliest basilicas built after Rome's fall.

    Tintoretto's *Last Supper* (*Ultima Cena*, 1568–69; immediately to left of entrance) is a different take on the scene than you'll see at Scuola San Rocco. The table is set on diagonal floor tiles. Only Christ is facing us—the others twist and turn, their body language following the left-to-right flow of the table and floor tiles . . . until the eye settles on brooding Judas on the right. (As Tintoretto and theater directors know, characters going "against the flow" attract our attention.)

G. B. Tiepolo's *Virgin Appearing to St. John of Nepomuk*, **1754** (opposite entry door, on the second altar on the left, as you face the main altar) was designed for this location by the master of 3-D perspective. He foreshortens the figures, knowing we're on church level looking up at it.

Turn 90 degrees right and compare Tiepolo with the work of the man he most admired, Paolo Veronese. In **Veronese's** *Betrothal of the Virgin, with Angels* (c. 1580, left corner, as you face the main altar), God the Father rides above it all, but at an odd perspective—he's looking "down" at Mary and Joseph, while we are looking "across" at him.

• *In an adjoining room, find the cycle of paintings by G. D. Tiepolo.*

G. D. Tiepolo, the son of the more famous G. B. Tiepolo, has a more sober, down-to-earth style. In his *Stations of the Cross* (*Via Crucis*, 1747–49), we follow Christ's last excruciating days (moving around the room clockwise from the entrance), from his death sentence to torture to crucifixion to removal of his body from the cross. The scenes are evenly lit in the glow of a luminous gray-sky background. We catch hints of the elder Tiepolo in the bright-colored robes, but these scenes are more understated... and ultimately more moving because of it.

• *From the Church of San Polo, continue southwest about 200 meters. Jog left when you have to, then right when you have to, onto Calle dei Nomboli. On the right, just before a small bridge, you'll see the...*

10. "Tragicomica" Mask Shop

One of Venice's best mask stores, it's also a workshop that lets you see mask-making in action. Venice's masks date from the celebration of Carnevale (the local pre-Lent blowout). Many masks are patterned after standard characters of the theater style known as commedia dell'arte: the famous trickster Harlequin, the beautiful and cunning Columbine, the country bumpkin Pulcinella (who later evolved into the wife-beating "Punch" of marionette shows), and the pompous, long-nosed Doctor (*dottore*).

• *Across the narrow street from the mask shop is...*

11. Casa Goldoni

Those with a hearty passion for theater (or with a Museum Pass, allowing free admission) will want to tour this small, sparse, Italian-language-only museum.

The playwright Carlo Goldoni (1707–1793) was born in this building, and it's now a museum to his life in theater. An established lawyer in Venice, Goldoni truly loved the stage. He wrote comedies along the lines of buffoonish commedia dell'arte, but he stripped off the masks, creating more realistic characters and plots, and pointing the way toward modern theater.

The museum is just three small rooms, one a makeshift theater for watching videos. The Murano glass chandelier, wood-beamed ceiling, and reflecting candle mirrors hint at the luxury of the social set Goldoni ran in and satirized. The room to the left displays marionettes of commedia dell'arte characters (Harlequin, the Doctor, etc.) and of colorful Venetians of Goldoni's day—well-dressed ladies, gentlemen, and Moors. The room to the right has early editions of his plays, a 3-D map of the many theaters of his day, and portraits of Goldoni.

Along one wall are engravings illustrating the major events in his life: 1) As a child, the diligent Carlo studied rhetoric and philosophy at a church boarding school. 2) At age 12, he saw a performance that entranced him, causing him to run away and join a traveling dell'arte troupe. 3) He returned to study law but was expelled for writing an indecent satire about the local girls. 4) At 25, Carlo finally passed his bar exams. 5–6) He kept his day job practicing law, while at night he wrote plays. 7) At age 27, Goldoni saw his first play performed on a Venetian stage. It was only the first of many triumphs in Venice, including *The Servant of Two Masters*, *The Good Wife*, and *The Artful Widow*. His last years were spent in Paris—then the center of the civilized world— making the King of France laugh.

• *Continue along, cross the bridge, and veer right. You'll see signs directing you to "Scuola Grande di San Rocco." A block later, you'll bump into the back end of the Frari Church (★ see Tour on page 112), with the Scuola next door (★ see Scuola San Rocco Tour on page 102).*

ST. MARK'S TO SAN ZACCARIA
WALK

San Zaccaria, the oldest church in Venice, with a submerged crypt and a Bellini altarpiece, is just a few minutes on foot from St. Mark's Square. Along the way, there's a great view of the Bridge of Sighs.

The Route

You can make a square circuit from St. Mark's Square to the Church of San Zaccaria to the waterfront, and back to St. Mark's Square.

- From St. Mark's Square, walk behind St. Mark's Basilica to the Church of San Zaccaria.
- Turn right at San Zaccaria and walk a block to the waterfront.
- Turn right and walk along the Riva, returning to St. Mark's Square.

Orientation

Church of San Zaccaria: Free. Daily 10:00–12:00 & 16:00–18:00. Admission to the crypt costs €1.

Start at St. Mark's Square

• *Facing St. Mark's Basilica, head east, circling behind the church on the left-hand side (past the stone lions that kids love to sit on).*

You'll reach a bridge with a . . .

1. View of the Bridge of Sighs

This lesser-known view of the Bridge of Sighs also lets you see the Church of San Giorgio Maggiore in the distance, framed by the arch of the Bridge of Sighs.

• *Continuing east, you'll cross another*

St. Mark's to San Zaccaria

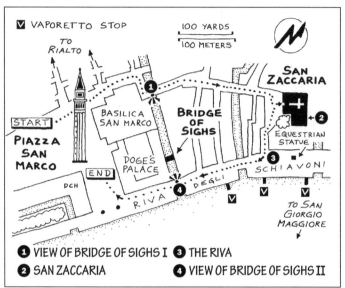

☑ VAPORETTO STOP   100 YARDS
          TO   100 METERS
       RIALTO

                              SAN
                              ZACCARIA

START   BASILICA   BRIDGE
               SAN MARCO   OF
PIAZZA   SIGHS   EQUESTRIAN
SAN   STATUE
MARCO   DOGE'S   SCHIAVONI
          END PALACE
     DCH   DEGLI
               RIVA   TO SAN
                                       GIORGIO
                                       MAGGIORE

❶ VIEW OF BRIDGE OF SIGHS I   ❸ THE RIVA
❷ SAN ZACCARIA   ❹ VIEW OF BRIDGE OF SIGHS II

bridge with a view of a "Modern Bridge of Sighs," which connects two wings of the exclusive Danieli Hotel. Continue east another 50 meters until you run into the...

2. Church of San Zaccaria

Back in the ninth century, when Venice was just a collection of wooden houses, back before there was a St. Mark's Basilica, a stone church and convent stood here. Here is where the doges worshiped, public spectacles occurred, and the most sacred relics were kept. Today's structure dates mostly from the 15th century.

The tall facade by Mauro Cardussi (who also did the clock tower in St. Mark's Square) is about as close to northern European–style Gothic as Venice gets. The "vertical" effect produced by the four support pillars that rise up to an arched crown is tempered by the horizontal, many-layered stories and curved shoulders.

• *Enter the church. The second chapel on the right holds the...*

Body of Zachariah (S. Zaccaria, Patris S. Jo: Baptista)

Of two bodies in the chapel, the upper one in the glass case,

supported by stone angels, is
the reputed body of Zachariah,
the father of John the Baptist.
Back when mortal remains were
venerated and thought to bring
miracles to the faithful, Venice
was proud to own these bones.

• *The church is virtually wallpapered with art. On the opposite side
of the nave (second chapel on the
left), you'll find . . .*

Giovanni Bellini's *Madonna and Child with Saints (Sacra Conversazione*, 1505)

Mary and the baby, under a pavilion, are surrounded by various
saints engaged in a "holy conversation," which is more like a
quiet meditation.

This is one of the last of Bellini's paintings in the *sacra
conversazione* formula (see his others in the Accademia and Frari
Church). The setting is an extension of the church—the pavilion's
columns match the real church columns. He establishes a 3-D
effect using floor tiles. We see a glimpse of trees and a cloudy
sky beyond. A violinist angel plays solo at Mary's feet. The four
saints pose symmetrically.

There's a harmony of big blocks of rich-colored robes—
blue, green, red, white, and yellow. The whole scene is enveloped
in a cool white light that casts no dark shadows. This is a meditative *Sacra*. The saints' mood is melancholy, with lidded eyes and
downturned faces. The 75-year-old Bellini was innovative and pro-
ductive until the end of his long life. The German artist Dürer said
of him: "He is very old, and still he is the best painter of them all."

• *On the right-hand side of the nave is the entrance (€1 entry fee) to . . .*

The Chapel of the Choir, the Chapel of Gold, and the Crypt

The first room contains **Tintoretto's *Birth of John the Baptist***
(on the altar). Mother Elizabeth lies in bed in the background,
while nurses hold and coo over little John. Zachariah, the father,
is nowhere to be seen.

The five **gold chairs** were once seats for doges. Every
Easter, the current doge would walk from St. Mark's Square to
this original religious center. After the doge took a seat in one
of these chairs, nuns from the San Zaccaria convent would give

him a pope's crown, one which had been given to Venice for saving an early pope's life. The ceremony celebrated proud Venice's independence from Rome.

The Chapel of Gold has a 12th-century mosaic fragment from the original church. In fact, these rooms were parts of the earlier churches.

Finally, go downstairs into the **crypt**—the foundation of a church built in the ninth century. The crypt is low and the water table high, so the room is often flooded, and you have to walk through on a raised path. It's a weird experience, calling up echoes of the Dark Ages. There's an altar, a statue of Mary, and, somewhere in the gloom, the tombs of eight early doges.

• *Emerge from the Church of San Zaccaria into the small square in front. Exit left to reach the waterfront.*

3. The Riva

The waterfront promenade known as the "Riva" gives a great view of the Church of San Giorgio Maggiore. If you want to head there next, catch vaporetto #82 from the "San Marco (M.V.E.)" stop to the left (past the equestrian statue).  ✪ See San Giorgio Maggiore Tour, page 148.

The Riva is lined with many of Venice's most famous luxury hotels, such as the Danieli.

• *Turn right and return to St. Mark's Square. The commotion atop a little bridge marks...*

4. The Famous View of the Bridge of Sighs

From this bridge, prisoners took one last look at Venice before entering the dark and dank prisons. And sighed. From here, you can take one last look at the lagoon before entering crowded and sweaty St. Mark's Square...and sigh.

For a more detailed description of the bridge, see page 52.

DAY TRIPS

Padua, Vicenza, Verona, and Ravenna

While Venice is just one of many towns in the Italian region of Veneto (VEN-eh-toh), few venture off the lagoon. Four important towns and possible side trips, in addition to the lakes and the Dolomites, make zipping directly from Venice to Milan or Florence a route strewn with temptation.

Planning Your Time

The towns of Padua, Vicenza, Verona, and Ravenna are all, for various reasons, good stops. Each town gives the visitor a low-key slice of Italy that complements the high-powered urbanity of Venice, Florence, and Rome. But none is an essential part of the best three weeks Italy has to offer.

Visiting Verona, Padua, and Vicenza couldn't be easier: All are 30 minutes apart on the Venice–Milan line (hrly, 3 hrs). Spending a day town-hopping between Venice and Bolzano or Milan—with 3-hour stops at Padua, Vicenza, and Verona—is exiting and efficient. Trains run frequently enough to allow flexibility and little wasted time. Of the towns discussed below, only Ravenna (2.5 hours from Padua or Florence) is not on the main Venice–Milan train line.

If you're Padua-bound, note that you need to reserve ahead to see the Scrovegni Chapel (see below). Most sights in Verona and Vicenza are closed on Monday.

PADUA (Padova)

Living under Venetian rule for four centuries seemed only to sharpen Padua's independent spirit. Nicknamed "the brain of Veneto," Padua has a prestigious university (founded 1222) that was home to Galileo, Copernicus, Dante, and Petrarch. The old town, even when packed with modern-day students, is

Day Trips from Venice

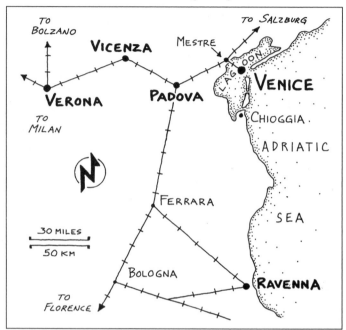

a colonnaded time-tunnel experience. And Padua's museums and churches hold their own in Italy's artistic big league. Note that you need to book ahead to visit the Scrovegni Chapel with its great Giotto paintings (see page 174).

Arrival in Padua: Enter the station lobby. To get oriented, turn around and face the tracks. Look for the two small offices next to each other, marked: *Biglietti e Prenotazioni Internazionali* (Tickets and International Reservations) and Tourist Information. To the left of these is an even smaller office, marked Bus Tickets, which sells city bus tickets (€0.85). At the **TI**, pick up a city map and list of sights (April–Sept Mon–Sat 8:30–19:00, Sun 8:30–12:30, Oct–March Mon–Sat 10:00–13:00 & 13:30–16:30, Sun 8:30–12:30, tel. 049-876-7927).

Day-trippers: The station has a baggage check office (€3.90, daily 6:00–24:00). If you have reservations for the Scrovegni Chapel, that will dictate the order of your sightseeing. But if you don't plan on seeing the chapel, here's an efficient plan: Take the bus from the station to the Basilica of St. Anthony, then walk through the old town, sightseeing your way back to the station (buy your €0.85 bus ticket at the Bus Ticket office in the station lobby or at a *tabacchi* stop; catch bus #8, #12, or #18 to Via Luca Belludi, next to Piazza del Santo and the Basilica of St. Anthony). A taxi into town costs about €5. (If you have any train business, such as reservations, note that a CIT travel agency is on the square in front of the station.)

Sights—Padua

▲▲**Basilica of St. Anthony**—Friar Anthony of Padua, "Christ's perfect follower and a tireless preacher of the Gospel," is buried here. For nearly 800 years, his remains and this impressive church (building started immediately after the death of the saint in 1231) have attracted pilgrims to Padua (daily in summer 6:30–19:45, winter 6:30–19:00, modest dress code enforced).

Nod to St. Anthony looking down from the facade, then start your visit at the information desk just inside the cloisters (daily 9:00–12:00 & 15:00–18:00, very helpful with an abundance of St. Anthony–related handouts). Wander around the various cloisters. In the far end, a fascinating little museum is filled with votives and folk art recounting miracles attributed to Anthony.

Entering the basilica, you gaze past the crowds and through the incense haze at Donatello's glorious crucifix hanging over the altar, and realize this is one of the most important pilgrimage sites in Christendom.

Along with the crucifix, Donatello's bronze statues—Mary with Padua's six favorite saints—grace the high altar.

On the left, pilgrims file slowly by the chapel containing **St. Anthony's tomb**. This Renaissance masterpiece from 1500 is circled by nine marble reliefs showing scenes and miracles from the life of the saint. The pilgrims believe Anthony is their protector—a confidant and intercessor of the poor. And they believe he works miracles. Votives placed here by the faithful ask for help or give thanks for miracles they believe he's performed. By putting their hand on his tomb while saying a silent prayer, pilgrims show devotion to Anthony and feel the saint's presence.

Next on the pilgrim route is the **Chapel of the Reliquaries** (behind the altar), where you can see St. Anthony's robe, vocal chords (discovered intact when his remains were examined in 1981), jaw . . . and "uncorrupted tongue" (discovered when the remains were examined in 1263). These relics—considered miraculously preserved—befit the saint who couldn't stop teaching, preaching, and praying.

Outside, on Piazza del Santo, stands Donatello's much-admired equestrian statue of the Venetian mercenary General Gattamelata. Even military commanders—such as this powerful

Padua

200 METERS
200 YARDS

N

400 METERS TO
TRAIN STATION
& ❸

V. GIOTTO
CORSO GARIBALDI
V. TRIESTE

SCROVEGNI
CHAPEL

BUS
STN.

CIVIC
MUSEUM

ERMITAGE
CHURCH

PIAZZA
INSURREZIONE

V. VERDI   V. EM. FIL.

VIA S. LUCIA

V. ZABARELLA
V. ALT.

❷

PIAZZA
SIGNORIA

P.
FRUTTA   ❽

⑩

❺

PIAZZA
CAVOUR

❼

POST

❾

V. MANIN

P.
ERBE

❻

DUOMO

V. VESCOVADO

V. SOLF.

V. 8 FEB.

❶

UNIVERSITY
& ANATOMY
THEATER
(PALAZZO BO)

V. TITO LIVIO

VIA DEL SANTO

VIA S. FRANCESCO

P.
ANT.

V. ROMA

R.

V. STAMPA

V. S. CHIARA

V. GALILEO

20 SETT.

VIA

RIV. RUZZANTE

RUDENA

VIA

H

VIA UMB.

❹

V. ALEARDI

V. SEM.

VIA   TORRESINO

V. BELLUDI

SAN
ANTONIO

MUSEUMS

DCH

PRATO
DELLE
VALLE

❶ MAJESTIC HOTEL TOSCANELLI
❷ HOTEL VERDI
❸ HOTEL GRAND' ITALIA &
   HOTEL MONACO
❹ OSTELLO CITTA DI PADOVA
❺ LA COVA RISTORANTE

❻ MARECHIARO PIZZERIA
❼ BREK CAFETERIA
❽ ISOLA DI CAPRERA REST.
❾ CAFE PEDROCCHI & T.I.
⑩ PALAZZO RAGIONE

Venetian—wanted to be close to St. Anthony. This statue is famous as the first statue of this size cast out of bronze since ancient Roman times. On the square, you'll find a handy **TI** and a couple of friendly cafés. A 10-minute stroll up Via del Santo takes you back into the center.

Palazzo della Ragione—This grand 13th-century palazzo once held the medieval law courts. The first floor consists of a huge hall—81 meters by 27 meters (265 feet by 90 feet)—that was once adorned with frescoes by Giotto. A fire in 1312 destroyed those paintings and the palazzo was then decorated with the 15th-century art you see today: a series of 123 frescoes depicting the signs of the zodiac, labors of the month, symbols representing characteristics of people born under each sign, and finally, figures of saints to legitimize the power of the courts in the eyes of the church. The hall is topped with a keel-shaped roof, which helps to support the structure without the use of columns—quite an architectural feat in its time, considering the building's dimensions. The curious stone in the right-hand corner near the entry is the "Stone of Shame," which was the seat of debtors being punished during the Middle Ages. Instead of being sentenced to death or prison (same thing back then), debtors sat upon this stone, renounced their possessions, and denounced themselves publicly before being exiled from the city. Exhibitions are often held in the palace (€3.60, Feb–Oct Tue–Sun 9:00–19:00, Nov–Jan closes at 18:00, closed Mon).

▲▲**Market Squares: Piazza Erbe and Piazza Frutta**—The stately Palazzo della Ragione (described above) provides a quintessentially Italian backdrop for Padua's almost exotic-feeling market, filling the surrounding squares—Piazza delle Erbe and Piazza della Frutta—each morning. Second only to the produce market in Italy's gastronomic capital of Bologna, this market has been renowned for centuries as having the freshest and greatest selection of herbs, fruits, and vegetables. Beneath the Palazzo della Ragione are various butchers, *salumerie* (delicatessens), cheese shops, bakeries, and fishmongers.

Make a point to explore this scene. Students gather here each evening, spilling out of colorful bars and cafés—drinks in hand—into the square. Their drink of choice is a *spritz*, an aperitif with Campari, Cynar (two bitter, alcoholic liqueurs), white wine, and sparkling water, garnished with an olive and a blood-orange wedge. **Bar Nazionale**, at #41 under the staircase of Palazzo della Ragione, offers outdoor seating for a ringside view of the action. **Bar degli Spritz** at #36 near the middle of the palazzo at the passageway is the students' hangout. Get your *spritz* to take away *(da portar via)* and join the young people out on the piazza. This is a classic opportunity to enjoy a real discussion with smart, English-speaking students who see tourists not as pests but as interesting people from far away. For an instant conversation starter, ask about the current political situation in Italy or the cultural differences between the north and the south.

Consider dropping by **Café Pedrocchi**, a sumptuously neo-classical café famous as the place where students plotted an uprising in 1848. You can still see a bullet hole in the wall of the Sala Bianca, where one of the insurgents was killed. Nowadays you get more foam than fervor, but the café is still a marvel of interior design. Each room is decorated in a different style, from simple color schemes (the red, white, and green rooms on the ground floor represent the colors of the Italian flag) to more elaborate Egyptian or Etruscan design. The Sala Verde (green room) is the only room where people can sit and enjoy the beautiful interior without ordering anything or having to pay (at intersection of Oberdan and Febbraio 8, between Piazza delle Erbe and Piazza Cavour, tel. 049-820-5007).

University of Padua—This prestigious university, which requires a reservation to tour, is just across the street from Café Pedrocchi. Founded in 1222, it's one of the first, greatest, and most progressive in Europe. Back when the Church controlled university curricula, a group of professors broke free and created this liberal school, independent of Catholic constraints and accessible to people of alternative faiths. A haven for free thinking, it attracted intellectuals from all over Europe. The great astronomer Copernicus made some of his most important discoveries here. And Galileo—notorious for disagreeing with the Church's views on science—called his 18 years on the faculty here the best of his life. Students gather in ancient courtyards, surrounded by memories of illustrious alumni—including the first woman ever to receive a university degree (in 1678).

And just upstairs, Europe's first great **anatomy theater**, from the 1500s, is worth a look. While strictly forbidden by the Church, students would pack this theater to watch professors dissect human cadavers. If the Church came a-knockin', the table could be flipped, allowing the corpse to fall into a river below and be replaced with an animal instead (€2.60, 1 tour daily except Sun, 45 min, request English, book ahead by calling 049-876-7927, university tel. 049-827-3047).

From Piazza Cavour, it's about a 10-minute walk to the station; en route you'll find the town's artistic wonder, the . . .

▲▲**Scrovegni Chapel (Cappella degli Scrovegni)**—Reserve in advance to see this glorious, recently renovated chapel. It's surrounded by the ruins of a Roman amphitheater, a reminder that Padua was an important Roman town. But the sightseeing thrill here is the chapel, wallpapered by Giotto's beautifully preserved cycle of nearly 40 frescoes, depicting scenes from the lives of Jesus and Mary. Painted by Giotto and his assistants from 1303 to 1305, and considered by many to be the first piece of modern art, this work makes it clear: Europe was breaking out of the Middle Ages. A sign of the Renaissance to come, Giotto placed real people in real scenes. These frescoes were radical for their 3-D nature, lively colors, light sources, emotion, and humanism.

To protect the paintings from excess humidity, only 25 people are allowed in the chapel at a time for a 15-minute visit. To reserve, call 049-201-0020 (Mon–Fri 9:00–19:00, Sat 9:00–13:00) or book online at www.cappelladegliscrovegni.it. Reserve at least four days in advance; earlier is better to guarantee a visit (€11, credit card only).

Arrive one hour before your appointed time to exchange your booking receipt for a ticket. Then consider visiting the neighboring Civic Museum (included with ticket; see below). Be at the chapel 15 minutes before your time slot; it's 100 meters from the ticket desk, outside, and well-signed (daily 9:00–19:00, maybe as late as 22:00, people allowed in every 15 min at :00, :15, :30, and :45 past the hr, last entry 15 min before closing, no photos allowed in chapel). Once you're admitted, you'll have to wait in the anteroom for 15 minutes to establish humidity levels before continuing into the chapel. During your enforced wait, you can watch a multimedia presentation (with English subtitles) on the frescoes, or study a guidebook that you purchased beforehand in the gift shop. Although you have only 15 minutes inside the chapel, it's divine. You're essentially inside a Giotto time capsule, looking back at an artist ahead of his time.

Civic Museum (Musei Civici Eremitani)—This museum, next to the Scrovegni Chapel, displays Roman and Etruscan archaeological finds, buckets of rare coins, and 15th- to 18th-century paintings. The highlight is a Giotto crucifix (€4.10, covered by €11 Scrovegni ticket, Tue–Sun 9:00–18:00, until 19:00 in summer, closed Mon, Piazza Eremitani, tel. 049-820-4500).

Sleeping in Padua
(€1 = about $1, country code: 39)

Many travelers make Padua a low-stress, low-price home base from which to tour Venice. I'd rather flip-flop it—sleeping in Venice and side-tripping to Padua, 30 minutes away by train.

S = Single, **D** = Double/Twin, **T** = Triple, **Q** = Quad, **b** = bathroom, **s** = shower only, **CC** = Credit Cards accepted, **no CC** = Credit Cards not accepted, **SE** = Speaks English, **NSE** = No English.

In the Center: **Majestic Hotel Toscanelli** is a big, fancy hotel with 32 pleasant rooms, a touch of charm, and a relatively quiet location on a side street (Sb-€96–116, Db-€140–165, CC, superior rooms and suites available at extra cost, includes a wonderful breakfast, Via dell' Arco 2, several blocks south of Piazza delle Erbe, tel. 049-663-244, fax 049-876-0025, e-mail: majestic@toscanelli.com).

Hotel Verdi, much cheaper, has 18 basic rooms and a good attitude (S-€23, D-€36, Via Dondi dell' Orologio 7, bus #10 from station to Teatro Verdi, about four zigzag blocks northwest of Piazza Signori, tel. 049-875-5744).

Down by the Station: For elegant four-star comfort, convenience, and prices, it's **Hotel Grand' Italia**. Housed in a palace, its 57 rooms are comfortable, and the breakfast room is bright and inviting (Db-€124–186 depending on season and size, includes breakfast, CC, elevator, air-con, Corso del Popolo 81, right outside train station, tel. 049-876-1111, fax 049-875-0850, www .hotelgranditalia.it, e-mail: info@hotelgranditalia.it).

Hotel Monaco, a three-star hotel a few doors away, is plain in comparison, with darkly decorated rooms, but it's a heck of lot cheaper (Db-€108, includes breakfast, CC, elevator, air-con, traffic noise, Piazzale Stazione 3, to the right as you leave the station, tel. 049-664-344, fax 049-664-669, www.monacohotel.it, e-mail: info@monacohotel.it).

Hostel: The well-run **Ostello Città di Padova** has four-, six-, and 16-bed rooms (€14 beds with sheets and breakfast, €14.50 in family rooms, bus #3, #8, #12, or #18 from station, Via Aleardi 30, tel. 049-875-2219).

Eating in Padua

These are all centrally located in the historic core. **La Cova Ristorante/Pizzeria**, at Piazza Cavour, offers a pleasing range of pizza and pasta (Wed–Mon 12:00–15:30 & 18:00–2:00, closed Tue, Piazza Cavour 20, Via P.F. Calvi, tel. 049-654-312). **Marechiaro Pizzeria/Trattoria** is another good bet, just off Piazza delle Erbe (Tue–Sun 12:00–15:00 & 18:00–24:00, closed Mon, Via D. Manin 37, tel. 049-875-8489). **Brek**, tucked into a corner of Piazza Cavour #20, is an easy self-service *ristorante* (daily 11:30–15:00 & 19:30–22:00, tel. 049-875-8489).

For more of a dining experience, consider **Isola di Caprera** for traditional Veneto cuisine (€21 menu, cheaper à la carte options, CC, Mon–Sat 12:00–15:00 & 19:30–23:00, closed Sun, air-con, Via Marsilio da Padova 11-15, a half block north of the eastern edge of Piazza della Frutta, tel. 049-876-0244; to reserve, call 664-282-876-0244).

VICENZA

To many architects, Vicenza is a pilgrimage site. Entire streets look like the back of a nickel. This is the city of Palladio, the 16th-century Renaissance architect who gave us the Palladian style that is so influential in countless British country homes. For the casual visitor, a quick stop offers plenty of Palladio (1508–1580)—the last great artist of the Renaissance. Note that Vicenza's major sights are closed on Monday.

Tourist Information: The main TI is at Piazza Matteotti 12 (Mon–Sat 9:00–13:00 & 14:30–18:00, Sun 9:00–13:00, tel. 0444-320-854, www.ascom.vi.it/aptvicenza—site has English translations). The train station sometimes has a bleak TI (Aug–Oct only, if at all). Pick up a map and, if staying the night, an entertainment guide. Architect fans will appreciate the free *Vicenza Città del Palladio* brochure in English. Guided **tours** are offered Saturday at 10:00 (€13, includes admissions to Olympic Theater and other sights—a super deal, April–Oct, 2 hrs, depart from TI on Piazza Matteotti, booking is required, call 0444-320-854 to reserve and confirm time).

Arrival in Vicenza: From the train station, it's a five-minute **walk** up wide Viale Roma to the bottom of Corso Palladio. Or it's a short **bus** ride to Piazza Matteotti and the top of Corso Palladio. For a day trip, consider catching the bus to Piazza Matteotti and doing your sightseeing on the way back to the station. From the station, catch bus #1, #2, or #5 (€0.90, tickets sold at *tabacchi* shop in station and at small white kiosk—marked *Vendita Biglietti*—across street in the bushes). Validate your ticket in the machine near the back of the bus. Get off at Piazza Matteotti, a skinny, park-like square in front of a white neoclassical building. A **taxi** to Piazza Matteotti costs about €5.50.

At the station, you can store luggage (baggage check-€3.90, daily 6:00–22:00 to the far right as you face the ticket booths) and rent bicycles (€1/hr, €8/day, daily 8:00–20:00).

Launderette: The self-service **Lava & Asciuga** is a 10- to 15-minute walk from either the station or central Piazza dei Signori (daily 7:30–22:30, Contra S. Tommaso 46).

Market Days: Vicenza hosts a Tuesday market on Piazza dei Signori and a larger Thursday market that also spills into Piazza Duomo, Piazza del Castello, and Viale Roma (8:00–13:00).

Sights—Vicenza

Most of Vicenza's sights are covered by a Biglietto Unico ticket for €7, sold only at the Olympic Theater. In addition to the theater, this combo-ticket includes the Pinacoteca (paintings, in Palazzo Chiericati on Piazza Matteotti), the Santa Corona

Vincenza

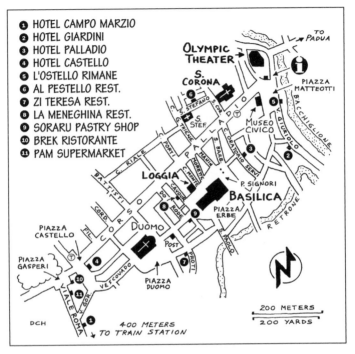

1. HOTEL CAMPO MARZIO
2. HOTEL GIARDINI
3. HOTEL PALLADIO
4. HOTEL CASTELLO
5. L'OSTELLO RIMANE
6. AL PESTELLO REST.
7. ZI TERESA REST.
8. LA MENEGHINA REST.
9. SORARU PASTRY SHOP
10. BREK RISTORANTE
11. PAM SUPERMARKET

Archaeological and Natural History Museum (next to the Church of Santa Corona), and the Basilica Palladiana (in Piazza dei Signori, ticket does not include exhibits held in the basilica).

▲▲**Olympic Theater (Teatro Olimpico)**—Palladio's last work is one of his greatest. Begun in 1580, shortly before Palladio died, the theater was actually completed by his pupil Scamozzi. Modeled after the theaters of antiquity, this is a wood-and-stucco festival of classical columns, statues, and an oh-wow stage bursting with perspective tricks. Behind the stage, framed by a triumphal arch, five streets recede at different angles. Many of the statues in niches are modeled after the people who funded the work. In contrast to the stunning stage, the audience's wooden benches are simple and crude. One of the oldest indoor theaters in Europe and considered one of the world's best, it's still used for performances (€7 Biglietto Unico ticket, Tue–Sun 9:00–17:00, July–Aug until 19:00, last entry 15 min before closing, closed Mon, hours can vary, tel. 0444-222-800, www.olimpico.vicenza.it, WC through entrance to the right).

▲**Church of Santa Corona (Church of the Holy Crown)**—
A block away from the Olympic Theater, this church was built in
the 13th century to house a thorn from the crown of thorns given
to the Bishop of Vicenza by the French king Louis IX (free, Mon
15:00–18:00, Tue–Sun 8:30–12:00 & 15:00–18:00). It has Giovanni Bellini's fine *Baptism of Christ* (c. 1500, put in a coin for
light, to the left of the altar). Study the incredible inlaid marble
and mother-of-pearl work on the high altar (1670) and the inlaid
wood complementing that in the stalls of the choir (1485).

Archaeological and Natural History Museum—Next door
to the Church of Santa Corona, this humble museum features
Roman antiquities (mosaics, statues, and swords) on its ground
floor; prehistoric scraps upstairs; and precious little English information throughout (€7 Biglietto Unico, Tue–Sun 9:00–17:00,
closed Mon).

Strolling Corso Palladio—From the Olympic Theater or Church
of Santa Corona, stroll down Vicenza's main drag, Corso Andrea
Palladio, and see why they call Vicenza "Venezia on terra firma."
A steady string of Renaissance palaces and Palladian architecture
is peopled by Vicenzans (considered by their neighbors to be as
uppity as most of their colonnades) and punctuated by upper-
class gelaterias.

After a few blocks, you'll see the commanding **Basilica
Palladiana,** under restoration in 2003. (This was not a church,
but a meeting place for local big shots.) With its 82-meter-tall,
13th-century tower, the basilica dominates the Piazza dei Signori,
the town center since Roman times. It was young Palladio's pro-
posal to redo Vicenza's dilapidated Gothic palace of justice in the
neo-Greek style that established him as Vicenza's favorite architect. The rest of Palladio's career was a one-man construction
boom. Opposite the basilica, the brick-columned **Loggia del
Capitaniato**—home of the Venetian governor and one of
Palladio's last works—gives you an easy chance to compare early
Palladio (the basilica) with late Palladio (the loggia). The ground
floor of the basilica is filled with shops. Climb up the 15th-century
stairs. You'll see the lion's mouth after a few steps; centuries ago,
people used to sneak notes into the mouth, anonymously reporting
neighbors suspected of carrying communicable diseases such as
the plague. The arcaded upper floor (with a WC in back) contains
the entrance to the huge basilica (€7 Biglietto Unico, Tue–Sun
9:00–17:00, closed Mon, frequent exhibitions, Piazza dei Signori).
The basilica's ceiling, shaped like an upside-down keel, has a
nautical feel, augmented by the porthole windows. Set in the wall
in front, the winged lion (symbol of St. Mark and Venice) set the
course for this little town in the 15th century.

Also in the Piazza dei Signori stand two tall 15th-century columns topped by Jesus and the winged lion. When Venice took over Vicenza in the early 1400s, these columns were added—à la St. Mark's Square—to give the city a Venetian feel. (A rare public WC is behind the basilica; face the belfry and go left through the arch and down the stairs.)

Finish your Corso Palladio stroll at Piazzale Gasperi (where the Pam supermarket is a handy place to grab a picnic for the train ride), dip into the park called Giardino Salvi (for one last Palladio loggia), and then walk five minutes down Viale Roma back to the station. Trains leave about every hour for Milan/Verona and Venice (less than an hour away).

Villa la Rotonda—Thomas Jefferson's Monticello was inspired by Palladio's Rotonda (a.k.a. Villa Almerico Capra). Started by Palladio in 1566, it was finished by his pupil, Scamozzi. The white, gently domed building, with grand colonnaded entries, seems to have popped out of the grassy slope. Palladio, who designed a number of country villas, had a knack for using the setting for dramatic effect. This private—but sometimes tourable—residence is on the edge of Vicenza (€3 for grounds, mid-March–Oct Tue–Sun 10:00–12:00 & 15:00–18:00, closed Mon; €6 for interior—open only Wed 10:00–12:00 & 15:00–18:00; everything closed Nov–mid-March, Via Rotunda 29, tel. 0444-321-793). To get to the villa from Vicenza's train station, hop a bus (#8, hrly) or take a taxi (about €5.50). For a quick round-trip any time of day, you can zip out by cab (5 min from train station) to see the building sitting regally atop its hill, and then ride the same cab back.

Sleeping in Vicenza
(€1 = about $1, country code: 39)

Hotel Campo Marzio, a four-star, American-style, modern place, faces a park on the main drag a few minutes' walk in front of the station (Db-€155–207 depending on season and size of room— "superior" means bigger, includes breakfast, CC, easy parking, air-con, elevator, Viale Roma 21, 36100 Vicenza, tel. 0444-545-700, fax 0444-320-495, www.hotelcampomarzio.com, e-mail: info@hotelcampomarzio.com).

Hotel Giardini, with three stars and 17 sleek rooms, has splashy pastel colors and a refreshing feel (Sb-€88, Db-€119, includes breakfast, CC, elevator, air-con, on busy street but has double-paned windows, within a block of Piazza Matteotti/ Olympic Theater on Via Giuriolo 10, tel. & fax 0444-326-458, www.hotelgiardini.com, e-mail: hgiardini.vi@iol.it).

Hotel Palladio has a shortage of matching bedspreads, but it's decent for a two-star hotel in the city center (25 rooms,

S-€36, Sb-€65, D-€62, Db-€72, Tb-€103, includes breakfast, CC, ask for quieter room, a block off Piazza dei Signori, Via Oratoria dei Servi 25, tel. 0444-321-072, fax 0444-547-328, e-mail: hotelpalladio@libero.it).

Hotel Castello, on Piazza Castello, has 18 dim, quiet rooms (Sb-€78–98, Db-€98–129, includes breakfast, CC, air-con, Contra Piazza del Castello 24, down alley to the right of Ristorante agli Schioppi, 5-min walk from station, tel. 0444-323-585, fax 0444-323-583, www.hotelcastello.net, e-mail: mail@hotelcastello.net).

Hostel: **L'Ostello Rimane,** just a few years old, has a great location on Piazza Matteotti (84 beds, €14 beds in 4–6 bed rooms, €15 beds in family room, €16.50 beds in doubles, closes from 9:30–15:30 and at 23:00, no breakfast, Internet access, best to reserve several weeks in advance by fax, tel. 0444-540-222, fax 0444-547-762).

Eating in Vicenza

The local specialty is marinated cod, called *baccala alla Vicentina*. **Al Pestello** serves typical *cucina Vicentina* a block from the Church of Santa Corona (Santo Stefano 3, Mon–Sat 12:30–14:30 & 19:30–22:30, closed Sun, tel. 0444-323-721). Locals like the romantic **Zi Teresa** for its moderately priced traditional cuisine and pizzas (Thu–Tue 11:30–15:30 & 18:30–24:00, closed Wed, a couple blocks southwest of Piazza dei Signori, Contra S. Antonio 1, at intersection with Contra Proti, tel. 0444-321-411).

La Meneghina is an atmospheric pastry shop (on Contra Cavour, a short street between Piazza dei Signori and Corso Palladio, daily 8:00–1:00, closed Mon off-season, tel. 0444-323-305). Nearby, on Piazza dei Signori, the tiny **Soraru** pastry shop has lots of sidewalk tables within tickling distance of the Palladio statue (Thu–Tue 8:30–13:00 & 15:30–20:00, closed Wed, next to basilica, at far end of square from the two tall columns).

A cheap, self-service **Brek Ristorante** is just off Piazza del Castello, in the shadow of the arch where Corso Palladio meets Viale Roma (Tue–Sun 11:30–15:00 & 18:30–22:00, closed Mon, Corso Palladio 12, tel. 0444-327-829). A few steps from that same arch is the **Pam supermarket**, perfect for picnics (daily 8:30–20:00, Wed only until 19:30, follow the curve of the road just outside the city wall).

VERONA

Romeo and Juliet made Verona a household word. But, alas, a visit here has nothing to do with those two star-crossed lovers. You can pay to visit the house falsely claiming to be Juliet's, with an almost believable balcony (and a courtyard slathered with tour groups), take part in the tradition of rubbing the breast of Juliet's statue to ensure finding a lover (or picking up the sweat of someone who can't), and even make a pilgrimage to what isn't "La Tomba di Giulietta." Despite the fiction, the town has been an important crossroads for 2,000 years and is therefore packed with genuine history. R and J fans will take some solace in the fact that two real feuding families, the Montecchi and the Capellis, were the models for Shakespeare's Montagues and Capulets. And, if R and J had existed and were alive today, they would recognize much of their "hometown."

Verona's main attractions are its wealth of Roman ruins; the remnants of its 13th- and 14th-century political and cultural boom; its 21st-century, quiet, pedestrian-only ambience; and a world-class opera festival each July and August (schedule at www.arena.it). After Venice's festival of tourism, Veneto's second city (in population and in artistic importance) is a cool and welcome sip of pure Italy, where dumpsters are painted by schoolchildren as class projects. If you like Italy but don't need great sights, this town is a joy.

Ask a Veronese to tell you about Papa del Gnoccho (NYOko). Every year someone from the San Zeno neighborhood is elected Papa del Gnoccho. On the Friday before Mardi Gras, he's dressed like a king. But instead of a scepter, he holds a huge fork piercing a *gnoccho* (potato dumpling). Lots of people wear costumes, including little kids who dress as gnocchi. The focal point is the Church of San Zeno; the origin is in medieval times. About 500 years ago, at a time when the Veronese were nearly starving, the prince handed out gnocchi to everyone. Even now it's customary for the Veronese to eat gnocchi on Friday during Lent.

Orientation

The most enjoyable core of Verona is along Via Mazzini between Piazza Bra and Piazza Erbe, Verona's market square since Roman times. Head straight for Piazza Bra—and stroll. All sights of importance are located within an easy walk through the old town, which is defined by a bend in the river. For a good day trip, see the Arena and take the self-guided "Introductory Old Town Walk," outlined below.

Tourist Information: Verona's TI offices are at the station (Mon–Sat 9:00–18:00, closed Sun, shorter hours off-season, tel. 045-800-0861, www.tourism.verona.it) and at Piazza Bra (July–Aug daily 9:00–19:00, shorter hours off-season; facing the large yellow-white building, TI is across street to your right, tel. 045-806-8680, public WC on Piazza Bra). Pick up the free city map that includes a list of sights, opening hours, and walking tours. Many sights are closed on Monday and are free on the first Sunday of every month.

If you're staying the night, ask for the free *Agenda di Verona*, the monthly entertainment guide (it's in Italian, but *concerto di musica classica* is darn close to English).

The **Verona Card** covers bus transportation and most of Verona's sights (€8/day or €12/3 days, sold at museums). A pricier version of the Verona Card (€19.50) includes Gardaland, an Italian Disneyland that's best reached by car.

Verona's historic **churches**—San Zeno, San Lorenzo, Sant' Anastasia, San Fermo, and the Duomo—charge admission (covered by Verona Card or €2 apiece, €5 for a combo-ticket sold at the churches, hours roughly Mon–Sat 9:00–18:00, Sun 13:00–18:00, no photos allowed, no touring during Mass, modest dress expected).

Opera: In July and August, Verona's opera festival brings crowds and higher hotel prices (tickets €19.50–154, book tickets either online at www.arena.it or by calling tel. 045-800-5151).

Internet Access: Try Internet Train on Via Roma 17a, a couple of blocks off Piazza Bra toward Castelvecchio (Mon–Fri 11:00–22:00, Sat 11:00–20:00, Sun 14:00–20:00, tel. 045-801-3394), Internetfast.it (Mon–Fri 10:00–22:00, Sat 10:00–20:00, Sun 14:00–20:00, Via Oberdan 16/b, just off Porta Borsari toward Piazza Bra, tel. 045-803-3212), or the tiny Realta Virtuale at platform 1 at the train station (Mon–Sat 7:30–19:00, closed Sun).

Private Guides: For private guides, consider Marina Menegoi (€95/hour, tel. 045-801-2174, e-mail: milanit@libero.it) or the Verona guide association (tel. 045-810-1322, e-mail: veronaguide@katamail.com).

Arrival in Verona

Arriving by train, get off at Verona's Porta Nuova station. The train station is modern, but so cluttered with shops it can be hard to get oriented. As you come out of the underground passage from the tracks, an ATM machine is to your right, pay toilets and phones to your left. In the lobby, with your back to the tracks, you'll find the baggage check to your far right (€2.60/12 hrs), and, if you search hard, you'll see the TI (tel. 045-800-861, hours vary), tucked inside an office labeled "Centro Accoglienza e Informazioni." Buses to Verona's airport shuttle you from the train station from 6:00–23:00, departing every 20 minutes.

The 15-minute walk from the station (on busy streets) to Piazza Bra is boring; take the **bus.** Buses leave from directly in front of the station. You need to buy a ticket before boarding (€0.95, from *tabacchi* shop inside station or at white bus kiosk outside at Platform A). Bus information will likely be posted in English on the window of the bus kiosk (or ask, *Che numero per centro?*; kay NOO-may-roh pehr CHEN-troh). You'll probably

have a choice of orange bus #11, #12, or #13, leaving from
Platform A. Validate your ticket on the bus by stamping it in
the machine in the middle of the bus (good for 60 min). Buses
stop on Piazza Bra, the square with the can't-miss-it Roman
Arena. The TI is just a few steps beyond the bus stop. Buses
return to the station from the bus stop just outside the city wall
(on the right), where Corso Porta Nuova hits Piazza Bra.

Taxis pick up only at taxi stands (at train station and
Piazza Bra) and cost about €5.50 for a ride between the train
station and Piazza Bra.

Sights—Verona

Arena—This elliptical 140-by-120-meter (466-by-400-foot)
amphitheater is the third-largest in the Roman world. Dating
from the first century A.D., it looks great in its pink marble. Over
the centuries, crowds of up to 25,000 spectators have cheered
Roman gladiator battles, medieval executions, and modern plays
(including the popular opera festival that takes advantage of the
famous acoustics every July and August). Climb to the top for a
fine city view (€3.10, Tue–Sun 9:00–18:30, closed Mon and at
15:00 during opera season, info boxes near entry, located on
Piazza Bra).

House of Juliet—This bogus house is a block off Piazza Erbe
(detour right to Via Cappello 23). The tiny, admittedly romantic
courtyard is a spectacle in itself, with Japanese posing from the balcony, Nebraskans polishing Juliet's bronze breast, and amorous
graffiti everywhere. The info boxes (€0.50 for 2) offer a good history. ("While no documentation has been discovered to prove the
truth of the legend, no documentation has disproved it either.") The
"museum" is only empty rooms and certainly not worth the €3.10
entry fee (Tue–Sun 9:00–19:00, closed Mon, tel. 045-803-4303).

▲**Piazza Erbe**—Verona's market square is a photographer's
delight, with pastel buildings corralling the stalls, fountains,
pigeons, and people that have come together here since Roman
times, when this was a forum. Notice the Venetian Lion hovering above the square, reminding locals since 1405 of their con-
querors. During medieval times, the stone canopy in the center
held the scales where merchants measured the weight of things
they bought and sold, such as silk, wool, even wood. The fountain
has bubbled here for 2,000 years. Its statue, originally Roman,
had lost its head and arms. After a sculptor added a new head and
arms—voilà—the statue became Verona's Madonna. She holds a
small banner that reads: "I want justice and I bring peace."

▲▲**Evening *Passeggiata***—For me, the highlight of Verona is the
passeggiata (stroll)—especially in the evening—from the elegant

Verona

- **1** BUS TO STATION
- **2** BUS FROM STATION
- **3** HOTEL TORCOLO
- **4** HOTEL EUROPA
- **5** LOCANDA CATULLO
- **6** HOTEL AURORA
- **7** HOTEL BOLOGNA
- **8** HOTEL GIULIETTA E ROMEO
- **9** TO YOUTH HOSTEL
- **10** OSTERIA AL DUCA
- **11** RISTORANTE GREPPIA & BOTTEGA DEL VINO
- **12** ORESTE DAL ZOVO CANTINA
- **13** PIZZERIA SALVATORE

cafés of Piazza Bra through the old town on Via Mazzini (one of Europe's many "first pedestrian-only streets") to the bustling and colorful market square, Piazza Erbe.

Roman Theater (Teatro Romano)—Dating from the first century A.D., this ancient theater was discovered in the 19th century and restored. To reach the worthwhile museum, high up in the building above the theater, you can take the stairs or the elevator (to find the elevator, start at the stage and walk up the middle set of stairs, then continue straight on the path through the bushes). The museum displays Roman artifacts (mosaic floors, busts, and clay and bronze votive figures) and a model of the theater; helpful English info sheets are in virtually every room (€2.60, free first Sun of month, Tue–Sun 8:30–19:30, Mon 13:30–19:30, across the river near Ponte Pietra, tel. 045-800-0360). Every summer, the theater stages Shakespeare plays—only a little more difficult to understand in Italian than in Old English.

Giardini Giusti—If you'd enjoy a Renaissance garden with manicured box hedges and towering cypress trees, you could find this worth the walk and fee (€4.10, daily 9:00–sunset, cross river at Ponte Nuovo, continue 8 blocks up Via Carducci).

Introductory Old Town Walk

This walk will take you from Piazza Erbe to the major sights and end at Piazza Bra. Allow an hour (including tower climb and dawdling but not detours).

From the center of Piazza Erbe, head toward the river on Via della Costa. The street is marked by an arch with a whale's rib suspended from it. When you pass through the arch, don't worry. The whale's rib has hung there a thousand years. According to legend, it will fall when someone who's never lied walks under it.

The street soon opens up to a square, **Piazza dei Signori**, which has a white statue of Dante center-stage. The pensive Dante seems to wonder why the tourists choose Juliet over him. Dante—expelled from Florence for political reasons—was granted exile in Verona by the Scaligeri family. With the whale's rib behind you, you're facing the brick, crenellated, 13th-century Scaligeri residence. Behind Dante is the yellowish 15th-century Venetian Renaissance-style Portico of the Counsel. In front of Dante—and to his right (follow the white "WC" signs) is the 12th-century Romanesque **Palazzo della Ragione**.

Enter the courtyard. The impressive staircase—which goes nowhere—is the only surviving Renaissance staircase in Verona. For a grand city view, you can climb to the top of the 13th-century **Torre dei Lamberti** (€1.50 for stairs, €2.10 elevator, Tue–Sun 9:30–21:00, closed Mon). The elevator saves you 245 steps—

but you'll need to climb about 45 more to get to the first view platform. It's not worth continuing up the endless spiral stairs to the second view platform.

Exit the courtyard the way you entered and turn right, continuing down the whale-rib street. Within a block you'll find the strange and very **Gothic tombs** of the Scaligeri family, who were to Verona what the Medici family were to Florence. Notice the dogs' heads near the top of the tombs. On the first tomb, the dogs peer over a shield displaying a ladder. The story goes that the Scaligeri family got rich making ladders, but money can't buy culture. When Marco Polo returned from Asia boasting of the wealthy Kublai Khan, the Scaligeris wanted to be associated with this powerful Khan by name. But misunderstanding "Khan" as "Cane" (dog), one Scaligeri changed his name to Can Grande (big dog) and another to Can Signori (lead dog).

Continue straight for one long block and turn left on San Pietro Martire (you'll need to step into the street to check the road sign). After one block, you'll reach Verona's largest church, the brick **Church of Sant' Anastasia**. It was built from the late 13th century through the 15th century, but the builders ran out of steam, for the facade was never finished. You can enter the church for €2 (or pay €5 for a combo-ticket that includes other churches, including the Duomo, which we'll stop at later; ask for English brochure), or just peek in over the screen to get a sense of its size. The highlights of the interior are the grimacing hunchbacks holding basins of holy water on their backs (near entrance at base of columns) and Pisanello's fragmented fresco of *St. George and the Princess* (above chapel to right of altar). The story of the church is available in English from the screen at the entry/exit.

Back to the walking tour. Face the church, then go right and walk along the length of it. Take a left on Via Sottoriva. In a block, you'll reach a small riverfront park that usually has a few modern-day Romeos and Juliets gazing at each other rather than the view. Get up on the sidewalk right next to the river. You'll see the red-and-white bridge, **Ponte Pietra**. The white stones are from the original Roman bridge that stood here. After the bridge was bombed in World War II, the Veronese fished the marble chunks out of the river to rebuild it.

You'll also see, across the river and built into the hillside, the **Roman Theater** (description in "Sights," above). Way above the theater is the fortress, Castello San Pietro. We'll be heading toward the Roman bridge. This is your chance to break away, cross the bridge, and visit the Roman Theater; or climb the stairs to the left of the theater for a city view; or take the little road Scalone

Castello S. Pietro and climb to the top of the hill to the Castello for an expansive view.

Me? I'm simply passing the bridge on the way to the next church. Leave the riverfront park and take the street to the right, toward the bridge. One block before you reach the bridge (bridge entry clearly marked by an arch in a tower), turn left on Via Cappelletta. After two long blocks, turn right on Via Duomo (the corner is marked by a little church). Straight ahead you'll see the striped **Duomo**. One of Verona's historic churches, it costs €2 to enter (€5 combo-ticket; English descriptions given at the entrance). Started in the 12th century, it was built over a period of centuries, showing with its bright interior the tremendous leaps made in architecture. (Okay, so the white paint helps.)

The highlights are Titian's *Assumption* and the ruins of an older church. To find the Titian, stand at the very back of the church, facing the altar; the painting is to your left. Mary calmly rides a cloud—direction up—to the shock and bewilderment of the crowd below.

To find the ruins of the older church, walk up toward the altar to the last wooden door on the left. If the door's not open, ask someone for help. Inside are the 10th-century foundations of the Church of St. Elena, turned intriguingly into a modern-day chapel.

Leave the church, returning down Via Duomo. Continue straight ahead on Via Duomo until you reach the Church of Sant' Anastasia. With your back to this church, walk down Corso S. Anastasia.

In five minutes (at a brisk pace), you'll reach the ghostly white **Porta Borsari**, stretching across the road. This sturdy first-century Roman gate was one of the original entrances to this ancient town.

Continue straight (the name of the street changes to Corso Cavour). In a little park next to the castle is a first-century Roman triumphal arch, **Arco dei Gavi**. After being destroyed by French revolutionary troops in 1796, it was rebuilt at this location in the 1900s.

Castelvecchio, the medieval castle next to the arch, is now a sprawling art museum displaying Christian statuary, some weaponry, and fine 15th- to 17th-century paintings (€4.20 unless there are special exhibits, free first Sun of month, Tue–Sun 8:30–19:30, last entrance 45 minutes before closing, closed Mon, audioguide-€3.65 or €5.20 for two). If you visit the castle, you'll pass outdoors between the museum's build-ings; look for the skinny stairway leading up to the ancient wall overlooking the river. Climb up. It's a dead end but offers a great opportunity to shoot arrows at medieval invaders.

From the castle, you have three options. For a view, you can walk out upon the grand bridge that leads from the castle over the river. To get back to Piazza Bra, take the castle's drawbridge; it points the way to Via Roma, taking you to Piazza Bra and a well-deserved rest at a sidewalk café (Brek is good).

Or: A few blocks from the castle is the 12th-century **Basilica of San Zeno Maggiore.** This offers not only a great example of Italian Romanesque but also Mantegna's *San Zeno Triptych* and a set of 48 paneled 11th-century bronze doors that are nicknamed "the poor man's Bible." Pretend you're an illiterate medieval peasant and do some reading. Facing the altar on the far right, you can see frescoes painted on top of other frescoes and graffiti from the 1300s (€2, €5 combo-ticket, March–Oct 8:30–16:00, Nov–Feb until 13:00).

Sleeping in Verona
(€1 = about $1, country code: 39, zip code: 37100)

Prices soar in July and August (during opera season) and any time of year for a trade fair or holiday. The first two are my favorites for their family-run feeling.

Near Piazza Erbe: **Hotel Aurora**, just off Piazza Erbe, has friendly family management, a terrace overlooking the piazza, and 19 fresh and newly renovated, air-conditioned rooms (S-€62, Sb-€104, Db-€117, Tb-€145, includes good buffet breakfast, lower prices off-season, reserve with traveler's check or personal check for deposit, CC, elevator, church bells ring the hour early, Piazza Erbe, 37121 Verona, tel. 045-594-717, fax 045-801-0860, www .hotelaurora.biz, SE). Their two quads (each with 2 rooms, a double bed, 2 twins, and bathroom; €191/night) are best for families because the bedrooms aren't private.

Near Piazza Bra: Several fine places are in the quiet streets just off Piazza Bra, within 200 meters of the bus stop and well marked with yellow signs.

Hotel Torcolo provides 19 comfortable, lovingly maintained rooms in a good location near Piazza Bra (Sb-€48–73, Db-€82–104, breakfast-€6.20–10.30, prices vary with season, CC, air-con, fridge in room, elevator, garage-€8–10.25/day, Vicolo Listone 3, with your back to the gardens and the Arena over your right shoulder, head down the alley to the right of #16 on Piazza Bra, tel. 045-800-7512, fax 045-800-4058, www.hoteltorcolo.it, well-run by Silvia Pomari, SE).

Hotel Europa offers sleek, modern comfort in the same great neighborhood. Nearly half of its 46 rooms are smoke-free, a rarity in Italy (Db-€132 but €160 July–Aug, includes breakfast, call to check for discounts, CC, air-con, elevator, Via Roma 8, 37121 Verona, tel. 045-594-744, fax 045-800-1852, e-mail: hoteleuropavr@tiscalinet.it, SE).

Hotel Bologna, within a half block of the Arena, has 30 bright, classy, and well-maintained rooms; attractive public areas; and an attached restaurant (Sb-€96–122, Db-€117–172, Tb-€148–218, includes breakfast, CC, air-con, Piazzetta Scalette Rubiani 3, tel. 045-800-6830, fax 045-801-0602, e-mail: hotelbologna@tin.it).

Hotel Giulietta e Romeo, just behind the Arena, is on a quiet side street. Its 30 decent rooms are decorated in dark colors, but on the plus side, they have non-smoking rooms (on first floor) and don't take tour groups (Sb-€62–103, Db-€77–160, includes breakfast, CC, free Internet access in lobby, bike rentals €5/ half day, €10/day, air-con, elevator, laundry service, garage-€17.00/day, Vicolo Tre Marchetti 3, tel. 045-800-3554, fax 045-801-0862, www.giuliettaeromeo.com).

***Between Piazza Bra and Piazza Erbe:* Locanda Catullo** is a cheaper, quiet, and quirky place deeper in the old town, with 21 good basic rooms up three flights of stairs (S-€39, D-€54, Db-€65, Qb-€124, no CC, no breakfast, left off Via Mazzini onto Via Catullo, down an alley between 1D and 3A at Via Valerio Catullo 1, tel. 045-800-2786, fax 045-596-987, e-mail: locandacatullo@tiscalinet.it, SE a little).

***Hostel:* Villa Francescatti** is a good hostel (8- to 10-bed rooms, some family rooms, €12 beds with breakfast, €7.25 dinners, launderette, bus #73 from station during the day or #90 at night and Sun, over the river beyond Ponte Nuovo at Salita Fontana del Ferro 15, tel. 045-590-360, fax 045-800-9127). During busy times, hostel members get priority over nonmembers.

Eating in Verona

***Near Piazza Erbe:* Osteria al Duca** has an affordable two-course menu (€13) and lots more options. For dessert, try the chocolate salami. Family-run with a lively atmosphere, it's popular—go early (Mon–Sat 12:00–14:15 & 18:45–22:00, closed Sun, Via Arche Scaligere 2, half block from Scaligeri Tombs, tel. 045-594-474). Its sister restaurant, **Osteria Giulietta e Romeo,** serves up the same menu a block away with fewer crowds (Corso Sant' Anastasia 27, tel. 045-800-9177).

More good choices include **Ristorante Greppia** (Vicolo Samaritana 3, tel. 045-800-4577) and the pricier **Bottega del Vino** (closed Tue, Via Scudo di Francia 3, tel. 045-800-4535);

to find these, head from Piazza Erbe up Via Mazzini—they're within a couple of blocks.

For a fun, local wine/grappa bar (no formal food but an abundance of fun and hearty bar snacks), try **Oreste Dal Zovo**, run by Oreste and his wife Beverly from Chicago (March–Dec 8:00–20:00, no chairs, just a couple of benches; it's on the alley—San Marco in Foro #7—off Porta Borsari, just a block from Piazza Erbe, tel. 045-803-4369).

On Piazza Bra: For fast food with a great view of Verona's main square, consider the self-service **Brek** (daily 11:30–15:00 & 18:30–22:00, indoor/outdoor seating, cheap salad plates, Piazza Bra 20, tel. 045-800-4561). **Enoteca Cangrande** serves great wine (such as the local *pasito bianco*) and delicious food (Tue–Sun 10:00–14:00 & 17:00–2:00, closed Mon, CC, Via Dietro Liston 19/D, one block off Piazza Bra and Via Roma, tel. 045-595-022).

Near Ponte Nuovo: **Pizzeria Salvatore**, just across the Ponte Nuovo bridge (and to the left), serves great pizza on funky, modern art tables (Tue–Sat 12:00–14:30 & 19:00–23:00, Sun 19:00–23:00, closed Mon, Piazza San Tomasso 6, tel. 045-803-0366).

Transportation Connections—Verona

By train to: Florence (5/day, 3 hrs, more with transfer in Bologna; note that all Rome-bound trains stop in Firenze), **Bologna** (nearly hrly, 2 hrs), **Milan** (hrly, 2 hrs), **Rome** (4/day, 4–6 hrs, more with transfer in Bologna), **Bolzano** (hrly, 90 min, note that Brennero-bound trains stop in Bolzano).

Parking in Verona: Drivers will find lots of free parking at the stadium or cheap long-term parking near the train station and city walls. The most central lot is behind the Arena on Piazza Cittadella (guarded, €1/hr). Street parking costs €0.80 for two hours (buy ticket at *tabacchi* shop to put on dashboard). The town center is closed to regular traffic.

RAVENNA

Ravenna is on the tourist map for one reason: Its 1,500-year-old churches, decorated with best-in-the-West Byzantine mosaics. Known in Roman times as Classe, the city was an imperial port for the large naval fleet. Briefly a capital of eastern Rome during its fall, Ravenna was taken by the barbarians. Then, in A.D. 540, the Byzantine emperor Justinian turned Ravenna into the western-most pillar of the Byzantine empire. A pinnacle of civilization in that age, Ravenna was a light in Europe's Dark Ages. Two hundred years later, the Lombards booted out the Byzantines, and Ravenna melted into the backwaters of medieval Italy, staying out of historical sight for a thousand years.

Today the local economy booms with a big chemical industry, the discovery of offshore gas deposits, and the construction of a new ship canal. The bustling town center is Italy's most bicycle-friendly (bike paths are in the middle of pedestrian streets, subtly indicated by white brick paving). Locals go about their business, while busloads of tourists slip quietly in and out of town for the best look at the glories of Byzantium this side of Istanbul.

Ravenna's only a 90-minute detour from the main Venice–Florence train line and worth the effort for those interested in old mosaics. While its sights don't merit an overnight stop, many find that the peaceful charm of this untouristy and classy town makes it a pleasant surprise in their Italian wandering.

Orientation

Central Ravenna is quiet, with a pedestrian-friendly core and more bikes than cars. On a quick visit to Ravenna, I'd see the Basilica di San Vitale and its adjacent Mausoleum of Galla Placidia, the Basilica of St. Apollinare Nuovo, the covered market, and Piazza del Popolo.

Tourist Information: The TI is a 20-minute walk (or a 5-minute pedal) from the train station (Mon–Sat 8:30–19:00, Sun 10:00–16:00, Via Salara 8, tel. 0544-35404, www.turismo .ravenna.it). For directions to the TI, see the section "Orientation Walk," below.

For a private guide, consider Claudia Frassineti (tel. 335-613-2996, www.abacoguide.it).

Combo-Tickets: Many top sights can only be seen by purchasing a combo-ticket (called *biglietto cumulativo* or Visit Card, €6, sold at the sights). It includes admission to the Basilica of San Vitale, Mausoleum of Galla Placidia, St. Apollinare Nuovo, Spirito Santo, Battistero Neoniano, and Cappella Arcivescoville. There are no individual admissions to these sights.

A different combo-ticket (€5) covers admissions to the National Museum and Mausoleum of Teodorico. Pay an extra €1.50 to include the Sant' Apollinare in Classe. Unlike with the other combo-ticket mentioned above, you can buy individual admissions to the sights (National Museum-€4, Tue–Sun 8:30–19:30, off-season until 18:00, closed Mon; Mausoleum of Teodorico-€2.10, daily 8:30–18:00, off-season until 17:30, last entry 30 min before closing; and Sant' Apollinare in Classe-€2.10, Mon–Sat 8:30–19:30; Sun 13:00–19:00).

Bike Rental: Bikes are available free from the TI (passport required) or for rent from Coop San Vitale on Piazza Farini (on the left just as you exit train station, tel. 0544-37031).

Sights—Ravenna

Orientation Walk—A visit to Ravenna can be as short as a three-hour loop from the train station. From the station, walk straight down Viale Farini to Piazza del Popolo. This square was built around 1500, during a 60-year period when the city was ruled by Venice. Under the Venetian architecture, the people of Ravenna gather here as they have for centuries. A right on Via IV Novembre takes you a block to the colorful covered market (Mercato Coperto, Mon–Sat 7:00–14:00, closed Sun, good for picnic fixings). The TI is a block away (on Via Salara 8). Ravenna's two most important sights, Basilica di San Vitale and the Mausoleum of Galla Placidia, are two blocks away down Via San Vitale. On the other side of Piazza del Popolo is the Basilica of St. Apollinare Nuovo, also worth a look. From there, you're about a 15-minute walk back to the station.

▲▲**Basilica di San Vitale**—Imagine... it's A.D. 540. The city of Rome had been looted, the land was crawling with barbarians, and the infrastructure of Rome's thousand-year empire was crumbling fast. Into this chaotic world came the emperor of the East, Justinian, bringing order and stability, briefly reassembling the empire, and making Ravenna a beacon of civilization. His church of San Vitale—standing as a sanctuary of order in the midst of that chaos—is covered with lavish mosaics: gold and glass chips the size of your fingernail. It's impressive enough to see a 1,400-year-old church. But to see one decorated in brilliant mosaics, still managing to convey the intended feeling that "this peace and stability was brought to you by your emperor and God," is rare indeed.

In a medieval frame of mind, study the scene: High above the altar, God is in heaven, portrayed as Christ sitting on a celestial orb. He oversees his glorious creation, symbolized by the four rivers. And running the show on earth is Justinian (left side), sporting both a halo and a crown to show he's leader of the church and the state. Here, Justinian brings together the military leaders and the church leaders, all united by the straight line of eyes. The bald bishop of Ravenna—the only person who was actually here—is portrayed most realistically.

Facing the emperor (from the right side) is his wife, Theodora, and her entourage. Decked out in jewels and pearls, the former dancer who became Justinian's mistress and then empress carries a chalice to consecrate the new church.

The walls and ceilings sparkle with colorful Bible scenes told with a sixth-century exuberance. This was a time of transition, and many consider the mosaics of Ravenna both the last ancient Roman and the first medieval European works of art. For instance, you'll see

Ravenna

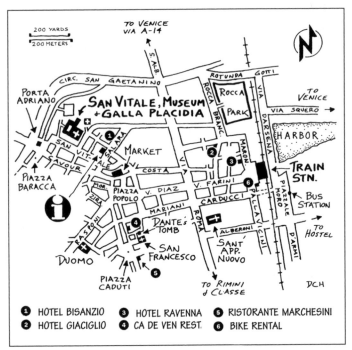

```
200 YARDS
200 METERS
```

TO VENICE VIA A-14

S. ALB.

N

CIRC. SAN GAETANINO

PORTA ADRIANO

SAN VITALE, MUSEUM + GALLA PLACIDIA

ROTUNDA · GOTTI

ROCCA BRANC.

ROCCA PARK

VIA DARSENA

TO VENICE

VIA SQUERO →

HARBOR

SAN VITALE

CAVOUR

MARKET

COSTA

MARONI

TRAIN STN.

PIAZZA BARACCA

MOR.

ZIRA.

PIAZZA POPOLO

V. DIAZ

FARINI

CARDUCCI

PIAZZALE FARRO

BUS STATION

PIAZZALE FARRO

MARIANI

PASSOLI

PORTA

CLAVALONI

TO HOSTEL

D'ARMI

DANTE'S TOMB

ALBERONI

SANT' APP. NUOVO

DUOMO

SAN FRANCESCO

PIAZZA CADUTI

TO RIMINI & CLASSE

DCH

| ❶ HOTEL BISANZIO | ❸ HOTEL RAVENNA | ❺ RISTORANTE MARCHESINI |
| ❷ HOTEL GIACIGLIO | ❹ CA DE VEN REST. | ❻ BIKE RENTAL |

a beardless Christ (as he was depicted by ancient Romans) next to a bearded Christ, his standard medieval portrayal.

The church's octagonal design—clearly Eastern—inspired the construction of the Hagia Sofia, built 10 years later in Constantinople. Charlemagne traveled here in about A.D. 800. He was so impressed that when he returned to his capital, Aix le Chapelle (present-day Aachen in Germany), he built what many consider the first great stone building in northern Europe—modeled after this church (€6 for combo-ticket, see above, daily 9:00–19:00, off-season until 16:30, tel. 0544-219-938).

▲▲**Mausoleum of Galla Placidia**—Just across the courtyard (and included in San Vitale admission) is this tiny, humble-looking mausoleum, with the oldest—and to many, the best—mosaics in Ravenna. The Mausoleum of Galla Placidia (plah-CHEE-dee-ah) is reputed to be the burial place of this daughter, sister, and mother of emperors, who died in A.D. 450. The little light that sneaks through the thin alabaster panels brings a glow and a twinkle to the very early Christian symbolism (Jesus the Good Shepherd,

Mark's lion, Luke's ox, John's eagle, the golden cross above every-thing) that fills the little room. Cover the light of the door with your hand to see the standard Roman portrayal of Christ—beard-less and as the Good Shepherd. The Eastern influence is apparent in the carpet-like decorative patterns (€6 for combo-ticket, daily 9:00–19:00, off-season until 17:30, reservations necessary, call 0544-219-938 to book ahead).

▲▲**Basilica of St. Apollinare Nuovo**—This austere sixth-century church, with a typical early-Christian basilica floor plan, has two huge and wonderfully preserved side panels. One is a procession of haloed virgins, each bringing gifts to the Madonna and the Christ Child. Opposite, Christ is on his throne with four angels, awaiting a solemn procession of 26 martyrs. Ignoring the Baroque altar from a thousand years later, we can clearly see the rectangular Roman hall of justice or basilica plan—which was adopted by churches and used throughout the Middle Ages (€6 for combo-ticket, daily 9:30–19:00, off-season until 17:30, tel. 0544-219-938).

▲**Church of Sant' Apollinare in Classe**—Featuring great Byzantine art, this church is a favorite among mosaic pilgrims (€2.10, or €6.50 combo-ticket with National Museum and Mausoleum of Teodorico, Mon–Sat 8:30–19:30, Sun 13:00–19:00, tel. 0544-473-661). It's five kilometers out of town. Catch bus #4 from the station or #44 from Piazza Caduti (3/hr, 10 min, €0.80, buy bus tickets from a tobacco shop).

Other Sights—The **Basilica San Francesco** is worth a look for its simple interior and flooded, mosaic-covered crypt below the main altar (daily 7:30–12:00 & 15:00–19:00). Nearby, the **Tomb of Dante** is the true site of his remains. The Dante memorial—often mistaken for a tomb—in Florence's Santa Croce Church is empty (daily 9:00–19:00, off-season daily 9:00–12:00 & 15:00–17:00).

Overrated Sight—The nearby beach town of Rimini is an over-crowded and polluted mess.

Sleeping in Ravenna
(€1 = about $1, country code: 39, zip code: 48100)
Hotel Bisanzio is a business-class splurge in the city center (Sb-€98, Db-€124, larger Db-€154, Via Salara 30, tel. 0544-217-111, fax 0544-32539).

Hotel Diana, with 33 cozy rooms, is an easy walk from San Vitale (Sb-€57, Db-€83, superior and deluxe rooms available, free parking nearby, Via G. Rossi 47, tel. 0544-39164, fax 0544-30001, www.ravennabedandbreakfast.it).

Two cheap hotels near the station are **Al Giaciglio** (S-€33, D-€42, Db-€51, reception closes at 24:00, Via R. Brancaleone 42, tel. & fax 0544-39403, SE) and **Hotel Ravenna** (S-€40, Sb-€45,

D-€50, Db-€62, CC, Via Maroncelli 12, tel. 0544-212-204, fax 0544-212-077, SE).

Hostel: **Ostello Dante** is a 20-minute walk from the station (€13 bed in 4–6 bed rooms, family rooms available, follow signs for Ostello Dante or catch bus #1 or #70 from the station, Via Nicolodi 12, tel. & fax 0544-421-164, SE).

Eating in Ravenna

The atmospheric **Ristorante-Enoteca Cá de Ven**—or House of Wine—fills a 16th-century warehouse with locals enjoying quality wine and traditional cuisine. *Piadina* (peeah-DEE-nah) dominates the menu. An unleavened bread that kids are raised on here, it's served with cheese and prosciutto (Tue–Sun 11:00–14:00 & 17:30–22:15, closed Mon, Via C. Ricca 24, 2-min walk from Piazza del Popolo, tel. 0544-30163).

Ristorante Marchesini has a classy, self-serve menu that includes some delicious salads (Mon–Fri 12:00–14:30, Sat 19:30–22:30, closed Sun, Via Mazzini 6, 5-min walk from Piazza del Popolo, near Piazza Caduti, tel. 0544-212-309).

Free Flow Bizantino, inside the covered market, is another self-serve (Mon–Fri open for lunch only). Or assemble a picnic at the market and enjoy your feast in the shady gardens of the **Rocca Brancaleone** fortress (5-min walk from the station).

For a cheap and traditional lunch or snack, try a *piadina* or *cresciolo* (vegetarian) sandwich from **Pizzeria Cupido** just up Via Cavour, past the covered market. These tasty sandwiches come stuffed with a variety of meats and cheeses for €2.85–4.15. Try the *squaquarella*, filled with a soft regional cheese (Tue–Sun 8:00–20:00, closed Mon, Via Cavour 43, through the archway, tel. 0544-37529).

Transportation Connections—Ravenna

By train to: Venice (3 hrs with transfer in Ferrara: Ravenna to Ferrara, every 2 hrs, 1 hr; Ferrara to Venice, hrly, 90 min), **Florence** (4 hrs with transfer in Bologna: Ravenna to Bologna, 8/day, 90 min; Bologna to Florence, hrly, 90 min). Train info: tel. 848-888-088.

SLEEPING

For hassle-free efficiency, I favor hotels handy to sightseeing activities. Virtually all of the hotels listed here are central. I've listed rooms in three neighborhoods: in the Rialto action, St. Mark's bustle, and the quiet Dorsoduro area behind the Accademia Gallery. If a hotel has a Web site, check it. Hotel Web sites are particularly valuable for Venice, because they often come with a map that at least gives you the illusion you can easily find the place.

Reserve a room as soon as you know when you'll be in town. Book direct—not through any tourist agency. If everything's full, don't despair. Call a day or two in advance and fill in a cancellation. It's possible to visit Venice without booking ahead, but given the high stakes and the quality of the gems I've found for this city guide, I'd highly recommend making reservations (see "Making Reservations," below).

I've listed prices for peak season: April, May, June, September, and October. *If a price range is listed, the higher end reflects peak-season and the lower end, off-season.* Prices can get soft in July, August, and winter.

Tourist information room-finding services cannot give opinions on quality. A major advantage of this book is its extensive listing of good-value rooms. I like places that are clean, small, central, relatively quiet at night, traditional, inexpensive, friendly, and come with firm beds. I also prefer those not listed in other guidebooks. (In Venice, for me, 6 out of 9 means it's a keeper.)

Hotels
The listings range in price from €20 bunks to plush €270 doubles with Grand Canal views. Double rooms range from about €60 (very simple, toilet and shower down the hall) to €270 (maximum

Sleep Code

To help you sort easily through these listings, I've divided the rooms into three categories based on the price for a standard double room with bath:

Higher Priced—Most rooms more than €180.
Moderately Priced—Most rooms less than €180.
Lower Priced—Most rooms less than €130.

To give maximum information in a minimum of space, I use the following code to describe the accommodations. Prices listed are per room, not per person. Unless otherwise noted, breakfast is included (but usually optional). English is generally spoken.

S = Single room (or price for one person in a double).

D = Double or Twin room. "Double beds" are often two twins sheeted together and are usually big enough for nonromantic couples.

T = Triple (generally a double bed with a single).

Q = Quad (usually two double beds).

b = Private bathroom with toilet and shower or tub.

s = Private shower or tub only (the toilet is down the hall).

CC = Accepts credit cards (Visa and MasterCard, rarely American Express).

no CC = Doesn't accept credit cards; pay in local cash.

SE = Speaks English. This code is used only when it seems predictable that you'll encounter English-speaking staff.

NSE = Does not speak English. Used only when it's unlikely you'll encounter English-speaking staff.

According to this code, a couple staying at a "Db-€140, CC, SE" hotel would pay a total of €140 (about $140) for a double room with a private bathroom. The hotel accepts credit cards or Italian cash (euros). The staff speaks English.

plumbing and more), with most clustering around €110 to €150 (with private bathrooms). Three or four people economize by sharing larger rooms. Solo travelers find that the cost of a *camera singola* (single room) is often only 25 percent less than a *camera doppia* (double room). Most listed hotels have rooms for anywhere from one to five people. If there's room for an extra cot, they'll cram it in for you.

You normally get close to what you pay for. Prices are fairly standard. Shopping around earns you a better location and more character, but rarely a cheaper price.

However, prices at nearly any hotel can get soft if you do any of the following: arrive direct (without using a pricey middleman like the TI), offer to pay cash, stay at least three nights, mention this book, or visit off-season. Breakfasts are legally optional (though some hotels insist they're not). Initial prices quoted often include a small breakfast and a private bathroom. Offer to skip breakfast for a better price. If you're on a budget, ask for a cheaper room or a discount. Always ask.

You'll save €20 to €30 if you request a room without a shower and just use the shower down the hall. Generally rooms with a bath or shower also have a toilet and a bidet (which Italians use for quick sponge baths). Tubs usually come with a frustrating "telephone shower" (handheld nozzle). If a shower has no curtain, the entire bathroom showers with you. The cord that dangles over the tub or shower is not a clothesline. You pull it when you've fallen and can't get up.

Double beds are called *matrimoniale*, even though hotels aren't interested in your marital status. Twins are *due letti singoli*.

Many hotel rooms have a TV and phone. Rooms in fancier hotels usually come with air-conditioning (sometimes you pay an extra per-day charge for this), a small safe, and a small stocked fridge called a *frigo bar* (FREE-goh bar).

If you arrive on an overnight train, your room may not be ready. Drop your bag at the hotel and dive right into Venice.

When you check in, the receptionist will normally ask for your passport and keep it for a couple of hours. Hotels are legally required to register each guest with the local police. Relax. Americans are notorious for making this chore more difficult than it needs to be.

The hotel breakfast, while convenient, is often a bad value—€9 for a roll, jelly, and usually unlimited *caffè latte*. You can request cheese or salami (€3 extra). I enjoy taking breakfast at the corner café. It's OK to supplement what you order with a few picnic goodies.

Rooms are safe. Still, zip cameras and keep money out of sight. More pillows and blankets are usually in the closet or available on request. In Italy, towels and linen aren't always replaced every day. Hang your towel up to dry.

To avoid the time-wasting line at the reception desk in the morning, settle up your bill the evening before you leave.

Country Code and Exchange Rate

If you're phoning Italy, you'll need to know its country code: 39. To call Italy from the U.S.A. or Canada, dial 011 - 39 - local number. If calling Italy from another European country, dial 00 - 39 - local number. To call from within Italy, dial the 10-digit number in its entirety.

The exchange rate: €1 = about $1.

Making Reservations

To reserve from home, telephone first to confirm availability, then fax or e-mail your formal request. It's easy to reserve by phone. (For detailed instructions on making calls, see "Telephones" in this book's introduction.) Most hotels listed are accustomed to English-only speakers. Fax costs are reasonable, e-mail's a steal, and simple English is usually fine. To fax, use the handy form in the appendix; for e-mailers, the form's online at www.ricksteves.com/reservation. If you don't get an answer to your fax request, consider that a "no." (Many little places get 20 faxes a day after they're full and can't afford to respond.)

A two-night stay for the nights of August 16 and 17 would be "2 nights, 16/8/03 to 18/8/03" (Europeans write the date day/month/year and hotel jargon uses your day of departure). You'll often receive a response back requesting one night's deposit. If your credit-card number is accepted as the deposit (which is usually the case), you can pay with your card or cash when you arrive; if you don't show up, you'll be billed for one night. Always reconfirm your reservations a day or two in advance by phone.

Honor (or cancel by phone) your reservations. Long distance is cheap and easy from public phone booths. Don't let these people down—I promised you'd call and cancel if for some reason you can't show up.

Sleeping between St. Mark's Square and Campo Santa Maria di Formosa
(zip code: 30122 unless otherwise noted)

MODERATELY PRICED

Locanda Piave, with 27 fine rooms above a bright and classy lobby, is fresh, modern, and comfortable (Db-€139–155, Tb-€190, Qb-€210, family suites-€250 for 4, €280 for 5–6, prices good through 2003 with this book, CC but discount with cash, air-con; vaporetto #51 or #1 to San Zaccaria, to left of Hotel Danieli is Calle de le Rasse—take it, turn left at end, turn right nearly immediately at square—S.S. Filippo e Giacomo—on Calle Rimpeto La Sacrestie, go over bridge, take second left, hotel is 2 short blocks ahead on Ruga Giuffa 4838/40, Castello, tel. 041-528-5174, fax 041-523-8512, www.elmoro.com/alpiave, e-mail: hotel.alpiave@iol.it, Mirella, Paolo, and Ilaria SE, faithful Molly NSE). They have two apartments for €200 to €232 (for 3–4 people, includes breakfast and kitchenette, cheaper in Aug).

Locanda Casa Querini, run by Patty, is a plush little six-room place on a quiet square tucked away behind St. Mark's (Db-€165, CC, 5 percent discount with this book, air-con, exactly halfway between San Zaccaria vaporetto stop and Campo Santa Maria Formosa at Campo San Giovanni Novo 4388, Castello, 30100 Venezia, tel. 041-241-1294, fax 041-241-4231, e-mail: casaquerini@hotmail.com, Silvia SE). Patty also runs a five-room annex (Db-€155, on the other side of the church at Calle Cavanella 4483, reception and breakfast at the locanda).

LOWER PRICED

Hotel Riva, with gleaming marble hallways and bright modern rooms, is romantically situated on a canal along the gondola serenade route. You could actually dunk your breakfast rolls in the canal (but don't). Sandro may hold a corner *(angolo)* room if you ask, and there are also a few rooms overlooking the canal. Confirm prices and reconfirm reservations, as readers have had trouble with both (Sb-€78, 2 D with adjacent showers-€95, Db-€110, Tb-€157, Qb-€190, Ponte dell' Angelo—also spelled Anzolo, Castello 5310, tel. 041-522-7034, fax 041-528-5551). Face St. Mark's Basilica, walk behind it on the left along Calle de la Canonica, take the first left (at blue "Pauly & C" mosaic in street), continue straight, go over the bridge, and angle right to the hotel.

Corte Campana has three comfy, quiet rooms just behind St. Mark's Square (Db-€70–130, Tb-€105–150, Qb-€140–200, buffet breakfast-€11; facing St. Mark's Basilica, take Calle Canonica—to the far left of the church—turn left on Calle dell' Anzolo and another right on Calle del Remedio, follow signs to Hotel Remedio and enter little courtyard to your right, go up three flights of steps and ring bell at Calle del Remedio 4410, Castello, tel. 041-523-3603, cellular 389-272-6500, e-mail: cortecampana70@hotmail.com, enthusiastic Riccardo SE).

Sleeping on or near the Waterfront, East of St. Mark's Square
(zip code: 30122)

These places, about one canal down from the Bridge of Sighs, on or just off the Riva degli Schiavoni waterfront promenade, rub drainpipes with Venice's most palatial five-star hotels. The first

Venice Center Hotels

- Vaporetti Stops
- Traghetto Routes

200 YARDS

200 METERS

TO GHETTO, TRAIN STN, ❶⁹
& TRONCHETTO

TO FONDAMENTA
NUOVE &
BOATS TO
MURANO &
BURANO

STRADA NUU D'ORO

CA
D'ORO

FISH
MKT.

NOVA

SS.
APOST.

HOSP.

LARGA

CAMPO S.
GIOVANNI
& PAOLO

MKT

ERBE

RIALTO

Post

RUGA VECCHIA

MARCELLO

CANAL

SAL. SAN
LIO

CAMPO
S.M.
FORMOSA

CARBON

CAMPO
S.LUCA

MERCERIA

FABBRI

CHIESA

FIUBERA

S.
ZAC.

CAMPO
MANIN

FUSERI

MANDOLA

VRONA

FREZZARIA

TRON

Post

CAMP.

SCHIAV.

DOGE'S
PAL.

LA
FENICE

WC

AMEX

LARGA XXII

SAN
MARCO

S. MOISÈ

CAMPO
S.MARIA
ZOBENIGO

ⓘ

❶ HOTEL RIVA
❷ LOCANDA PIAVE
❸ LOCANDA CASA QUERINI
❹ HOTEL CAMPIELLO
❺ ALBERGO PAGANELLI
❻ ALBERGO DONI
❼ HOTEL FONTANA
❽ ALBERGO CORONA
❾ HOTEL ASTORIA

❿ LOCANDA GAMBERO
⓫ HOTEL BEL SITO
⓬ ALLOGGI ALLA SCALA
⓭ LOCANDA STURION &
   HOTEL LOCANDA OVIDIUS
⓮ ALBERGO GUERRATO
⓯ HOTEL CANADA
⓰ HOTEL GIORGIONE
⓱ LOCANDA LA CORTE
⓲ FORESTERIA DELLA
   CHIESA VALDESE
⓳ TO HOTEL GEREMIA

two, while a bit pricey because of their location, are professional and comfortable. Ride the vaporetto to San Zaccaria (#51 from train station, #82 from Tronchetto car park).

MODERATELY PRICED

Hotel Campiello, a lacy and bright little 16-room, air-conditioned place, was once part of a 19th-century convent. It's ideally located 50 meters off the waterfront (Sb-€119, Db-€119–180, CC, 8 percent discount with cash, 30 percent discount mid-Nov–Feb excluding Christmas and Carnevale; behind Hotel Savoia, up Calle del Vin off the waterfront street—Riva degli Schiavoni 4647, San Zaccaria, tel. 041-520-5764, fax 041-520-5798, www.hcampiello.it, e-mail: campiello@hcampiello.it, family-run for 4 generations, sisters Monica and Nicoletta).

Albergo Paganelli is right on the waterfront—on Riva degli Schiavoni—and has a few incredible view rooms (S-€90, Sb-€125, Db-€150–181, Db with view-€200, request *con vista* for view, CC, air-con, prices often soft, at San Zaccaria vaporetto stop, Riva degli Schiavoni 4182, Castello, tel. 041-522-4324, fax 041-523-9267, www.hotelpaganelli.com, e-mail: hotelpag@tin.it). With spacious rooms, carved and gilded headboards, chandeliers, and hair dryers, this elegant place is a good value. Seven of their 22 rooms are in a less interesting but equally comfortable *dipendenza* (annex), a block off the canal.

Hotel Fontana is a cozy, two-star, family-run place with 14 rooms and lots of stairs on a touristy square two bridges behind St. Mark's Square (Sb-€55–110, Db-€85–170, family rooms, fans, 10 percent discount with cash, quieter rooms on canal side, piazza views can be noisier, 2 rooms have terraces, see Web site for off-season deals, CC; vaporetto #51 to San Zaccaria, find Calle de le Rasse—to left of Hotel Danieli—take it, turn right at end, continue to first square, Campo San Provolo 4701, Castello, tel. 041-522-0579, fax 041-523-1040, www.hotelfontana.it, e-mail: htlcasa@gpnet.it).

LOWER PRICED

Albergo Doni is a dark, hardwood, clean, and quiet place with 12 dim but classy rooms run by a likable smart aleck named Gina (D-€80, Db-€107, T-€108, Tb-€142, ceiling fans, secure telephone reservations with CC but must pay in cash, Riva degli Schiavoni, Calle del Vin 4656, San Zaccaria N., tel. & fax 041-522-4267, e-mail: albergodoni@libero.it, Nicolo and Gina SE). Leave Riva degli Schiavoni on Calle del Vin and go 100 meters with a left jog.

Albergo Corona is a homey, confusing, Old World place

with eight basic rooms, lots of stairs, and no breakfast (D-€63, vaporetto #1 to San Zaccaria dock, take Calle de le Rasse—to left of Hotel Danieli, turn left at end, take right at square—Campo S.S. Filippo e Giacomo—on Calle Rimpeto La Sacrestie, take first right, then next left on Calle Corona to #4464, tel. 041-522-9174).

Sleeping North of St. Mark's Square
(zip code: 30124)

MODERATELY PRICED

Locanda Gambero, with 32 rooms, is a comfortable and very central three-star hotel run by Sandro (Sb-€77–140, Db-€115–180, Tb-€155–249, CC, Internet in lobby, air-con, 5 percent discount for payment in cash; from Rialto vaporetto #1 dock, go straight inland on Calle le Bembo, which becomes Calle dei Fabbri; or from St. Mark's Square go through Sotoportego dei Dai then down Calle dei Fabbri to #4687, at intersection with Calle del Gambero, tel. 041-522-4384, fax 041-520-0431, e-mail: hotelgambero@tin.it, Christian and Luciana run the day shift, cheery Giorgio the night shift, all SE). Gambero runs the pleasant, Art Deco–style La Bistrot on the corner, which serves old-time Venetian cuisine.

LOWER PRICED

Hotel Astoria has 24 simple rooms tucked away a few blocks off St. Mark's Square (D-€103, Db-€124, some suites available, €10 discount July–Aug if you pay cash, closed mid-Nov–mid-March, CC, 2 blocks from San Zulian Church at Calle Fiubera 951; from Rialto vaporetto #1 dock, go straight inland on Calle le Bembo, which becomes Calle dei Fabbri, turn left on Calle Fiubera, tel. 041-522-5381, fax 041-528-8981, www.hotelastoriavenezia.it, e-mail: info@hotelastoriavenezia.it, Alberto and Enrico SE).

Sleeping West of St. Mark's Square
(zip code: 30124)

HIGHER PRICED

Hotel Bel Sito, friendly for a three-star hotel, has Old World character and a picturesque location—facing a church on a small square between St. Mark's Square and the Accademia. With solid wood furniture, its rooms feel elegant (Sb-€130, Db-€195, CC, air-con, elevator, some rooms with canal or church views; vaporetto #1 to Santa Maria del Giglio stop, take narrow alley to square, hotel at far end to your right, Santa Maria del Giglio 2517, San Marco, tel. 041-522-3365, fax 041-520-4083, e-mail: belsito@iol.it).

Flexible Floors

All over town, from palaces to cheap old hotels, you'll find speckled floors *(pavimento alla Veneziana)*. While they may look like cheap linoleum, these are historic—protected by the government and a pain for local landlords to maintain. As Venice was built, it needed flexible flooring to absorb the inevitable settling of the buildings. Through an expensive and laborious process, several layers of material are built up and finished with a broken marble top that is shaved and polished to what you'll see today. While patterns were sometimes designed into the flooring, it's often just a speckled hodgepodge. Keep an eye open for this. Craftspeople still give landlords fits when repairs are needed.

Sleeping Northwest of St. Mark's Square
(zip code: 30124)

LOWER PRICED

Alloggi alla Scala, a seven-room place run by Signora Andreina della Fiorentina, is homey, central, and tucked away on a quiet square that features a famous spiral stairway called Scala Contarini del Bovolo (small Db-€77, big Db-€87, extra bed-€26, breakfast-€7.75, CC, 5 percent discount for payment in cash, tell her when you reserve if you'll be paying by credit card, sometimes overbooks and sends overflow to her sister's lesser accommodations, Campo Manin 4306, San Marco, tel. 041-521-0629, fax 041-522-6451, daughter Emma SE). To find the hotel from Campo Manin, follow signs to (on statue's left) "Scala Contarini del Bovolo" (€2.10, daily 10:00–17:30, views from top).

Sleeping near the Rialto Bridge
(zip code: 30125)

The first three hotels are on the west side of the Rialto Bridge (away from St. Mark's Square) and the last three are on the east side of the bridge (on St. Mark's side). Vaporetto #82 quickly connects the Rialto with both the train station and the Tronchetto car park.

On West Side of Rialto Bridge
HIGHER PRICED

Hotel Locanda Ovidius, with an elegant Grand Canal view terrace, a breakfast room with a wood-beam ceiling, and nine bright, comfortable rooms, is on the Grand Canal (Sb-€77–155, Db-€130–210,

Db with view-€185–260, check Web site for special offers, CC, air-con, Calle del Sturion 677a, tel. 041-523-7970, fax 041-520-4101, www.hotelovidius.com, e-mail: info@hotelovidius.com).

Locanda Sturion, with air-conditioning and all the modern comforts, is pricey because it overlooks the Grand Canal (Db-€132–202, Tb-€195–265, family deals, canal-view rooms cost about €16 extra, CC, piles of stairs, 100 meters from Rialto Bridge, opposite vaporetto dock, Calle Sturion 679, San Polo, Rialto, tel. 041-523-6243, fax 041-522-8378, www.locandasturion.com, e-mail: info@locandasturion.com, SE). They require a personal check or traveler's check for a deposit.

LOWER PRICED
Albergo Guerrato, overlooking a handy and colorful produce market one minute from the Rialto action, is run by friendly, creative, and hardworking Roberto and Piero. Giorgio takes the night shift. Their 800-year-old building is Old World simple, airy, and wonderfully characteristic (D-€82, Db-€106, big top floor Db-€127, T-€103, Tb-€133, Qb-€153, prices promised through 2003 with this book in hand, cash only; €2 maps sold in their lobby; walk over the Rialto away from St. Mark's Square, go straight about 3 blocks, turn right on Calle drio la Scimia— not Scimia, the block before—and you'll see the hotel sign, Calle drio la Scimia 240a, tel. 041-522-7131 or 041-528-5927, fax 041-241-1408, e-mail: hguerrat@tin.it, SE). My tour groups book this place for 50 nights each year. Sorry. If you fax without calling first, no reply within three days means they are booked up. (It's best to call first.) They rent family apartments in the old center (great for groups of 4–8) for around €55 per person.

On East Side of Rialto Bridge
HIGHER PRICED
Hotel Giorgione, a four-star hotel in a 15th-century palace on a quiet lane, is super-professional, with plush public spaces, pool tables, Internet access, a garden terrace, and 72 spacious, over-the-top rooms with all the comforts (Sb-€90–150, Db-€130–255, pricier superior rooms and suites available, extra bed-€60, 10 percent discount with Web reservations, CC, elevator, air-con, Campo S.S. Apostoli 4587, 30131 Venezia, tel. 041-522-5810, fax 041-523-9092, www.hotelgiorgione.com).

MODERATELY PRICED
Hotel Canada has 25 small and pleasant rooms (S-€87, Sb-€119, D-€129, Db-€153, Tb-€189, Qb-€236, CC, air-con-€7.75 extra per night; rooms on canal come with view and aroma; rooms

facing church are noisier but fresh; Castello San Lio 5659, 30122
Venezia, tel. 041-522-9912, fax 041-523-5852, SE). This hotel is
ideally located on a small, lively square, just off Campo San Lio
between the Rialto and St. Mark's Square.

LOWER PRICED
Locanda Novo Venezia, a charming eight-room place in a
15th-century palazzo run by industrious Claudio and Ivan, is just
off a super square—Campo dei S.S. Apostoli, just north of the
Rialto Bridge (Db-€130 with this book, family deals for up to
6 in a room, CC, air-con, Calle dei Preti 4529, Cannaregio,
30121 Venezia, tel. 041-241-1496, fax 041-241-5989, www
.locandanovo.com, e-mail: info@locandanovo.com).

Sleeping near S.S. Giovanni e Paoli
(zip code: 30122)
MODERATELY PRICED
Locanda la Corte, a three-star hotel, has 18 attractive, high-
ceilinged, wood-beamed rooms—done in pastels—bordering a
small, quiet courtyard (Sb-€104, standard Db-€175, superior
Db-€185, suites available, CC, air-con; vaporetto #52 from train
station to Fondamente Nove, exit boat to your left, follow waterfront, turn right after second bridge to get to S.S. Giovanni e
Paolo square; facing Rosa Salva bar, take street to left—Calle
Bressana, hotel is a short block away at #6317 bridge; Castello,
tel. 041-241-1300, fax 041-241-5982, www.locandalacorte.it,
e-mail: info@locandalacorte.it).

Sleeping near the Accademia Bridge
(zip code: 30123 unless otherwise noted)
When you step over the Accademia Bridge, the commotion of
touristy Venice is replaced by a sleepy village laced with canals.
This quiet area, next to the best painting gallery in town, is a
10-minute walk from St. Mark's Square and a 15-minute walk
from the Rialto. The fast vaporetto #82 connects the Accademia
Bridge with both the train station (in about 15 min) and St. Mark's
Square (5 min). The hotels are located near the south end of the
Accademia Bridge, except for the last listing (Fondazione Levi),
which is at the north end of the bridge (St. Mark's side).

On South Side of Accademia Bridge
HIGHER PRICED
Hotel American is a small, cushy, three-star hotel on a lazy canal
next to the delightful Campo San Vio (a tiny overlooked square

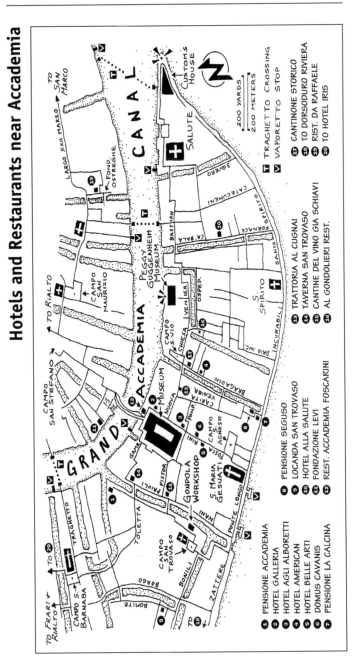

Hotels and Restaurants near Accademia

1. PENSIONE ACCADEMIA
2. HOTEL GALLERIA
3. HOTEL AGLI ALBORETTI
4. HOTEL AMERICAN
5. HOTEL BELLE ARTI
6. DOMUS CAVANIS
7. PENSIONE LA CALCINA
8. PENSIONE SEGUSO
9. LOCANDA SAN TROVASO
10. HOTEL ALLA SALUTE
11. FONDAZIONE LEVI
12. REST. ACCADEMIA FOSCARINI
13. TRATTORIA AL CUGNAI
14. TAVERNA SAN TROVASO
15. CANTINE DEL VINO GIA SCHIAVI
16. AL GONDOLIERI REST.
17. CANTINONE STORICO
18. TO DORSODURO RIVIERA
19. RIST. DA RAFFAELE
20. TO HOTEL IRIS

- **T** TRAGHETTO CROSSING
- **V** VAPORETTO STOP

200 YARDS
200 METERS

facing the Grand Canal). At this Old World hotel with 30 rooms, you'll get better rates Sundays through Thursdays (Sb-€171, Db-€233, Db with view-€268, extra bed-€26–52, CC, air-con, free Internet access in the lobby, 30 meters off Campo San Vio and 200 meters from Accademia Gallery; facing Accademia Gallery, go left, forced right, take second left—following yellow sign to Guggenheim Museum, cross bridge, take immediate right to #628, Accademia, tel. 041-520-4733, fax 041-520-4048, check www.hotelamerican.com for deals, e-mail: reception@hotelamerican.com, Marco SE).

Hotel Belle Arti is a good bet if you want to be in the old center without the tourist hordes. With a grand entry and all the American hotel comforts, it's a big, 67-room, modern, three-star place sitting on a former schoolyard (Sb-€114–150, Db-€145–210, Tb-€186–255, the cheaper rates apply to July–Aug and winter, CC, plush public areas, air-con, elevator, 100 meters behind Accademia Gallery; facing Gallery, take left, then forced right, Via Dorsoduro 912, tel. 041-522-6230, fax 041-528-0043, www.hotelbellearti.com, e-mail: info@hotelbellearti.com, SE).

MODERATELY PRICED

Pensione Accademia fills the 17th-century Villa Maravege. While its 27 comfortable and air-conditioned rooms are nothing extraordinary, you'll feel aristocratic gliding through its grand public spaces and lounging in its breezy garden (Sb-€83–123, standard Db-€129–181, superior Db-€155–227, one big family-of-5 room with grand canal view, family deals, CC; facing Accademia Gallery, take first right, cross first bridge, go right, Dorsoduro 1058, tel. 041-523-7846, fax 041-523-9152, www.pensioneaccademia.it, e-mail: info@pensioneaccademia.it).

Hotel Galleria has 10 compact and velvety rooms, most with views of the Grand Canal. Some rooms are quite narrow; ask for a larger room (S-€66–90, D-€90–97, Db-€110–140, 2 big canal-view Db-€135, includes breakfast in room, CC, fans, near Accademia Gallery, and next to recommended Foscarini restaurant, 4 extra rooms available near Peggy Guggenheim Museum with varying prices—ask, Dorsoduro 878a, tel. 041-523-2489, tel. & fax 041-520-4172, www.hotelgalleria.it, e-mail: galleria@tin.it, SE).

Hotel Agli Alboretti is a cozy, family-run, 24-room place in a quiet neighborhood a block behind the Accademia Gallery. With red carpeting and wood-beamed ceilings, it feels elegant (Sb-€96, 2 small Db-€123, Db-€150, Tb-€180, Qb-€210, CC, air-con; 100 meters from the Accademia vaporetto stop on Rio Terra a Foscarini at Accademia 884; facing Accademia Gallery, go left, then forced right, tel. 041-523-0058, fax 041-521-0158, www.aglialboretti.com, e-mail: alborett@gpnet.it, SE).

Pensione La Calcina, the home of English writer John Ruskin in 1876, comes with all the three-star comforts in a professional yet intimate package. Its 29 rooms are squeaky clean, with good wood furniture, hardwood floors, and a peaceful canalside setting facing Giudecca (S-€65–77, Sb-€97, Sb with view-€110, Db-€130–145, Db with view-€160–185, prices vary with room size and season, CC, air-con, rooftop terrace, killer sundeck on canal and canalside buffet-breakfast terrace, Dorsoduro 780, at south end of Rio di San Vio, tel. 041-520-6466, fax 041-522-7045, e-mail: la.calcina@libero.it). They also rent apartments nearby (max 2 people, from €140–250, air-con and amenities). From the Tronchetto car park or station, catch vaporetto #51 or #82 to Zattere (at vaporetto stop, exit right and walk along canal to hotel).

Pensione Seguso, next door to Pensione La Calcina, is almost an Addams-Family-on-vacation time warp. Signora Seguso runs her place as her parents did, with the beds, free-standing closets, lamps, and drapes all feeling like your great-grandmother's. The upside is the commanding canalside setting. The downside is that dinner is required during high season (Db with dinner-€210, maximum price for 2 people, slow season Db-€140 without dinner, CC, elevator, Zattere 779, tel. 041-522-2340, fax 041-528-6096, e-mail: what's that?).

Hotel Alla Salute, a basic retreat buried deep in Dorsoduro, is ideal for those wanting a quiet Venice with three-star comforts (Db-€135, facing the canal Rio delle Fornace near La Salute church, tel. 041-523-5404, fax 041-522-2271, e-mail: hotel.salute.dacici@iol.it).

LOWER PRICED

Domus Cavanis, across the street from—and owned by—Hotel Belle Arti, is a big, practical, plain place with a garden, renting 30 quiet and simple rooms (Db-€103, extra bed-€50, includes breakfast at Hotel Belle Arti, elevator, TV, phones, reception closes at 23:00, Dorsoduro 895, tel. 041-522-7374, fax 041-522-8505, e-mail: info@hotelbellearti.com).

Locanda San Trovaso is sparkling new, with seven classy, spacious rooms—three with canal views—and a peaceful location on a small canal (Sb-€77–95, Db-€115–130, CC, small roof terrace, Dorsoduro 1351; take vaporetto #82 from Tronchetto or #51 from Piazzale Roma or train station, get off at Zattere, exit left, cross bridge, turn right at tiny Calle Trevisan, cross bridge, cross adjacent bridge, take immediate right, then first left, tel. 041-277-1146, fax 041-277-7190, www.locandasantrovaso.com, e-mail: s.trovaso@tin.it, Mark and his son Alessandro SE).

On North Side of Accademia Bridge
LOWER PRICED
Fondazione Levi, a guest house run by a foundation that pro-
motes research on Venetian music, offers 21 quiet, institutional
yet comfortable rooms (Sb-€57, Db-€93, Tb-€108, Qb-€127,
twin beds only, elevator; 80 meters from base of Accademia
Bridge on St. Mark's side; from Accademia vaporetto stop, cross
Accademia Bridge, take immediate left—crossing the bridge
Ponte Giustinian and going down Calle Giustinian directly to
the Fondazione, buzz the "Foresteria" door to the right, San
Vidal 2893, 30124 Venezia, tel. 041-786-711, fax 041-786-766,
e-mail: foresterialevi@libero.it, SE).

Sleeping between Frari Church and the Grand Canal
(zip code: 30125)

MODERATELY PRICED
Hotel Iris is a cozy respite with 19 rooms off the beaten path
(S-€70, Sb-€93, D-€99, Db-€135, includes breakfast, air-con,
CC; from Campo dei Frari, head south to Campo San Tomá, then
take right on Calle del Campanile to Rio della Frescada, hotel is on
other side of Ristorante Giardinetto before first bridge to the right,
San Polo 2910/A, tel. & fax 041-522-2882, www.irishotel.com).

Sleeping near the Train Station
(zip code: 30121)

MODERATELY PRICED
Hotel San Geremia, a three-minute walk from the station,
offers 20 rooms at decent prices near a self-service laundry,
Internet café, and the Ferrovia vaporetto stop. Head left outside
the station and follow Lista di Spagna to Campo San Geremia.
With the bridge in front of you, the hotel is to your left at
Campo San Geremia 290/A (Db-€110–145, the higher price
is for weekends, CC, tel. 041-716-245, fax 041-524-2342,
e-mail: sangeremia@yahoo.it, Claudio SE).

Cheap Dormitory Accommodations
Foresteria della Chiesa Valdese, warmly run by the Methodist
church, offers dorms and doubles, halfway between St. Mark's
Square and the Rialto Bridge. This run-down but charming old
place has elegant ceiling paintings (dorm bed-€18, D-€52, Db-€67,
family apartment-€103 for 5, must check in and out when office
is open: 9:00–13:00 & 18:00–20:00, from Campo Santa Maria di

Formosa, walk past Bar all' Orologio to end of Calle Lunga and cross bridge, Castello 5170, 30122 Venezia, tel. & fax 041-528-6797, fax 041-241-6328, e-mail: veneziaforesteria@chiesavaldese.org).

Venice's **youth hostel** on Giudecca Island is crowded and inexpensive (€16 beds with sheets and breakfast in 10- to 16-bed rooms, membership required, office open daily 7:00–9:30 & 13:30–23:00, catch vaporetto #82 from station to Zittele, tel. 041-523-8211). The budget cafeteria welcomes non-hostelers (nightly 17:00–23:30).

EATING

The Italians are masters of the art of fine living. That means eating...long and well. Lengthy, multicourse lunches and dinners and endless hours sitting in outdoor cafés are the norm. Americans eat on their way to an evening event and complain if the check is slow in coming. For Italians, the meal is an end in itself, and only rude waiters rush you. When you want the bill, mime-scribble on your raised palm or ask for it: "*Il conto?*"

Even those of us who liked dorm food will find that the local cafés, cuisine, and wines become a highlight of our Italian adventure. Trust me, this is sightseeing for your palate, and even if the rest of you is sleeping in cheap hotels, your taste buds will relish an occasional first-class splurge. You can eat well without going broke. But be careful; you're just as likely to blow a small fortune on a disappointing meal as you are to dine wonderfully for €20.

Restaurants

When restaurant-hunting, choose places filled with locals, not the place with the big neon signs boasting, "We speak English and accept credit cards." Restaurants parked on famous squares generally serve tourists bad food at high prices. Locals eat better at lower-rent locales. Family-run places operate without hired help and can offer cheaper meals. The word *osteria* (normally a simple local-style restaurant) makes me salivate. For unexciting but basic values, look for a *menù turistico*, a three- or four-course, set-price menu. Galloping gourmets order à la carte with the help of a menu translator. (The *Marling Menu Master for Italy* is excellent. *Rick Steves' Italian Phrase Book* has enough phrases for intermediate eaters.)

A full meal consists of an appetizer (antipasto, €3–6), a first course (*primo piatto*, pasta or soup, €4.50–7.50), and a second course *(secondo piatto,* expensive meat and fish dishes, €5.50–11). Vegetables *(contorni, verdure)* may come with the *secondo* or cost extra (€3.50) as a side dish. The euros can add up in a hurry. Light and budget eaters get a *primo piatto* each and share an antipasto.

Restaurants normally pad the bill with a cover charge *(pane e coperto*—"bread and cover charge," around €1) and a service charge *(servizio,* 15 percent, see Tipping, below); these charges are listed on the menu.

Tipping

Tipping is an issue only at restaurants that have waiters and waitresses. If you order your food at a counter, don't tip.

If the menu states that service is included *(servizio incluso),* there's no need to tip beyond that, but if you like to tip and you're pleased with the service, throw in €1 to €2 euros per person.

If service is not included, tip 5 to 10 percent by rounding up or leaving the change from your bill. Leave the tip on the table or hand it to your server. It's best to tip in cash even if you pay with your credit card. Otherwise the tip may never reach your waiter.

Pizzerias

Pizza is cheap and everywhere. Key pizza vocabulary: *capricciosa* (generally ham, mushrooms, olives, and artichokes), *funghi* (mushrooms), *marinara* (tomato sauce, oregano, garlic, no cheese), *quattro formaggi* (4 different cheeses), and *quattro stagioni* (different toppings on each of the four quarters for those who can't choose just one menu item). If you ask for pepperoni on your pizza, you'll get green or red peppers, not sausage. Kids like *diavola* (closest thing in Italy to American "pepperoni") and *margherita* (tomato and cheese) pizzas.

Bars/Cafés

Italian "bars" are not taverns but cafés. These local hangouts serve coffee, mini-pizzas, sandwiches, and cartons of milk from the cooler. Many dish up plates of fried cheese and vegetables from under the glass counter, ready to reheat. This is my budget choice, the Italian equivalent of English pub grub.

For quick meals, bars usually have trays of cheap ready-made sandwiches *(panini* or *tramezzini)*—some kinds are delightful grilled. To get food "to go," say, *"Da portar via"* (for the road). All bars have a WC *(toilette, bagno)* in the back, and the public is entitled to use it.

Bars serve great drinks—hot, cold, sweet, or alcoholic. Chilled bottled water *(natural* or *frizzante)* is sold cheap to go.

Coffee: If you ask for *"un caffè,"* you'll get espresso.

Cappuccino is served to locals before noon and tourists any time of day. (To an Italian, cappuccino is a breakfast drink and a travesty after anything with tomatoes.) Italians like it only warm. To get it hot, request *"Molto caldo"* (very hot) or *"Più caldo, per favore"* (hotter, please; pronounced pew KAHL-doh, pehr fah-VOH-ray).

Experiment with a few of the options...

* *caffè freddo:* sweet and iced espresso
* *cappuccino freddo:* iced cappuccino
* *caffè hag:* espresso decaf (decaf is easily available for any coffee drink)
* *macchiato:* espresso with only a little milk
* *caffè latte:* coffee with lots of hot milk, no foam
* *caffè Americano:* espresso diluted with water
* *caffè corretto:* espresso with a shot of liqueur

Beer: Beer on tap is *"alla spina."* Get it *piccola* (33 cl), *media* (50 cl), or *grande* (a liter).

Wine: To order a glass *(bicchiere;* pron. bee-kee-AY-ree) of red *(rosso)* or white *(bianco)* wine say, *"Un bicchiere di vino rosso/bianco."* *Corposo* means full-bodied. House wine often comes in a quarter-liter carafe *(un quarto).*

Prices: You'll notice a two-tiered price system. Drinking a cup of coffee while standing at the bar is cheaper than drinking it at a table. If you're on a budget, don't sit without first checking out the financial consequences.

If the bar isn't busy, you'll often just order and pay when you leave. Otherwise: 1) decide what you want; 2) find out the price by checking the price list on the wall, the prices posted near the food, or by asking the barman; 3) pay the cashier; and 4) give the receipt to the barman (whose clean fingers handle no dirty euros) and tell him what you want.

Picnics

In Venice, picnicking saves lots of euros and is a great way to sample local specialties. For a colorful experience, gather your ingredients in the morning at Venice's produce market (near the Rialto Bridge); you'll probably visit several market stalls to put together a complete meal. A local *alimentari* is your one-stop corner grocery store (most will slice and stuff your sandwich for you if you buy the ingredients there).

Juice-lovers can get a liter of O.J. for the price of a Coke or coffee. Look for "100% *succo*" (juice) on the label. Hang onto the half-liter mineral-water bottles (sold everywhere for about €0.50). Buy juice in cheap liter boxes, drink some, and store the extra in your water bottle. (I drink the tap water—*acqua del rubinetto*.)

Picnics can be an adventure in high cuisine. Be daring. Try

Eating with the Seasons

Italian cooks love to serve you fresh produce and seafood at its tastiest. If you must have porcini mushrooms outside of October and November, they'll be frozen. To get the freshest veggies at a fine restaurant, request *"Un piatto di verdure della stagione, per favore."* (A plate of what's seasonal, please). Here are a few examples of what's fresh when:

April–May:	Calamari, squid, green beans, artichokes and zucchini flowers
April, May, Sept, Oct:	Black truffles
May–June:	Mussels, asparagus, zucchini, cantaloupe, and strawberries
May–Aug:	Eggplant
Oct–Nov:	Mushrooms and white truffles
Fresh year-round:	Clams, meats, and cheese

the fresh mozzarella, *presto* pesto, shriveled olives, and any UFOs the locals are excited about. Shopkeepers are happy to sell small quantities of produce. But in a busy market, a merchant may not want to weigh and sell small, three-carrot-type quantities. In this case, estimate generously what you think it should cost, and hold out the coins in one hand and the produce in the other. Wear a smile that says, "If you take the money, I'll go." He will usually grab the money. A typical picnic for two might be fresh rolls, 100 grams of cheese, 100 grams of meat (100 grams = about a quarter pound, called *un etto* in Italy), two tomatoes, three carrots, two apples, yogurt, and a liter box of juice. Total cost—about €10.

VENETIAN CUISINE

Venetian cuisine relies more heavily on fish, shellfish, risotto, and polenta than the rest of Italy. Note that seafood and steak may be sold by weight (if you see "100 g" or "*l'etto*" by the price on the menu, you'll pay that price *per* 100 grams—about a quarter pound). Some special dishes come in large quantities meant for two people; the shorthand way of showing this on a menu is "x2" (meaning "times two"). Along with the usual pizza and pasta fare, here are some typical foods you'll encounter:

Bar Snacks

Venetians often eat a snack—*cicchetti* or *panini*—standing at a bar. (Remember, you'll usually pay more if you sit, rather than stand.) *Cicchetti:* Generic name for various small finger foods served in some pubs—like tapas, Venetian style. Designed as a quick meal for working people, the selection and ambience is best on workdays (Mon–Sat lunch and early dinner). See "The Stand-Up Progressive Venetian Pub-Crawl Dinner," below.

Panini: Sandwiches made with rustic bread, filled with meat, vegetables, and cheese, served cold or toasted (you can eat in or take away).

Tramezzini: Crustless, white bread sandwiches served cold and stuffed with a variety of fillings (often seafood, such as shrimp), mixed with a mayonnaise dressing.

Appetizers *(Antipasti)*

Antipasto di mare: A marinated mix of fish and shellfish served chilled.

Asiago **cheese:** The Veneto region's specialty, a cow's-milk cheese that's either *mezzano*—young, firm, and creamy; or *stravecchio*—aged, pungent, and granular.

Sarde in saor: Sardines marinated with onions.

Rice *(Riso)*, Pasta, and Polenta

Risotto: Short-grain rice, simmered in broth and often flavored with fish and seafood. For example, *risotto nero* is risotto made with octopus and it's ink, or *risotto ai porcini* with porcini mushrooms.

Risi e bisi: Rice and peas.

Pasta e fagioli: White bean and pasta soup.

Bigoli in salsa: A long, thin, whole-wheat noodle (one of the few traditional pastas) with anchovy sauce.

Polenta: Cornmeal boiled into a mush and served soft or cut into firm slabs and grilled. Polenta is a standard accompaniment with cod *(baccala)* or calf liver and onions *(fegato alla Veneziana)*.

Seafood *(Frutti di Mare)*

Some sea creatures found in the Adriatic are slightly different from their American cousins. Generally, Venetian fish are smaller than American salmon and trout (think sardines and anchovies). The shellfish are more exotic. The weirder the animal (eels, octopus, frog-fisher), the more local it is. Remember that seafood may be sold by weight (per *etto*, or 100 grams, rather than per portion).

Baccala: Salt cod served with polenta, or chopped up and mixed with mayonnaise as a topping for *cicchetti* (appetizers).

Branzino: Sea bass, served whole (head and tail) and grilled.

Calamari: Squid, usually cut into rings and either deep-fried or marinated.

Cozze: Mussels steamed in an herb broth with tomato.

Gamberi: The generic name for shrimp. *Gamberetti* are small shrimp, and *Gamberoni* are large shrimp. (Language tip: *-etti* and *-oni* signify little and big.)

Moleche col pien: Fried soft-shell crabs.

Pesce fritto misto: Assorted deep-fried seafood (often calamari and prawns).

Seppie: Cuttlefish (squid-like creature that sprays black ink when threatened).

Sogliola: Sole, served poached or oven-roasted.

Vitello di mare: "Sea veal," like swordfish, firm, pink, mild, and grilled.

Vongole: Small clams steamed with fresh herbs and wine, or served as a first course, such as *spaghetti alla vongole*.

Zuppa di pesce: Seafood stew.

Dessert *(Dolci)*

Tiramisu: Spongy ladyfingers soaked in coffee and marsala, layered with mascarpone cheese and bitter chocolate. Arguably Venetian in origin, the literal meaning of the word is "pick-me-up."

Venetian cookies: There are numerous varieties, due perhaps to Venice's position in trade (spices) and the Venetians' love of celebrations. Many treats were created for certain feast days and religious holidays. *Pinza*, a sweet made with corn, wheat flour, and raisins (and sometimes figs, almonds, and lemon) is made for Epiphany, January 6. *Fritole* are tiny doughnuts associated with Carnevale (Mardi Gras). *Bussola* rings are made for Easter. Other popular treats are *bisse* (seahorse-shaped cookies) and *croccante* (made with toasted corn and almonds, similar in texture to peanut brittle).

Wine *(Vino)* and Stronger

Valpolicella: Light, dry, fruity red from the hills north of Verona. It's likely what you're drinking if you ordered the house wine *(vino della casa)*.

Bardolino: Also made from valpolicella grapes, it's a similar wine but grown near Lake Garda.

Amarone: Rich, intense red, with alcohol content around 16 percent, made from valpolicella grapes.

Soave: Crisp white (great with seafood) from near Verona. Soave Classico designates a higher quality.

Prosecco: Dry champagne, rather neutral-tasting, making it easy to drink too much.

Bellini: A cocktail of *prosecco* and white-peach puree; invented at pricey Harry's Bar (near San Marco vaporetto stop).

Tiziano: Grape juice and *prosecco*.

Grappa: Distilled *vinacce* (grape skins and stems left over from winemaking) make this powerful local firewater.

RESTAURANTS IN VENICE

While touristy restaurants are the scourge of Venice, and most restaurateurs believe you can't survive in Venice without catering to tourists, there are plenty of places that are still popular with locals and respect the tourists who happen in. First trick: Walk away from triple-language menus. Second trick: Order the daily special. Third trick: Most seafood dishes are the local catch-of-the-day.

For romantic—and usually pricey—meals along the water, see "Eating with a Romantic Canalside Setting," below. For dessert, it's gelato (see end of this chapter).

Eating between Campo Santi Apostoli and Campo S.S. Giovanni e Paolo

Antiche Cantine Ardenghi de Lucia e Michael is a leap of local faith and an excellent splurge. Effervescent Michael and his wife, Lucia, proudly cook Venetian for a handful of people each night by reservation only. You must call first. You pay €50 per person and trust them to wine, dine, and serenade you with Venetian class. The evening can be quiet or raucous depending on who and how many are eating. While the menu is heavy on crustaceans, Michael promises to serve plenty of veggies and fruit as well. Find #6369. There's no sign, the door's locked, and the place looks closed. But knock, say the password (*La Repubblica Serenissima*), and you'll be admitted. From Campo S.S. Giovanni e Paolo, pass the church-like hospital (notice the illusions painted on its facade), go over the bridge to the left, and take the first right on Calle della Testa to #6369 (you must reserve the day before, Tue–Sat 20:00–24:00, closed Sun–Mon, tel. 041-523-7691, cellular 389-523-7691).

The following two colorful *osterias* are good for *cicchetti* (munchies), wine-tasting, or a simple, rustic, sit-down meal surrounded by a boisterous local ambience:

Osteria da Alberto has the best variety of *cicchetti* (18:15–19:30) and great sit-down meals from 19:30 to 23:00 (CC, closed Sun, midway between Campo Santi Apostoli and Campo S.S. Giovanni e Paolo, next to Ponte de la Panada on Calle Larga Giacinto Gallina, tel. 041-523-8153).

Osteria al Promessi Sposi does *cicchetti* with gusto and offers a little garden for sit-down meals (great cod and polenta). This fun place is proud to be Venetian (Thu–Tue 9:00–23:00, closed Wed, a block off Campo S.S. Apostoli and a block inland from Strada Nova at Calle dell' Oca, tel. 041-522-8609).

You'll find pubs in the side streets opposite Campo St. Sofia across Strada Nova.

Eating in Dorsoduro, near the Accademia

For location, see map on page 224.

Restaurant/Pizzeria Accademia Foscarini, next to the Accademia Bridge and Galleria, offers decent €5–7 pizzas in a great canalside setting (Wed–Mon 7:00–23:00 in summer, until 21:00 in winter, closed Tue, Dorsoduro 878C, tel. 041-522-7281).

Trattoria al Cugnai is an unpretentious place run by three gruff sisters serving decent food at a good price (Tue–Sun 12:00–15:00 & 19:00–21:30, closed Mon, midway between Accademia Gallery and the forgotten and peaceful Campo San Vio, tel. 041-528-9238). Enjoy a quiet sit on Campo San Vio (benches with Grand Canal view) for dessert.

Taverna San Trovaso is an understandably popular restaurant/pizzeria. Arrive early or wait (CC, Tue–Sun 12:00–14:50 & 19:00–21:50, closed Mon, air-con, 100 meters from Accademia Gallery on San Trovaso canal; facing Accademia, take a right and then a forced left at canal). On the same canal, **Enoteca Cantine del Vino Gia Schiavi**—much loved for its *cicchetti*—is a good place for a glass of wine and appetizers (Mon–Sat 8:00–14:30 & 15:30–20:00, closed Sun, S. Trovaso 992, tel. 041-523-0034). You're welcome to enjoy your wine and finger-food while sitting on the bridge.

Al Gondolieri is considered one of the best restaurants for meat—not fish—in Venice. Its sauces are heavy and prices are high, but carnivores love it (Wed–Mon 12:00–13:00 & 19:00–22:00, closed Tue and for lunch Jul–Aug, reservations smart, Dorsoduro 366 San Vio, behind Guggenheim Museum on west end of Rio delle Torreselle, tel. 041-528-6396).

Cantinone Storico, also in this neighborhood, is described below under "Romantic Canalside Settings."

Eating near St. Mark's Square

Osteria da Carla, two blocks west of St. Mark's Square, is a fun and very local hole-in-the-wall where the food is good and the price is right. They have hearty tuna salads and a daily pasta special along with traditional antipasti, polenta, and decent wine by the glass. While you can eat outside, you don't want table #3 (Mon–Sat 8:00–22:00, closed Sun; from American Express head toward St. Mark's Square, first left down Frezzeria, first left again through "Contarina" tunnel, at Sotoportego e Corte Contarina, sign over door says "Pietro Panizzolo"—it's historic and can't be removed, tel. 041-523-7855, Carlo SE).

Eating on Campo S. Angelo

Ristorante Aqua Pazza (literally, "crazy water") provides good pizza in a wonderful setting on a square (check out the leaning tower over your shoulder) midway between the Rialto, Accademia, and St. Mark's. The owner is from Naples and he delights locals with Amalfi/Naples cuisine. That means perhaps the best—and most expensive—pizza in Venice (Tue–Sun 12:00–15:00 & 19:00–23:00, closed Mon, Campo S. Angelo 3809, tel. 041-277-0688).

Eating in Cannaregio

For great local cuisine, far beyond the crowds in a rustic Venetian setting, hike to **Osteria al Bacco** (closed Mon, reservations recommended, Fondamenta Cappuccine, Cannaregio 3054, halfway between train station and northernmost tip of Venice, tel. 041-717-493).

Near the train station, consider **Brek**, a popular self-service cafeteria (at Lista di Spagna 124; with back to station, facing canal, go left on Rio Terra—it becomes Lista di Spagna in 2 short blocks, tel. 041-244-0158).

Eating with a Romantic Canalside Setting

Of course, if you want a canal view, it comes with lower quality or a higher price. But the memory is sometimes most important.

Restaurant al Vagon is popular with tourists because nearly everyone gets a seat right on the canal. The food and prices are acceptable and the ambience glows (moderate prices, Wed–Mon 19:00–22:00, closed Tue, 3-min walk north of Rialto just before Campo S.S. Apostoli, overlooking canal called Rio dei Santi Apostoli, tel. 041-523-7558).

Ristorante da Raffaele is *the* place for classy food on a quiet canal. It's filled with top-end tourists and locals who want to pay well for the best seafood. The place was a haunt of the avant-garde a few generations ago. Today it's on a main gondolier thoroughfare—in fact, many guests arrive or depart by gondola. Make a reservation if you want a canalside table (you do). While the multilingual menu is designed for the tourists, locals stick with the daily specials (expensive, CC, Fri–Wed 18:30–22:30, closed Thu, exactly halfway between Piazza San Marco and the Accademia Bridge at Ponte delle Ostreghe, tel. 041-523-2317). Before leaving, wander around inside to see the owner's fabulous old weapons collection.

Ristorante Cantinone Storico sits on a peaceful canal in Dorsoduro between the Accademia Bridge and the Peggy Guggenheim Museum. It's dressy, specializes in fish, has six or eight tables on the canal, and is worth the splurge (daily 12:30–14:30 & 19:30–21:30, reservations wise, on the canal Rio de S. Vio, tel. 041-523-9577).

The "Dorsoduro Riviera," the long promenade along the south side of the Dorsoduro (a 5-min walk south of Accademia

Bridge), is lined with canalside restaurants away from the crush of touristic Venice. Places immediately south of the Accademia Bridge (near the Zattere vaporetto stop) are decent but more touristic. At the west end (near the S. Basilio vaporetto stop), try **Trattoria B. Basilio** and **Pizzeria Riviera** (a local fave for pizza); both come with local crowds and wet views.

For a Grand Canal view from the Rialto Bridge, consider **Al Buso**, at the northeast end of the Rialto Bridge. Of the several touristy restaurants that hug the canal near the Rialto, this is recommended by locals as offering the best value (daily 9:00–24:00, dine from 11:00–23:00, Ponte di Rialto 5338, tel. 041-528-9078).

The Stand-Up Progressive Venetian Pub-Crawl Dinner

My favorite Venetian dinner is a pub crawl. A *giro di ombra* (pub crawl) is a tradition unique to Venice—ideal in a city with no cars. *(Ombra* means shade, from the old days when a portable wine bar scooted with the shadow of the Campanile across St. Mark's Square.)

Venice's residential back streets hide plenty of characteristic bars with countless trays of interesting tooth-pick munchies *(cicchetti)*. This is a great way to mingle and have fun with the Venetians. Real *cicchetti* (chi-KET-tee) pubs are getting rare in these fast-food days, but locals appreciate the ones that survive.

I've listed plenty of pubs in walking order for a quick or extended crawl below. If you've crawled enough, most of these bars make a fine one-stop, sit-down dinner.

Try fried mozzarella cheese, gorgonzola, calamari, artichoke hearts, and anything ugly on a toothpick. Meat and fish *(pesce;* PESH-shay) munchies can be expensive; veggies *(verdure)* are cheap, around €3 for a meal-sized plate. In many places, there's a set price per food item (e.g., €1). To get a plate of assorted appetizers for €5 (or more, depending on how hungry you are), ask for: *"Un piatto classico di cicchetti misti da €5."*(Pron. oon pee-AH-toh KLAH-see-koh dee cheh-KET-tee MEE-stee da CHING-kway ay-OO-roh). Bread sticks *(grissini)* are free for the asking.

Drink the house wines. A small glass of house red or white wine *(ombra rosso* or *ombra bianco)* or a small beer *(birrino)* costs about €1. A liter of house wine costs around €3.60. *Vin bon,*

Venetian for fine wine, may run you from €1.60 to €2.60 per little glass. *Corposo* means full-bodied. A good last drink is *fragolino*, the local sweet wine—*bianco* or *rosso*. It often comes with a little cookie *(biscotti)* for dipping.

Bars don't stay open very late, and the *cicchetti* selection is best early, so start your evening by 18:00. Most bars are closed on Sunday. When just munching appetizers, you can stand around the bar or grab a table in the back—usually for the same price.

Cicchetteria West of the Rialto Bridge

Cantina do Mori is famous with locals (since 1462) and savvy travelers (since 1982) as a classy place for fine wine and *francobollo* (a spicy selection of 20 tiny sandwiches called "stamps"). Choose from the featured wines in the barrel on the bar. Order carefully or they'll rip you off. From Rialto Bridge, walk 200 meters down Ruga degli Orefici away from St. Mark's Square—then ask (Mon–Sat 17:00–20:30, closed Sun, stand-up only, arrive early before the *cicchetti* are gone, San Polo 429, tel. 041-522-5401).

A few steps from the Rialto fish market, you'll find Campo delle Beccarie and two little places serving traditional munchies. On this square, as you face the restaurant Vini da Pinto, **Osteria Sora al Ponte** is to your right, just over the bridge (each item €0.75, assemble by pointing, Tue–Sun until 22:00, closed Mon, Jul and Aug closed Sun), and **Cantina do Spade** is in the alley directly behind Vini da Pinto (head around building to your left, take a right through archway; closed Sun).

Eating near the Rialto Bridge

Eating East of the Rialto Bridge, near Campo San Bartolomeo

Osteria "Alla Botte" Cicchetteria is an atmospheric place packed with a young, local, bohemian-jazz clientele. It's good for a *cicchetti* snack with wine at the bar (see the posted, enticing selection of wines by the glass) or for a light meal in the small, smoke-free room in the back (Fri–Tue 10:00–15:00 & 18:00–23:00, closed Wed–Thu and Sun afternoons, 2 short blocks off Campo San Bartolomeo in the corner behind the statue—down Calle de la Bissa, notice the "day after" photo showing a debris-covered Venice after the notorious 1989 Pink Floyd open-air concert, tel. 041-520-9775).

If the statue on the Campo San Bartolomeo walked backward 20 meters, turned left, and went under a passageway, he'd hit **Rosticceria San Bartolomeo**. This cheap—if confusing—self-service restaurant has a likeably surly staff (good €5–6 pasta,

Restaurants in Venice

- ❶ CANTINA DO MORI
- ❷ OSTERIA SORA AL PONTE
- ❸ CANTINA DO SPADE
- ❹ OSTARIA ALLA BOTTE
- ❺ ROSTICCERIA SAN BARTOLOMEO
- ❻ PASTICCERIA PONTE DELLE PASTE
- ❼ OSTERIA AL PORTEGO
- ❽ DEVIL'S FOREST PUB & BORA BORA PIZZERIA
- ❾ OSTERIA AL DIAVOLO E L'AQUASANTA
- ❿ BAR ALL'OROLOGIO
- ⓫ CIP CIAP PIZZA
- ⓬ OSTERIA AL MASCARON
- ⓭ ENOTECA MASCARETA
- ⓮ GELATERIA
- ⓯ LA BOUTIQUE GELATERIA
- ⓰ ANTICHE CANTINE ARDENGHI
- ⓱ OSTERIA DA ALBERTO
- ⓲ OSTERIA AL PROMESSI SPOSI
- ⓳ REST. AL VAGON
- ⓴ BENITO'S HAIR SALON
- ㉑ MICHIELANGELO GELATERIA

great fried *mozzarella al prosciutto* for €1.40, delightful fruit salad, and €1 glasses of wine, prices listed on wall behind counter, no cover or service charge, daily 9:30–21:30, tel. 041-522-3569). Take out or grab a table.

From Rosticceria San Bartolomeo, continue over a bridge to Campo San Lio (a good landmark). Here, turn left, passing Hotel Canada and following Calle Carminati straight about 50 meters over another bridge. On the right is the pastry shop *(pasticceria)* and straight ahead is Osteria Al Portego (at #6015). Both are listed below:

Pasticceria Ponte delle Paste is a feminine and pastel *salon de tè*, popular for its pastries and aperitifs. Italians love taking

15-minute breaks to sip a *spritz* aperitif with friends after a long day's work, before heading home. Ask sprightly Monica for a *spritz al bitter* (white wine, *amaro*, and soda water, €1.30; or choose from the menu on the wall) and munch some of the free goodies on the bar around 18:00 (daily 7:00–20:30, Ponte delle Paste).

Osteria al Portego is a friendly, local-style bar serving great *cicchetti* and good meals (Mon–Fri 9:00–22:00, closed Sat–Sun, tel. 041-522-9038). The *cicchetti* here can make a great meal, but you should also consider sitting down for an actual dinner. They have a fine little menu.

The **Devil's Forest Pub**, an air-conditioned bit of England tucked away a block from the crowds, is—strangely—more Venetian these days than the *tipico* places. Locals come here for good English and Irish beer on tap, big salads (€6.70, lunch only), hot bar snacks, and an easygoing ambience (daily 8:00–24:00, meals 12:00–15:30, bar snacks all the time, closed Sun in Aug, no cover or service charge, fine prices, backgammon and chess boards available-€2.10, a block off Campo San Bartolomeo on Calle dei Stagneri, tel. 041-520-0623). Across the street, **Bora Bora Pizzeria** serves pizza and salads from an entertaining menu (Thu–Tue 12:00–15:00 & 19:15–22:30, closed Wed, CC, tel. 041-523-6583).

Eating West of the Rialto Bridge

Osteria al Diavolo e l'Aquasanta, three blocks west of the Rialto, serves good pasta and makes a handy lunch stop for sightseers (Wed–Mon 12:00–15:00 & 18:00–24:00, closed Mon eve and all day Tue, hiding on a quiet street just off Rua Vecchia S. Giovanni, on Calle della Madonna, tel. 041-277-0307).

La Rivetta Ristorante offers several Venetian specialties under €10 apiece. Scenically located on a canal, it's on the main drag between the Rialto Bridge and Campo San Polo—see the Rialto to Frari Church Walk, page 159 (open daily, San Polo 1479, tel. 041-523-1481).

Eating on or near Campo Santa Maria di Formosa

Campo Santa Maria di Formosa is just plain atmospheric (as most squares with a Socialist Party office seem to be). For a balmy outdoor meal, you could split a pizza with wine on the square. **Bar all' Orologio** has a good setting and friendly service but mediocre "freezer" pizza (happy to split a pizza for pub crawlers, Mon–Sat 6:00–23:00, closed Sun and in winter at 18:00). For a picnic pizza snack on the square, cross the bridge behind the canalside *gelateria* and grab a slice to go from **Cip Ciap Pizza** (Wed–Mon 9:00–21:00, closed Tue; facing *gelateria*, take bridge to the right; Calle del Mondo Novo). Pub-crawlers get a salad course at the fruit-and-vegetable stand next to the water fountain (Mon–Sat, closes about 19:30 and on Sun).

From Campo Santa Maria di Formosa, follow the yellow sign to "S.S. Giov e Paolo" down Calle Longa Santa Maria di Formosa, and head down the street to **Osteria al Mascaron**, a delightful little restaurant seemingly made to order for pirates gone good (#5225, Mon–Sat 11:30–15:00 & 19:00–23:30, closed Sun, reservations smart, tel. 041-522-5995). Their *antipasto della casa* (a €13 plate of mixed appetizers) is fun, and the *Pasta Scogliera* (€26, rockfish spaghetti for 2) makes a grand meal.

Enoteca Mascareta, a wine bar with much less focus on food, is 30 meters farther down the same street (#5183, Mon–Sat 18:00–24:00, closed Sun, tel. 041-523-0744).

The *gelateria* Zanzibar on the canal at Campo Santa Maria di Formosa is handy (open 7:00–24:00 in summer, 8:00–21:00 winter; for more, see "Gelato," below).

Cheap Meals

A key to cheap eating in Venice is **bar snacks** (see page 216), especially stand-up mini-meals in out-of-the-way bars. Order by pointing. *Panini* (sandwiches) are sold fast and cheap at bars everywhere. Basic reliable ham-and-cheese sandwiches (white bread, crusts trimmed) come toasted—simply ask for "toast"; these make a great supplement to Venice's skimpy hotel breakfasts.

For budget eating, I like small *cicchetti* bars (see "Pub-Crawl Dinner," above); for speed, value, and ambience, you can get a filling plate of local appetizers at nearly any of the bars.

Pizzerias are cheap and easy—try for a sidewalk table at a scenic location. If you want a fast-food pizza place, try **Spizzico** on Campo San Luca.

The **produce market** that sprawls for a few blocks just past the Rialto Bridge (best 8:00–13:00, closed Sun) is a great place to assemble a picnic. The adjacent fish market is wonderfully slimy. Side lanes in this area are speckled with fine little hole-in-the-wall munchie bars, bakeries, and cheese shops.

The **Mensa DLF**, the public transportation workers' cafeteria, is cheap and open to the public (daily 11:00–14:30 & 18:00–22:00). Leaving the train station, turn right on the Grand Canal, walk about 150 meters along the canal, up eight steps, and through the unmarked door.

Gelato

La Boutique del Gelato is one of the best *gelaterias* in Venice (daily 10:00–21:30, closed Dec–Jan, 2 blocks off Campo Santa Maria di Formosa on corner of Salizada San Lio and Calle Paradiso, next to Hotel Bruno, #5727—just look for the crowd).

For late-night gelato at Rialto, try **Michielangelo**, just off Campo San Bartolomeo, on the St. Mark's side of the Rialto Bridge on Salizada Pio X (daily 10:00–22:00). At St. Mark's Square, the **Al Todaro** *gelateria* opposite the Doge's Palace is open late (daily 8:00–24:00, 8:00–20:00 in winter, closed Mon in winter).

VENICE WITH CHILDREN

Some of the best kid fun I've had with my family has been in Venice. The city doesn't need an amusement park...it's one big fantasy world. It's safe and like nothing else your kids have ever seen. While there's lots of pavement and few parks or playgrounds, just being there—and free to wander—can be lots of fun. Consider these tips:

- Don't overdo it. Tackle just one or two key sights each day and mix in a healthy dose of fun activities. A vaporetto ride is a great way to start your visit.
- Follow this book's crowd-beating tips. Kids dislike long lines even more than you do.
- Eat dinner early (19:00 at restaurants). Skip romantic places. Try out-of-the-way bars or fast-food restaurants where kids can move around without bothering others. Picnics work well.
- Give your kid a cheap camera. Venice turns anyone into a photographer.
- Involve your children in the trip. Let them lead you through the maze of Venice's back streets. Get lost together.

Sights and Activities

In Venice, the parent/guide needs to be a little creative. Here are some suggestions:

Feed the pigeons on St. Mark's Square. If you yell, the birds will just ignore you, but tossing a sweater into the air kicks off a pigeon evacuation.

Ride the elevator to the top of the **Campanile** (St. Mark's bell tower) to enjoy the grand view, and be there as the huge bells whip into ear-shattering action at the top of each hour (open until 21:00 in summer, see page 49).

Take in a **glass-blowing demonstration** (just off St. Mark's

Square, see page 231). Part of the **Doge's Palace** tour includes the dark, dank prison and a creative armory (see page 63).

Ride lots of **boats** (vaporetto, gondola, *traghetto*, or speedboat tours of lagoon). Sit in the front seat of a vaporetto for the Grand Canal Cruise (see page 37) and let your child be the guide. See how many kinds of service boats you can spot during your time on the canal (UPS, police, fire, and so on).

The Rialto **fish market** is as fishy as they get (closed Sun–Mon; it's canalside, 2 blocks west of Rialto Bridge). Watch the people unload the boats at the market. You can leave by *traghetto* and cross the Grand Canal *(traghetto* dock at market).

A **children's park** is near the train station (facing the canal with your back to station, walk down the stairs and a block left past the shops to a small opening in wall on left—you'll see the playground inside). The bigger **Public Garden** *(Giardini Pubblici)* has swings and playground equipment (on far end of town—in Venice's "fishtail," near Giardini vaporetto stop). The **Lido** (beach) may sound intriguing, but it's filled with cars and offers only congested, dirty beaches.

Make a point to include some **Venetian history**. Taking advantage of the information in this book, explain St. Mark (look for winged lions; page 48), the birth of the city (page 242), how and why the city floods (page 30), and the story of the gondolas (page 234).

For fast and kid-friendly **meals** in the center, you'll find a couple of American hamburger joints between the Rialto Bridge and St. Mark's Square, great pizzerias on squares everywhere, and plenty of gelato.

SHOPPING

Long a city of aristocrats, luxury goods, and merchants, Venice was built to entice. While no one claims it's great for bargains, it has a shopping charm that makes paying too much strangely enjoyable. Carnevale masks, lace, glass, antique paper products, designer clothing, fancy accessories, and paintings are all popular with tourists visiting Venice.

Shops are generally open from 9:00 to 13:00 and from 15:00 to 19:30. In touristy Venice, more shops are open on Sunday than the Italian norm. If you're buying a substantial amount from nearly any shop, bargain. It's accepted and almost expected. Offer less and offer to pay cash; merchants are very conscious of the bite taken by credit-card companies. Anything not made locally is expensive to bring in and therefore generally more expensive than elsewhere in Italy. The shops near St. Mark's Square are most expensive.

Shopping Streets

Venice, which prides itself on being a cosmopolitan trendsetter, is a fun (if not cheap) place to shop for designer clothes, jewelry, antiques, and original art.

The best route to kick off your Venetian shopping spree is:

- **St. Mark's Square**—Walk the entire colonnaded square past pricey jewelry, glass, lace, and clothing stores, continuing down the...
- **Mercerie**—This is the main street between St. Mark's Square and the Rialto, noted for its high rent, high prices, fancy windows, and designer labels. Then, go over the...
- **Rialto Bridge**—The streets at either side are a cancan of shopping temptations. (From here you can follow the Rialto to Frari Church Walk, page 159.) Continue down the street...

- **Ruga Vecchia San Giovanni**—Away from the intensity of the tourist center, you'll enter a neighborhood with plenty of inviting shops, but fewer crowds and better prices.

  Elsewhere in Venice: Art-lovers browse the **art galleries** between the Accademia and the Peggy Guggenheim Museum.

  Salizada San Samuele is a nontouristy street with several artsy shops. **Livio de Marchi's** wood-sculpture shop is delightful, even when it's closed. Check out the window displays for his latest creations: socks, folded shirts, teddy bears, and "paper" sacks, all carved from wood (Mon–Fri 9:30–12:30 & 13:30–18:30, nearest major landmark is Accademia Bridge—on St. Mark's side, Salizada San Samuele 3157, vaporetto stop: San Samuele; if approaching by foot, follow signs to Palazzo Grassi, tel. 041-528-5694, www.liviodemarchi.com).

Venetian Glass

Popular Venetian glass is available in many forms: vases, tea sets, decanters, glasses, jewelry, lamps, mod sculptures (such as solid-glass aquariums), and on and on. Shops will ship it home for you (snap a photo of it before it's packed up). For a cheap, packable souvenir, consider the glass-bead necklaces sold at vendors' stalls throughout Venice.

If you're serious about glass, visit the small shops on **Murano Island**. Murano's glass-blowing demonstrations are fun; you'll usually see a vase and a "leetle 'orse" made from molten glass.

Various companies offer glass-blowing demos for tour groups around St. Mark's Square. **Galleria San Marco**, a tour-group staple, offers great demos just off St. Mark's Square every few minutes. They have agreed to let individual travelers flashing this book sneak in with tour groups to see the show (and sales pitch). And, if you buy anything, show this book and they'll take 20 percent off the listed price. (The gallery faces the square behind the orchestra nearest the church at #153, go through the arcade facing the square, cross the alley, get in good with the guard, and climb the stairs with the next group, daily 9:30–12:00 & 14:00–17:00, manager Adriano Veronese, tel. 041-271-8650.)

Souvenir Ideas

The most popular souvenirs and gifts are Murano glass (see above), Burano lace (fun lace umbrellas for little girls), Carnevale masks (fine shops and local artisans all over town), art reproductions (posters,

Getting a VAT Refund

Wrapped into the purchase price of your Venetian souvenirs is a Value Added Tax (VAT) that's generally about 17 percent. If you purchase more than €155 worth of goods at a store that participates in the VAT refund scheme, you're entitled to get most of that tax back. Personally I've never felt that VAT refunds are worth the hassle, but if you do, here's the scoop.

If you're lucky, the merchant will subtract the tax when you make your purchase (this is more likely to occur if the store ships the goods to your home). Otherwise, you'll need to:

Get the paperwork. Have the merchant completely fill out the necessary refund document, called a "cheque." You'll have to present your passport.

Get your stamp at the border. Process your cheque(s) at your last stop in the EU with the customs agent who deals with VAT refunds. It's best to keep your purchases in your carry-on for viewing, but if they're too large or dangerous (such as knives) to carry on, then track down the proper customs agent to inspect them before you check your bag. You're not supposed to use your purchased goods before you leave. If you show up at customs wearing your new shoes, officials might look the other way—or deny you a refund.

Collect your refund. You'll need to return your stamped document to the retailer or its representative. Many merchants work with a service, such as Global Refund or Cashback, which have offices at major airports, ports, or border crossings. These services, which extract a four percent fee, can refund your money immediately in your currency of choice or credit your card (within two billing cycles). If you have to deal directly with the retailer, mail the store your stamped documents, and then wait. It could take months.

postcards, and books), prints of Venice scenes, traditional stationery (pens and marbled paper products of all kinds), calendars with Venice scenes, silk ties, scarves, and plenty of goofy knickknacks (Titian mousepads, gondolier T-shirts, and little plastic gondolas).

Along Venice's many shopping streets, you'll notice fly-by-night vendors selling knockoffs of famous-maker handbags (Louis Vuitton, Gucci, etc.). These vendors are willing to bargain, but . . . buyer beware.

NIGHTLIFE

You must experience Venice after dark. The city is quiet at night, as tour groups are back in the cheaper hotels of Mestre on the mainland, and the masses of day-trippers return to their beach resorts. By 22:00, restaurants are winding down; by 23:00, many bars are closing; and by midnight, the city is virtually shut tight. But darkness brings a special romance to Venice. As during the day, it's the city itself that is the star. Venice—even the dark and distant back lanes—is considered very safe after nightfall.

Schedule of Events
Venice has a busy schedule of events, festivals, and entertainment. Check at the TI for listings in publications such as the free *Leo Bussola* magazine (bimonthly, in Italian and English) and in the free *Un Ospite di Venezia* magazine (monthly, bilingual, also available at top-end hotels).

Sightseeing
You can stretch your sightseeing day at the Doge's Palace (open daily until 19:00 April–Oct), Accademia (open Tue–Sun until 19:15), St. Mark's Campanile (open daily until 21:00 in summer), and the Peggy Guggenheim Museum (open Sat until 22:00 April–Oct).

Gondola Rides
Gondolas cost nearly double after dark but are triply romantic and relaxing under the moon. A rip-off for some, this is a traditional must for romantics. Gondoliers charge about €62 for a 50-minute ride during the day; from 20:00 on, figure on €77 to €105 (for *musica*—singer and accordionist—it's an additional

Gondolas

From the start, boats were *the* way to get around the island communities of the lagoon. To navigate over the countless shifting sandbars, the boats were flat (with no keel or rudder) and the captains stood up to see. Today's gondolas are prettier, but they work the same way.

Single oars are used both to propel and to steer the boats, which are built curved a bit so that an oar thrusting from the side sends the gondola in a straight line.

Through the early Middle Ages, the aristocracy preferred horses to boats. But beginning in the 14th century, when horses were outlawed from the streets of Venice, the noble class embraced gondolas as a respectable form of transportation and these sleek yet ornate boats appeared that we recognize today.

You can see the most picturesque gondola workshop in Venice in the Accademia neighborhood (walk down the Accademia side of the canal called Rio San Trovaso; as you approach Giudecca Canal you'll see the beached gondolas on your right across the canal). The workmen, traditionally from Italy's mountainous Dolomite region (because they need to be good with wood), maintain this refreshingly alpine-feeling little corner of Venice.

€88 during day, €98 after 20:00). You can divide the cost—and the romance—among up to six people per boat. Note that only two seats (the ones in back) are side by side.

Glide through nighttime Venice with your head on someone else's shoulder. Follow the moon as it sails past otherwise unseen buildings. Silhouettes gaze down from bridges while window glitter spills onto the black water. You're anonymous in the city of masks as the rhythmic thrust of your striped-shirted gondolier turns old crows into songbirds. This is extremely relaxing (and I think worth the extra cost to experience at night). Since you might get a narration plus conversation with your gondolier, talk with several and choose one you like who speaks English well. Women, beware...while gondoliers can be extremely

charming, local women say anyone who falls for one of these Romeos "has slices of ham over her eyes."

For cheap gondola thrills during the day, stick to the €1.60 one-minute ferry ride on a Grand Canal *traghetto*. At night, vaporettos are nearly empty, and it's a great time to cruise the Grand Canal on the slow boat #1. Or hang out on a bridge along the gondola route and wave at (or drop leftover pigeon seed on) romantics.

Dining

Locals and those spending the night in Venice fill the piazzas, restaurants, and bars. *The* local way to spend an evening is to simply enjoy a slow and late dinner in a romantic canalside or piazza setting (see Eating chapter, page 213).

Caffè Florian, on St. Mark's Square, is the most famous Venetian café and one of the first places in Europe to serve coffee. It has been *the* place for a discreet rendezvous in Venice since 1720. Today, it's most famous for its outdoor seating and orchestra (see below), but do walk inside through the richly decorated, 18th-century rooms where Casanova, Lord Byron, Charles Dickens, and Woody Allen have all paid too much for a drink (reasonable prices at bar in back, tel. 041-520-5641).

St. Mark's Square

For tourists, St. Mark's Square is the highlight, with lantern light and live music echoing from the cafés. Just being here after dark is a thrill, as **dueling café orchestras** entertain. Every night, enthusiastic musicians play the same songs, creating the same irresistible magic. Hang out for free behind the tables (which allows you to easily move on to the next orchestra when the musicians take a break) or spring for a seat and enjoy a fun and gorgeously set concert. If you sit a while, it can be €10 well spent (€6 drink plus a one-time €4 fee for entertainment). Dancing on the square is free (and encouraged).

Streetlamp halos, live music, floodlit history, and a ceiling of stars make St. Mark's magic at midnight. You're not a tourist, you're a living part of a soft Venetian night...an alley cat with money. In the misty light, the moon has a golden hue. Shine with the old lanterns on the gondola piers where the sloppy lagoon splashes at the Doge's Palace...reminiscing.

More Music

Baroque Concerts: Take your pick of traditional Vivaldi concerts in churches throughout town. Home-grown Vivaldi is as trendy here as Strauss in Vienna and Mozart in Salzburg. In fact, you'll find frilly young Vivaldis all over town hawk-ing concert tickets. The TI has a list of this week's Baroque concerts (tickets from €18, shows start at 21:00 and generally last 90 min). If you see a concert at **Scuola San Rocco**, you can enjoy the art (which you're likely to pay €5.20 for during the day) for free during the intermission. The general rule of thumb: musicians in wigs and tights offer better spectacle, musicians in black and white suits are better performers. Consider the venue carefully.

   Special Concerts: Another unique music experience is a Rondo Veneziano concert—classically inspired music with a modern electronic sound.

Movies

Venetian cinema is rarely in the original language; expect to hear it in Italian. **Outdoor cinema** on Campo San Polo is a fun scene (July–Aug). Every September, the Venice **film festival** (with some English-language films) doubles the viewing choices and brings out the stars.

Theater

Venice's two most famous theaters are Teatro Goldoni (mostly Italian live theater) and La Fenice (grand old opera house, closed since 1996 fire). Opera performances still take place at different venues in Venice from late November through the end of June. For the latest, see *Leo Bussola* or *Un Ospite de Venezia* magazines (both free at TI).

Pubs, Discos, and Late-Night Spots

While a pub-crawl dinner (see page 222) is fun and colorful, most serious eating is finished early to make way for drinking.

Campo Santa Margherita, the university student zone, is likely to be lively late. This popular-with-locals square has a good restaurant, café, and bar scene (Bar Rosso is particularly popular).

Other places likely to be open after 23:00 include: the **Al Todaro** *gelateria*, on the waterfront across from the Doge's Palace; the **American Bar**, under the clock tower on St. Mark's Square; and the **Vino Vino** wine bar, a few blocks west of St. Mark's Square (see St. Mark's to Rialto Walk, on page 153). I like the little no-name portable wooden **wine bar** tucked on a street corner along the Grand Canal, several blocks south of the west side of the Rialto Bridge; take your glass for a canalside walk and return it later.

Also open late are Irish pubs, such as the **Devil's Forest Pub** (until 1:00, closed Sun in Aug, east of Rialto Bridge, see page 225) and Irishark Pub (until 1:30, just west of Campo Santa Maria Formosa on Calle Mondo Nuovo). While Irish pubs are popular with locals rather than tourists, the venerable **Harry's Bar** (serving expensive food and American cocktails to dressy tourists at the St. Mark's vaporetto stop) is just the opposite.

Venice is not a good **disco** scene. Most discos are overpriced clubs (€22 entry) with expensive drinks (€11) and little actual dancing. Still, for a cultural experience and a throbbing techno beat, check out **Casanova** disco in Cannaregio #158/A, Lista di Spagna, open daily 21:00–4:00 (locals won't show up until at least 23:30 or midnight).

TRANSPORTATION
CONNECTIONS

A three-kilometer-long causeway (with both highway and train lines) connects Venice to the mainland. Mestre, the sprawling mainland industrial base, has fewer crowds, cheaper hotels, and plenty of parking lots, but no charm. Don't stop here, unless you're parking your car in a lot.

SANTA LUCIA TRAIN STATION

Trains to Venice stop at either Venezia Mestre (on the mainland) or at the Santa Lucia station on the island of Venice itself. But if your train dead-ends at Mestre, worry not. Shuttle trains regularly connect Mestre's station with Venice's Santa Lucia station (6/hr, 5 min).

Venice's **Santa Lucia train station** plops you right into the old town on the Grand Canal, an easy vaporetto ride or fascinating 40-minute walk to St. Mark's Square. Upon arrival, skip the station's crowded TI because the two TIs at St. Mark's Square are better, and it's not worth a long wait for a minimal map (buy a good one from a newsstand with no wait; the new €6.20 "Illustrated Venice Map" by Magnetic North is super). Confirm your departure plan (stop by train info desk or just study the *partenze*—departure—posters on walls).

Consider storing unnecessary heavy bags, even though lines for **baggage check** may be very long (platform 14, €2.60/12 hrs, €5.20/24 hrs, daily 5:00–24:00; there are no lockers).

Then walk straight out of the station to the canal. The dock for **vaporetti** #1 and #82 is on your left (for downtown Venice; most recommended hotels; and Grand Canal Cruise—see page 37); the dock for #51 and #52 is on your right (for some recommended hotels). Buy a €3.10 ticket (or €9.30 all-day pass) at the ticket window and hop on a boat for downtown (direction: Rialto or San Marco). Some boats only go as far as Rialto *(solo Rialto)*, so confirm with the conductor.

Italy's Public Transportation

KEY: — RAIL   - - - BUS   · · · · SHIP
NOT TO SCALE   ● GOOD OVERNIGHT STOPS

Types of Trains

You'll encounter several different kinds of trains in Italy. Along with the various milk-run trains, there are the slow IR (Interregional) and *diretto* trains, the medium *espresso*, the fast IC (Intercity), and the bullet-train T.A.V.—Treno Alta Velocita (supplement costs around €16, even with train pass). Fast trains, even with supplements, are affordable (e.g., including the express supplement, a first-class Venice-to-Florence ticket costs about €44; second-class about €28).

Buying supplements on the train comes with a nasty penalty. Buying them at the station usually involves a long wait in line. Try to buy supplements, train tickets, and *couchette* reservations (about €18) at downtown travel agencies—such as Kele & Teo Viaggi e Turismo (CC for train tickets only, Mon–Fri 8:30–19:00, Sat 9:00–19:00, Sat afternoons and Sun no train tickets available, at Ponte dei Bareteri on Mercerie halfway between Rialto Bridge and St. Mark's Square, tel. 041-520-8722). The cost is the same, the lines and language barrier are smaller, and you'll save time.

SCHEDULES

Newsstands sell up-to-date regional and all-Italy timetables (€4, ask for the *orario ferroviaro*). There is now a single all-Italy telephone number for train information: 848-888-088 (daily 7:00–21:00, automated Italian recording, have an Italian speaker listen for you). On the Web, check http://bahn.hafas.de/bin /query.exe/en or www.fs-on-line.com.

Strikes are common. They generally last a day, and train employees will simply say, *"sciopero"* (strike). Still, sporadic trains—following no particular schedule—lumber down the tracks during most strikes.

By train to: Padua (1/hr, 30 min), **Vicenza** (1/hr, 1 hr), **Verona** (1/hr, 90 min), **Ravenna** (1/hr, 3–4 hrs, transfer in Ferrara or Bologna), **Florence** (7/day, 3 hrs), **Dolomites** (8/day to Bolzano, about hourly, 4 hrs with 1 transfer; catch bus from Bolzano into mountains), **Milan** (1/hr, 3–4 hrs), **Monterosso/Cinque Terre** (2/day, 6 hrs, departs Venice at 10:00 and 15:00), **Rome** (7/day, 5 hrs, slower overnight), **Naples** (change in Rome, plus 2–3 hrs), **Brindisi** (3/day, 11 hrs, change in Bologna), **Bern** (3/day, change in Milan, 8 hrs), **Munich** (2/day, 8 hrs), **Paris** (4/day, 11 hrs), and **Vienna** (4/day, 9 hrs).

MARCO POLO AIRPORT

Venice's airport on the mainland, 10 kilometers north of the city, has a TI, cash machines, car-rental agencies, a few shops and eateries, and easy connections by bus and speedboat to the city center. Airport info: tel. 041-260-611, flight info: tel. 041-260-9260.

Romantics can jet to St. Mark's Square by Alilaguna **speedboat** (easiest transportation to historical center, €9.80, 1/hr, 70 min, runs 6:15–24:00 from airport; 4:50–22:50 from St. Mark's Square, generally departing airport 10 min after the hour, www.alilaguna.com). A **water taxi** zips you directly to your hotel in 30 minutes for €80. **Buses** connect the airport and the Piazzale Roma vaporetto stop: Catch either the blue ATVO shuttle bus (€2.60, 2/hr, 20 min, 5:30–20:40 to airport, 8:30–24:00 from airport, www.atvo.it) or the cheaper orange ACTV bus #5 (€0.75, 1–3/hr, 20–40 min, 4:40–1:00).

Driving in Italy

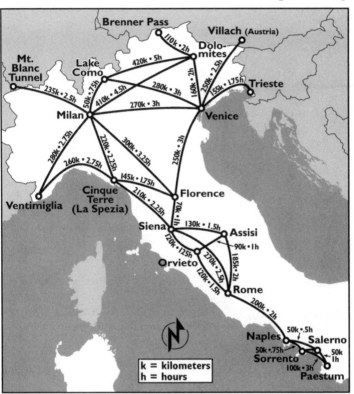

Brenner Pass
Villach (Austria)
Dolo-mites
Mt. Blanc Tunnel
Lake Como
110k • 2h
420k • 5h
250k • 2.5h
155k • 1.75h
Trieste
235k • 2.5h
50k • .75h
410k • 4.5h
280k • 3h
160k • 2h
Milan
270k • 3h
Venice
200k • 2.75h
210k • 2.25h
300k • 3.25h
250k • 3h
260k • 2.75h
145k • 1.75h
Cinque Terre (La Spezia)
210k • 2.25h
Florence
Ventimiglia
70k • 1h
Siena
130k • 1.5h
Assisi
90k • 1h
120k • 1.25h
270k • 2.5h
185k • 2h
Orvieto
120k • 1.5h
Rome
200k • 2h
50k • .5h
Naples
Salerno
50k • .75h
50k 1h
Sorrento
100k • 3h
Paestum

k = kilometers
h = hours

TIPS FOR DRIVERS

The freeway ends at Venice in a parking lot on the edge of the island. Follow the green lights directing you to a parking lot with space, probably Tronchetto (across the causeway and on the right), which has a huge, multistoried garage (€15.50/day, half price with discount coupon from your hotel, tel. 041-520-7555). From there, you'll find travel agencies masquerading as TIs and vaporetto docks for the boat connection (#82) to the town center. Don't let taxi boatmen con you out of the cheap €3.10 vaporetto ride. Parking in Mestre is easy and cheap (open-air lots €4.10/day, €5.20/day garage across from Mestre train station, easy shuttle-train connections to Venice's Santa Lucia Station—6/hr, 5 min).

VENETIAN HISTORY

CAPSULE HISTORY OF VENICE

A.D. 500–1000: Born in Mud

With Rome's infrastructure crumbling and Italy crawling with barbarians, coastal folk fled to marshy islands in the Adriatic. They sank pilings in the mud to build. Fishermen became sea traders.

Sights:
- The network of canals; gondolas
- Old crypt under San Zaccaria Church
- San Moisé Church
- Church on Torcello island

1000–1500: Medieval Growth and Expansion

Well-located between northern Europe and the eastern Mediterranean, Venetian sea traders established trading outposts in Byzantine and Muslim territories to the east. At home, a stable, constitutional government ran an efficient, state-operated multinational corporation. Grand buildings reflected Venice's wealth.

Sights:
- Doge's Palace
- St. Mark's Basilica

- Frari Church
- Buildings decorated in ornate Venetian-Gothic style
- Doge paraphernalia and city history at Correr Museum
- Glass and lace industries
- Arsenale shipbuilding complex
- Jewish Ghetto and Jewish Museum

1500–1600: Renaissance

Europe's richest city-state poured money into the arts...
even as her power was waning. Venice established a reputation
as a luxury-loving, exotic, cosmopolitan playground.

Sights:

- St. Mark's Square facades and other work by Sansovino
- Palladio's classical facades on churches of San Giorgio Maggiore and Il Redentore
- Titian paintings (Accademia, Frari Church, Doge's Palace, etc.)
- Giovanni Bellini (Accademia, Frari Church, San Zaccaria Church, Correr Museum)
- Giorgione (Accademia)
- Tintoretto (Accademia, Scuola San Rocco, many churches)

1600–1800: Elegant Decline

New trade routes, new European powers, and belligerent Turks drained Venice's economy and shrank its trading empire. At home, Venice's reputation for luxury—and now decadence—still made it a popular tourist destination for Europe's French-speaking gentry.

Sights:

- Ca' Rezzonico (Museum of 18th-Century Venice)
- La Salute Church
- Masks of the Carnevale tradition

- Old cafés (e.g., the Florian and the Quadri)
- La Fenice opera house, Teatro Goldoni
- Baroque interiors in many churches
- Canova sculpture (Correr Museum, Frari Church)
- Tiepolo paintings (Accademia, Doge's Palace, Ca' Rezzonico)
- Paintings of Canaletto, Guardi, G. D. Tiepolo (Ca' Rezzonico)

1800–2000: Modern Venice

Conquered by Napoleon, then placed under Austrian rule, the Venetians joined Italy's Risorgimento movement, resulting in the unified, democratic nation of Italy. Since little new building was done in the city, it remained a museum piece for foreigners—one increasingly threatened by mainland pollution, floods, and hordes of tourists.

Sights:
- Correr Museum's Risorgimento wing
- Statue of Daniele Manin
- Motorized vaporettos and taxis
- Train Station (1954)
- Peggy Guggenheim Museum
- The Biennale International Art Exhibition
- Pollution from Mestre, Burger King

SAILING THE SEVEN SEAS— FROM BIRTH TO UNIFICATION WITH ITALY

In Roman times, people didn't live in the Venetian lagoon. But the region had many important mainland cities. Convoys of Roman ships would connect the major ports of Ravenna and Aquileia (the fourth-largest Roman city) by navigating a series of lagoons they called "the Seven Seas" (hence the term we use today).

In the fifth century, when Rome fell, barbarian Visigoths and Huns ravaged the farmers of this area. Hoping the barbarians didn't like water, the first "Venetians" took refuge in the lagoon. For centuries there was no "Venice" as such . . . just a series of about a dozen principal refuge settlements in and around the Venetian lagoon.

The lagoon is a delta littered with tiny, muddy islands created by sediment dropped by rivers. As refugees squatted on this wet and miserable land, they kept certain streams from silting, and these streams eventually became canals. A motley collection of about 120 natural islands eventually became Venice.

From the start, these former farmers harvested salt and fish for their livelihood. Later, using the trading savvy gained from the salt-and-fish business, they began trading up the rivers. With the rise of Byzantium, there was more East–West trade, and Venetians were there as ready middlemen, selling goods from the East to consumers in the West.

In the sixth century, another wave of barbarians (the Longobards) plundered the mainland. Attacking cities this time, they sent a new kind of refugee into the lagoon: shopkeepers, clergy, artisans, and nobles.

Previously, the farmers had subsisted without much need to organize. But with the arrival of aggressive noble families, the lagoon became political. To sort out the squabbles, the Byzantine emperor appointed a local duke, or doge, in 697. This began a 1,100-year-long period of doge rule, ending only with the arrival of Napoleon in 1797.

The doge needed a capital, and he chose the town of Rialto (future Venice) for its easy-to-defend position. Over time, the most important trading nobles built their palaces in Rialto to be near the doge.

Because nobles settled on their own little islets, palaces are scattered all over the current city. Eventually, island communities decided to join, or literally "bridge," with others. Building bridges required shoring up the canals. Soon, paved canalside walks appeared. And by the 12th century, the government provided oil and required that streets be lit—a first in Europe.

Since feudalism didn't really work in the lagoon economy, the natural entrepreneurial energy of the nobility created the "noble merchant." Trade, which became the exclusive privilege of the upper classes, grew, thus supporting a larger, wealthier population. Suddenly, people (like both the Byzantine and Holy Roman emperors) were noticing Venice. Charlemagne, the Holy Roman Emperor (c. 800), looked hungrily at Venice.

Venetians wanted to keep their freedom, but knew they would have to choose: Byzantium or the Holy Roman Empire. Byzantium was preferable because as a distant fringe of that empire, Venice would be subjugated only in name. Arranging an alignment with Byzantium also involved Church politics.

Noteworthy Residents of Venice

1000–1400
Dandolo, Enrico (ruled 1192–1205)—Doge during the Fourth Crusade, when Venetian crusaders looted Constantinople, helping enrich Venice.

Polo, Marco (1254–1324)—Traveler to faraway China whose journal, *The Book of Marvels*, was dismissed by many as fiction.

Veneziano, Paolo (1310–1358)—Painter who mastered the Byzantine gold-icon style, then added touches of Western realism.

1400s
Foscari, Francesco (1373–1457)—Doge at Venice's peak of power, whose disastrous wars against Milan and Turks started the Republic's slow fade.

Bellini, Jacopo (c. 1400–1470)—Father of painting family. His training in Renaissance Florence brought 3-D realism to Venice.

Bellini, Gentile (c. 1429–1507)—Elder son of painting family, known for straightforward historical scenes of Venice.

Bellini, Giovanni (c. 1430–1516)—The most famous son in the painting family, whose glowing, colorful, 3-D Madonna-and-Childs started the Venetian Renaissance. Teacher of Titian and Giorgione.

Carpaccio, Vittore (c. 1460–1525)—Painter of realistic, secular scenes.

1500s
Giorgione (c. 1478–1511)—Innovative painter whose moody realism influenced Bellini (his teacher) and Titian (his friend and fellow painter).

Titian (Tiziano Vecellio, 1488–1576)—Premier Venetian Renaissance painter. Master of many styles, from teenage Madonnas to sober state portraits to exuberant mythological scenes to centerfold nudes.

Sansovino, Jacopo (1486–1570)—Renaissance architect who redid the face of Venice (especially St. Mark's Square), introducing sober, classical columns and arches to a city previously full of ornate Gothic.

Palladio, Andrea (1508–1580)—Influential architect whose classical style was much-imitated around the world, resulting in villas, government buildings, and banks that look like Greek temples.

Tintoretto (Jacopo Robusti, c. 1518–1594)—Painter of dramatic religious scenes, using strong 3-D, diagonal compositions, twisting poses, sharp contrast of light and shadow, and bright, "black velvet" colors (late Renaissance/Mannerist style).

Veronese, Paolo (1528–1588)—Painter of big, colorful canvases, capturing the exuberance and luxury of Renaissance Venice.

1600s

Monteverdi, Claudio (1567–1643)—The composer and *Capelmeister* at St. Mark's Basilica who wrote in a budding new medium—opera.

Longhena, Baldassare (1598–1682)—Architect of the Baroque-style La Salute Church.

1700s

Vivaldi, Antonio (c. 1677–1741)—Composer of "Four Seasons" ("Dah dunt-dunt-duh dutta dah-ah-ah").

Canaletto, Antonio (1697–1768)—Painter of photo-realist Venice views.

Guardi, Francesco (1712–1793)—Painter of proto-Impressionist Venice views.

Goldoni, Carlo (1707–1793)—Comic playwright who brought refinement to commedia dell'arte buffoonery.

Tiepolo, Gian Battista (1696–1770)—Painter of mythological subjects in colorful Rococo ceilings.

Tiepolo, Gian Domenico (1727–1804)—Painter son of the famous Tiepolo.

Casanova, Giacomo (1725–1798)—Gambler, womanizer, and adventurer whose exaggerated memoirs inspired Romantics.

Canova, Antonio (1757–1822)—Neoclassical sculptor whose polished, white, beautiful statues were especially popular in Napoleon's France.

Da Ponte, Lorenzo (1749–1838)—Mozart's librettist popularized Venice's sophisticated and decadent high society.

1800s

Manin, Daniele (1804–1857)—Led Venetian revolt (1848) against the city's Austrian rulers, eventually leading to united, democratic, modern Italy.

1900s

Guggenheim, Peggy (1898–1979)—American-born art collector, gallery owner, and friend of modern art and artists.

In A.D. 800, the bishop residing in the mainland city of Aquileia and loyal to the Holy Roman Emperor included Venice in his domain. This made the people of the lagoon subjects of the Holy Roman Emperor. To avoid this, the Venetians accepted an obscure bishop loyal to Byzantium.

To legitimize their bogus Byzantine bishop, the Venetians of the lagoon decided they needed just the right holy relics. This area had a strong affinity for St. Mark (he traveled here as Peter's translator), the man credited with bringing Christianity to the region. Knowing the power of actually possessing the relics of St. Mark, the Venetians managed to smuggle his remains from Egypt to Rialto in 828. Overnight, it became clear: The Venice bishop was legit. This established Venice as part of the Byzantine Empire, saving it from European control. To seal the city's oriental orientation, Venetian leaders had the grand St. Mark's Basilica built in a distinctly Eastern style.

As home of both the doge and St. Mark, and with its easily defensible position, Venice emerged as a regional powerhouse. The miscellaneous communities in the lagoon coalesced around what is now Venice. Though technically part of the Byzantine Empire, the city was so remote that, in practice, it was virtually free.

Venetian merchants ran a profitable trading triangle: timber from Venice's mainland to Egypt for gold to Byzantium for luxury goods to Venice. As this went round and round, Venice amassed lots of capital, and its merchant fleet grew to be the biggest in the Mediterranean. Back then, a fleet was essentially the same as a navy, making Venice a military power. Cleverly, Venice agreed to defend Byzantine and Crusader ports in return for free trade privileges. This made the eastern Mediterranean a virtual free-trade zone for a very aggressive Venetian trading community to exploit.

As Venetian nobles grew wealthy, they built lavish palaces. While their mainland counterparts fortified compounds with tall towers, Venetian merchants built palazzos—with a natural lagoon defense—that were luxurious rather than fortified. Palaces in Venice came complete with loading docks, warehouses, and, eventually, chandeliered ballrooms.

Later, Venice expanded its economy beyond trade. Picking up techniques from the East, it established strong local industries. Venice was the leading optical center. Understanding medicine as a chemical rather than an herbal business, the city developed Europe's first real pharmaceutical industry. Making Europe's first cheap paper from rags rather than sheepskins (parchment) and offering the first copyright protection (in 1474), the Venetian paper and printing industry boomed. Already clever at trading products from other countries, now Venice peddled its own stuff...more profitably than ever.

By 1100, Venice was running Europe's first industrial complex, the Arsenale. With more than 1,000 workers using an early form of assembly-line production, the Arsenale could produce about one warship a day. This put the "fear of Venice" into visiting rulers. When France's King Henry III dropped by the Arsenale, Venice entertained him with a shipbuilding spectacle: from ribs to finished product in four hours. Then the ship was completely outfitted before gliding down the exit canal.

With mountains of capital, plenty of traders with ready ships, a sophisticated system of insurance, joint ventures, and money drafts, Venice's traveling merchants eventually became resident merchants and bankers. By the 15th century, Venice was a commercial powerhouse—among the six biggest cities in Europe. Of its estimated 180,000 citizens, nearly 1,000 were of Rockefeller-esque wealth and power.

But Venice's power peaked. With the Ottoman defeat of the Byzantine emperor (messing up established trading partners and patterns), Vasco da Gama's voyage to India (opening up trade routes that skirted Venetian control), the appearance of English and Dutch shipping in the Mediterranean, and devastating plagues, Venice began to decline.

When Napoleon invaded Venetian territory, French ideas of citizens' rights caused the populace to reevaluate its 1,000-year-long aristocratic rule. In 1797, the last doge abdicated. A period of French and Austrian rule lasted until 1866, when Venice joined the kingdom of Italy.

VENICE TIMELINE
A.D. 400–900: Rome Falls,
Venice as an Isolated Sanctuary

A.D. 476 The last Roman emperor abdicates. Italy is full of "barbarians."

568 Lombards invade northern Italy, driving mainlanders onto sparsely populated islands of the lagoon. The Byzantine Empire in Constantinople gives aid and protection to the refugees.

697 The first doge is elected by leading families.

800 Charlemagne controls northern Italy.

828 Venice acquires St. Mark's relics from Alexandria. Possession of the famous relics legitimizes their self-appointed bishop, establishing their independence from the Holy Roman Empire's control.

c. 850 Tiny Venice is effectively an independent, self-ruling country.

Venetian History in a Seashell

In the Middle Ages, the Venetians, becoming Europe's clever middlemen for East–West trade, created a great trading empire ruled by a series of doges. By smuggling in the bones of St. Mark (San Marco, A.D. 828), Venice gained religious importance as well. With the discovery of America and new trading routes to the Orient, Venetian power ebbed. But as Venice fell, her appetite for decadence grew. Through the 17th and 18th centuries, Venice partied on the wealth accumulated through earlier centuries as a trading power.

1000–1300: Medieval Growth as a Seafaring Trading Power

1063 The current St. Mark's Basilica houses Mark's relics, after the old church burns down.

1095 In the First Crusade, Venice sides with Byzantium against overzealous Norman Crusaders. In return, Byzantium grants free trade throughout the empire to Venetians.

c. 1150 Constitutional limits are placed on the doges. The Republic is ruled by a Senate of wealthy families.

1204 During the Fourth Crusade, Venetian troops join other Crusaders in attacking and looting Christian Constantinople (partly to retaliate against Byzantine harassment of Venetian merchants). The booty boosts Venice further.

1261 Venice's seafaring rival, Genoa, helps the Byzantines retake Constantinople. Genoa is rewarded with trading rights in the Byzantine Empire, thus sparking two centuries of war over markets with Venice.

c. 1300 To avoid political coups d'état, the Venetian Senate sets constitutional limits restricting political power to only established (read: wealthy) families.

1300–1400: Peak of Power

1381 Venetian ships rout Genoa's fleet at Chioggia (on the south end of the lagoon). Venice rules the waves and the sea-trade of the eastern Mediterranean.

1416 Venice defeats the Muslim Turks at Gallipoli.

c. 1420 After military victories in northern Italy, Venice is at the height of its power, with mainland possessions and a powerful overseas trading empire to the east.

1400–1500: Turks to the East, Jealous Enemies to the West = War

1423 Doge Francesco Foscari starts disastrous, money-draining wars against Milan, while the Turks chip away at Venice's trading cities on the eastern front.

1453 Turks take Constantinople. Venice suffers major losses in its eastern markets.

1454 Venice finally makes peace with Milan. Other European powers join to prey on a weakened Venice.

1492 Columbus sails the ocean blue, establishing trade in a World that's New.

1498 Vasco da Gama circles around Africa's Cape Horn, finding a new sea-trade route to eastern markets. Venice's sea-trade monopoly is threatened.

1500–Present: Venice's Slow Fade

c. 1500– Though waning in power, Venice is a Renaissance
1570 cultural capital as home to Titian, Tintoretto, Sansovino, Palladio, and others.

1508 Pig pile on Venice—a European alliance of the pope, northern Italians, and northern Europeans defeat Venice at Agnadello. Meanwhile, the Turks keep pecking away in the east.

1571 At the Battle of Lepanto, Venice and European allies score a temporary victory over the Turks. Unfortunately, it's only a moral victory, as Venice's navy suffers major damage, and the city loses more trading rights. Spain, England, and Holland, with their oceangoing vessels, emerge as superior traders in a more global economy.

1669 Crete, the last major Venetian outpost, falls to the Turks.

1718 The Turks drive Venetians from southern Greece. Venice's once-great trading empire in the eastern Mediterranean is over.

1797 Napoleon invades Venice, deposes the last doge, and establishes something of a democracy along the lines of French Revolution ideals.

1815 After the Battle of Waterloo, Europe's kings put Venice under Austrian rule.

1846 A three-kilometer-long railroad causeway links Venice to the mainland.

1848 Daniele Manin, an influential lawyer, briefly establishes an independent, democratic Venetian Republic, but the revolution is soon crushed by Austrian troops.

1866 After Austria is defeated by Prussia, Venice is freed to join the new, modern, democratic kingdom of Italy.

1932 A highway running parallel to the causeway is built, bringing cars to Venice's edge.

c. 1950 Unbridled industrialization on the mainland produces pollution (sulfuric acid) and threatens Venice's stone monuments.

1966 Venice suffers a disastrous flood.

c. 1985 Plans are made to control flooding with a sea barrier, but no building is undertaken.

2003 You arrive in Venice to add to the city's illustrious history.

APPENDIX

Let's Talk Telephones

Here's a primer on making phone calls. For information specific to Italy, see "Telephones" in the Introduction.

Making Calls within a European Country: About half of all European countries use area codes; the other half use a direct-dial system without area codes.

To make calls within a country that uses a direct-dial telephone system (Italy, Belgium, the Czech Republic, Denmark, France, Portugal, Norway, Spain, and Switzerland), you dial the same number whether you're calling across the country or across the street.

In countries that use area codes (such as Austria, Britain, Finland, Germany, Ireland, the Netherlands, and Sweden), you dial the local number when calling within a city, and you add the area code if calling long distance within the country.

Making International Calls: You always start with the international access code (011 if you're calling from the U.S. or Canada, or 00 from Europe), then dial the country code of the country you're calling (see chart below).

What you dial next depends on the phone system of the country you're calling. If the country uses area codes (and remember that some do not), drop the initial zero of the area code, then dial the rest of the number.

Countries that use direct-dial systems (no area codes) vary in how they're accessed internationally by phone. For instance, if you're making an international call to Italy, Denmark, Norway, Portugal, or Spain, simply dial the international access code, country code, and phone number. But if you're calling Belgium, the Czech Republic, France, or Switzerland, drop the initial zero of the phone number.

European Calling Chart

Just smile and dial, using this key:
AC = Area Code, LN = Local Number.

European Country	Calling long distance within...	Calling from the U.S.A./ Canada to...	Calling from another European country to...
Austria	AC (Area Code) + LN (Local Number)	011 + 43 + AC (without the initial zero) + LN	00 + 43 + AC (without the initial zero) + LN
Belgium	LN	011 + 32 + LN (without initial zero)	00 + 32 + LN (without initial zero)
Britain	AC + LN	011 + 44 + AC (without initial zero) + LN	00 + 44 + AC . (without initial zero) + LN
Czech Republic	LN	011 + 420 + LN	00 + 420 + LN
Denmark	LN	011 + 45 + LN	00 + 45 + LN
Estonia	LN	011 + 372 + LN	00 + 372 + LN
Finland	AC + LN	011 + 358 + AC (without initial zero) + LN	00 + 358 + AC (without initial zero) + LN
France	LN	011 + 33 + LN (without initial zero)	00 + 33 + LN (without initial zero)
Germany	AC + LN	011 + 49 + AC (without initial zero) + LN	00 + 49 + AC (without initial zero) + LN
Gibraltar	LN	011 + 350 + LN	00 + 350 + LN From Spain: 9567 + LN
Greece	LN	011 + 30 + LN	00 + 30 + LN

European Country	Calling long distance within...	Calling from the U.S.A./ Canada to...	Calling from another European country to...
Ireland	AC + LN	011 + 353 + AC (without initial zero) + LN	00 + 353 + AC (without initial zero) + LN
Italy	LN	011 + 39 + LN	00 + 39 + LN
Morocco	LN	011 + 212 + LN (without initial zero)	00 + 212 + LN (without initial zero)
Netherlands	AC + LN	011 + 31 + AC (without initial zero) + LN	00 + 31 + AC (without initial zero) + LN
Norway	LN	011 + 47 + LN	00 + 47 + LN
Portugal	LN	011 + 351 + LN	00 + 351 + LN
Spain	LN	011 + 34 + LN	00 + 34 + LN
Sweden	AC + LN	011 + 46 + AC (without initial zero) + LN	00 + 46 + AC (without initial zero) + LN
Switzerland	LN	011 + 41 + LN (without initial zero)	00 + 41 + LN (without initial zero)
Turkey	AC (if no initial zero is included, add one) + LN	011 + 90 + AC (without initial zero) + LN	00 + 90 + AC (without initial zero) + LN

- The instructions above apply whether you're calling a fixed phone or cell phone.
- The international access codes (the first numbers you dial when making an international call) are 011 if you're calling from the U.S.A./Canada, or 00 if you're calling from virtually anywhere in Europe. Finland and Lithuania are the only exceptions. If calling from either of these countries, replace the 00 with 990 in Finland and 810 in Lithuania.
- To call the U.S.A. or Canada from Europe, dial 00 (unless you're calling from Finland or Lithuania), then 1 (the country code for the U.S.A. and Canada), then the area code and number. In short, 00 + 1 + AC + LN = Hi, mom!

International Access Codes

When dialing direct, first dial the international access code (00 if calling from Europe, 011 if calling from the U.S. or Canada). Virtually all European countries—including Italy—use "00" as their international access code; the only exceptions are Finland (990) and Lithuania (810).

Country Codes

After you've dialed the international access code, dial the code of the country you're calling.

Austria—43	Ireland—353
Belgium—32	Italy—39
Britain—44	Morocco—212
Canada—1	Netherlands—31
Czech Rep.—420	Norway—47
Denmark—45	Portugal—351
Estonia—372	Spain—34
Finland—358	Sweden—46
France—33	Switzerland—41
Germany—49	Turkey—90
Gibraltar—350	United States—1
Greece—30	

Useful Italian Phone Numbers

Emergency (English-speaking police help): 113
Emergency (military police): 112
Road Service: 116
Directory Assistance (for €0.50, an Italian-speaking robot gives the number twice, very clearly): 12
Telephone help (in English; free directory assistance): 170

Festivals in Venice

Venice's most famous festival is **Carnevale** (Feb 21–March 4 in 2003), the celebration Americans call Mardi Gras. Carnevale, which means "farewell to meat," originated centuries ago as a wild two-month-long party leading up to the austerity of Lent. In Carnevale's heyday—the 1600s and 1700s—you could do pretty much anything with anybody from any social class if you were wearing a mask. These days it's a tamer 10-day celebration, culminating in a huge dance lit with fireworks on St. Mark's Square. Sporting masks and costumes, Venetians from kids to businessmen join in the fun. Drawing the biggest crowds of the year, Carnevale has nearly been a victim of its own success, driving away many Venetians (who skip out on the craziness to go ski in the Dolomites).

2003

JANUARY
S	M	T	W	T	F	S
			1	2	3	4
5	6	7	8	9	10	11
12	13	14	15	16	17	18
19	20	21	22	23	24	25
26	27	28	29	30	31	

FEBRUARY
S	M	T	W	T	F	S
						1
2	3	4	5	6	7	8
9	10	11	12	13	14	15
16	17	18	19	20	21	22
23	24	25	26	27	28	

MARCH
S	M	T	W	T	F	S
						1
2	3	4	5	6	7	8
9	10	11	12	13	14	15
16	17	18	19	20	21	22
23/30	24/31	25	26	27	28	29

APRIL
S	M	T	W	T	F	S
		1	2	3	4	5
6	7	8	9	10	11	12
13	14	15	16	17	18	19
20	21	22	23	24	25	26
27	28	29	30			

MAY
S	M	T	W	T	F	S
				1	2	3
4	5	6	7	8	9	10
11	12	13	14	15	16	17
18	19	20	21	22	23	24
25	26	27	28	29	30	31

JUNE
S	M	T	W	T	F	S
1	2	3	4	5	6	7
8	9	10	11	12	13	14
15	16	17	18	19	20	21
22	23	24	25	26	27	28
29	30					

JULY
S	M	T	W	T	F	S
		1	2	3	4	5
6	7	8	9	10	11	12
13	14	15	16	17	18	19
20	21	22	23	24	25	26
27	28	29	30	31		

AUGUST
S	M	T	W	T	F	S
					1	2
3	4	5	6	7	8	9
10	11	12	13	14	15	16
17	18	19	20	21	22	23
24/31	25	26	27	28	29	30

SEPTEMBER
S	M	T	W	T	F	S
	1	2	3	4	5	6
7	8	9	10	11	12	13
14	15	16	17	18	19	20
21	22	23	24	25	26	27
28	29	30				

OCTOBER
S	M	T	W	T	F	S
			1	2	3	4
5	6	7	8	9	10	11
12	13	14	15	16	17	18
19	20	21	22	23	24	25
26	27	28	29	30	31	

NOVEMBER
S	M	T	W	T	F	S
						1
2	3	4	5	6	7	8
9	10	11	12	13	14	15
16	17	18	19	20	21	22
23/30	24	25	26	27	28	29

DECEMBER
S	M	T	W	T	F	S
	1	2	3	4	5	6
7	8	9	10	11	12	13
14	15	16	17	18	19	20
21	22	23	24	25	26	27
28	29	30	31			

In 2003, the city hosts the **Venice Biennale International Art Exhibition**, a world-class contemporary fair spread over the Arsenale and sprawling Castello Gardens. Artists representing 65 nations from around the world offer the latest in contemporary art forms: video, computer art, performance art, and digital photography, along with painting and sculpture (€13, daily generally March–Nov 10:00–18:00, Sat until 22:00; vaporetto stop: Giardini/Biennale; for details, see www.labiennale.org).

Other typically Venetian festival days filling the city's hotels with visitors and its canals with decked-out boats are: **Feast of the Ascension Day** (mid-May), **Feast and Regatta of the Redeemer** (parade and fireworks, July 19–20, 2003), and the **Historical Regatta** (old-time boats and pageantry, Sept 1–7, 2003). Smaller regattas include the **Murano Regatta** (early July) and the **Burano Regatta** (in September).

Venice's patron saint, **St. Mark**, is commemorated every April 25. Venetian men celebrate the day by presenting roses to the women in their lives (mothers, wives, and lovers).

Every November 21 is the **Feast of Our Lady of Good Health**. On this local "Thanksgiving," a bridge is built over the Grand Canal so the city can pile into the Salute Church and remember how this city survived the gruesome plague of 1630. On this day, Venetians eat smoked lamb from Dalmatia (which was the cargo of the first ship let in when the plague lifted).

Venice is always busy with special musical and artistic events. The free monthly *Un Ospite de Venezia* lists all the latest in English (free at TI or from fancy hotels). For a comprehensive list of festivals, contact the Italian tourist information office in the United States (see page 7) and visit www.whatsonwhen.com, www.festivals.com, and www.hostetler.net.

National Holidays in Italy

These national holidays (when many sights close) are observed throughout Italy. Note that this isn't a complete list; holidays strike without warning.

Jan 1: New Year's Day
Jan 6: Epiphany
April 20: Easter Sunday (2003)
April 21: Easter Monday (2003)
April 25: Liberation Day
May 1: Labor Day
May 9: Ascension Day
Aug 15: Assumption of Mary
Nov 1: All Saints' Day
Dec 8: Feast of the Immaculate Conception
Dec 25: Christmas
Dec 26: St. Stephen's Day

Numbers and Stumblers

- Europeans write a few of their numbers differently than we do. $1 = 1$, $4 = 4$, $7 = 7$. Learn the difference or miss your train.
- In Europe, dates appear as day/month/year, so Christmas is 25/12/03.
- Commas are decimal points and decimals commas. A dollar and a half is 1,50 and there are 5.280 feet in a mile.
- When pointing, use your whole hand, palm down.
- When counting with fingers, start with your thumb. If you hold up your first finger to request one item, you'll probably get two.

- What Americans call the second floor of a building is the first floor in Europe.
- Europeans keep the left "lane" open for passing on escalators and moving sidewalks. Keep to the right.

Metric Conversion (approximate)

1 inch = 25 millimeters	32 degrees F = 0 degrees C
1 foot = 0.3 meter	82 degrees F = about 28 degrees C
1 yard = 0.9 meter	1 ounce = 28 grams
1 mile = 1.6 kilometers	1 kilogram = 2.2 pounds
1 centimeter = 0.4 inch	1 quart = 0.95 liter
1 meter = 39.4 inches	1 square yard = 0.8 square meter
1 kilometer = .62 mile	1 acre = 0.4 hectare

Venice's Climate Chart

First line, average daily low; second line, average daily high; third line, days of no rain.

J	F	M	A	M	J	J	A	S	O	N	D
33°	35°	41°	49°	56°	63°	66°	65°	61°	53°	44°	37°
42°	46°	53°	62°	70°	76°	81°	80°	75°	65°	53°	46°
25	21	24	21	23	22	24	24	25	24	21	23

Basic Italian Survival Phrases

Good day.	**Buon giorno.**	bwohn **jor**-noh
Do you speak English?	**Parla inglese?**	**par**-lah een-**glay**-zay
Yes. / No.	**Si. / No.**	see / noh
I (don't) understand.	**(Non) capito.**	(nohn) kah-**pee**-toh
Please.	**Per favore.**	pehr fah-**voh**-ray
Thank you.	**Grazie.**	**graht**-seeay
I'm sorry.	**Mi dispiace.**	mee dee-spee**ah**-chay
Excuse me.	**Mi scusi.**	mee **skoo**-zee
(No) problem.	**(Non) c'è un problema.**	(nohn) cheh oon proh-**blay**-mah
Good.	**Va bene.**	vah **behn**-ay
Goodbye.	**Arrivederci.**	ah-ree-vay-**dehr**-chee
one / two	**uno / due**	**oo**-noh / **doo**-ay
three / four	**tre / quattro**	tray / **kwah**-troh
five / six	**cinque / sei**	**cheeng**-kway / **seh**ee
seven / eight	**sette / otto**	**seht**-tay / **ot**-toh
nine / ten	**nove / dieci**	**nov**-ay / dee**eay**-chee
How much is it?	**Quanto costa?**	**kwahn**-toh **kos**-tah
Write it?	**Me lo scrive?**	may loh **skree**-vay
Is it free?	**È gratis?**	eh **grah**-tees
Included?	**È incluso?**	eh een-**kloo**-zoh
Where can I buy / find...?	**Dove posso comprare / trovare...?**	**doh**-vay **pos**-soh kohm-**prah**-ray / troh-**vah**-ray
I'd like / We'd like...	**Vorrei / Vorremo...**	vor-**reh**ee / vor-**ray**-moh
...a room.	**...una camera.**	**oo**-nah kah-meh-rah
...the bill.	**...il conto.**	eel **kohn**-toh
...a ticket to ___.	**...un biglietto per___.**	oon beel-**yeht**-toh per
Is it possible?	**È possibile?**	eh poh-**see**-bee-lay
Where is...?	**Dov'è...?**	**doh**-veh
...the train station	**...la stazione**	lah staht-see**oh**-nay
...the bus station	**...la stazione degli autobus**	lah staht-see**oh**-nay **dayl**-yee ow-toh-boos
...tourist information	**...informazioni per turisti**	een-for-maht-see**oh**-nee pehr too-**ree**-stee
...toilet	**...la toilette**	lah twah-**leht**-tay
men	**uomini, signori**	**woh**-mee-nee, seen-**yoh**-ree
women	**donne, signore**	**don**-nay, seen-**yoh**-ray
left / right	**sinistra / destra**	see-**nee**-strah / **dehs**-trah
straight	**sempre diritto**	**sehm**-pray dee-**ree**-toh
When do you open / close?	**A che ora aprite / chiudete?**	ah kay oh-rah ah-**pree**-tay / keeoo-**day**-tay
At what time?	**A che ora?**	ah kay **oh**-rah
Just a moment.	**Un momento.**	oon moh-**mayn**-toh
now / soon / later	**adesso / presto / tardi**	ah-**dehs**-soh / **prehs**-toh / **tar**-dee
today / tomorrow	**oggi / domani**	**oh**-jee / doh-**mah**-nee

For more user-friendly Italian phrases, check out *Rick Steves' Italian Phrase Book and Dictionary* or *Rick Steves' French, Italian & German Phrase Book and Dictionary*.

Road Scholar Feedback for VENICE 2003

We're all in the same travelers' school of hard knocks. Your feedback helps us improve this guidebook for future travelers. Please fill this out (or use the online version at www.ricksteves.com/feedback), attach more info or any tips/favorite discoveries if you like, and send it to us. As thanks for your help, we'll send you our quarterly travel newsletter free for one year. Thanks! **Rick**

Of the recommended accommodations/restaurants used, which was:

Best _____

     Why? _____

Worst _____

     Why? _____

Of the sights/experiences/destinations recommended by this book, which was:

Most overrated _____

     Why? _____

Most underrated _____

     Why? _____

Best ways to improve this book:

_____

_____

I'd like a free newsletter subscription:

_____ Yes   _____ No   _____ Already on list

_____
Name

_____
Address

_____
City, State, Zip

_____
E-mail Address

    Please send to: ETBD, Box 2009, Edmonds, WA 98020

Faxing Your Hotel Reservation

Use this handy form for your fax or find it online at
www.ricksteves.com/reservation. Photocopy and fax away.

One-Page Fax

To: _____ @ _____
                     hotel   *fax*

From: _____ @ _____
                     name   *fax*

Today's date: ____ /_____ /____
                day   *month* *year*

Dear Hotel _____,

Please make this reservation for me:

Name: _____

Total # of people: _____   # of rooms: _____   # of nights: _____

Arriving: ____ /_____ /____ My time of arrival (24-hr clock): _____
            day *month* *year*   (I will telephone if I will be late)

Departing: ____ /_____ /____
              day *month* *year*

Room(s): Single___ Double___ Twin___ Triple___ Quad___

With: Toilet___ Shower___ Bath___ Sink only___

Special needs: View___ Quiet___ Cheapest___ Ground Floor___

Credit card: Visa___ MasterCard___ American Express___

Card #: _____

Expiration date:_____

Name on card: _____

You may charge me for the first night as a deposit. Please fax, e-mail, or
mail me confirmation of my reservation, along with the type of room
reserved, the price, and whether the price includes breakfast. Please also
inform me of your cancellation policy. Thank you.

_____
Signature

_____
Name

_____
Address

_____
City   *State*   *Zip Code*   *Country*

_____
E-mail Address

INDEX

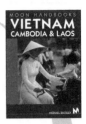

ℱOGHORN OUTDOORS®

Campers, hikers, boaters, and anglers agree:
With Foghorn, you'll spend less time planning and more time enjoying the outdoors.

www.foghorn.com

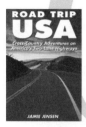

ROAD TRIP USA

Road Trip USA guides take you off
the beaten path, onto classic blacktop,
and into the soul of America.

www.roadtripusa.com

THE DOG LOVER'S COMPANION

A special breed of guidebook for
travelers and residents who don't want
to leave their canine pals behind.

www.dogloverscompanion.com

ADAPTER KIT

Adapter Kit helps travelers extend their journey
and live like the locals, with the help of authors
who have taken the plunge themselves.

www.adapterkit.com

AVALON TRAVEL PUBLISHING
www.travelmatters.com

Avalon Travel Publishing guides are available at your favorite book or travel store.

FREE-SPIRITED TOURS FROM

Rick Steves

FREE TRAVEL GOODIES FROM

Rick Steves

EUROPEAN TRAVEL NEWSLETTER

My *Europe Through the Back Door* travel company will help you travel better *because* you're on a budget—not in spite of it. To see how, ask for my 64-page *travel newsletter* packed full of savvy travel tips, readers' discoveries, and your best bets for railpasses, guidebooks, videos, travel accessories and free-spirited tours.

2003 GUIDE TO EUROPEAN RAILPASSES

With hundreds of railpasses to choose from in 2003, finding the right pass for your trip has never been more confusing. To cut through the complexity, visit www.ricksteves.com for my online *2003 Guide to European Railpasses*. Once you've narrowed down your choices, we give you unbeatable prices, including important extras with every Eurailpass, **free:** my 90-minute *Travel Skills Special* video or DVD and your choice of one of my 24 guidebooks.

RICK STEVES' 2003 TOURS

We offer 20 different one, two, and three-week tours (200 departures in 2003) for those who want to experience Europe in Rick Steves' Back Door style, but without the transportation and hotel hassles. If a tour with a small group, modest family-run hotels, lots of exercise, great guides, and no tips or hidden charges sounds like your idea of fun, ask for my 48-page 2003 Tours booklet.

YEAR-ROUND GUIDEBOOK UPDATES

Even though the information in my guidebooks is the freshest around, things do change in Europe between book printings. I've set aside a special section at my website (www.ricksteves.com/update) listing *up-to-the-minute changes* for every Rick Steves guidebook.

Visit www.ricksteves.com to get your...

☑ **FREE EUROPEAN TRAVEL NEWSLETTER**
☑ **FREE 2003 GUIDE TO EUROPEAN RAILPASSES**
☑ **FREE RICK STEVES' 2003 TOURS BOOKLET**

Rick Steves' Europe Through the Back Door

130 Fourth Avenue North, PO Box 2009, Edmonds, WA 98020 USA
Phone: (425) 771-8303 ■ Fax: (425) 771-0833 ■ www.ricksteves.com